The True
Ulysses S. Grant

THE "TRUE" BIOGRAPHIES AND HISTORIES

GRANT AS MAJOR-GENERAL COMMANDING IN THE WEST

Enlarged from a *carte de visite* photograph by J. E. McClees,
Philadelphia, in the collection of Charles H. Stephens

The True
Ulysses S. Grant

By
Charles King
Brig.-General U. S. V., 1898-99

With Twenty-eight Illustrations

Philadelphia and London
J. B. Lippincott Company
1914

PRINTED BY J. B. LIPPINCOTT COMPANY
AT THE WASHINGTON SQUARE PRESS
PHILADELPHIA, U. S. A.

TO
WEST POINT

THE
SCHOOL WHICH IN SPITE OF HIS AVERSION
TO THE SWORD GAVE TO THE NATION THE
INCOMPARABLE SERVICES

OF

ULYSSES S. GRANT
THESE PAGES ARE DEDICATED

PREFACE

When invited to prepare the manuscript for this work the writer's first impulse was to decline. The subject, however, had for long years commanded his deep interest and much investigation. His admiration of the character and his study of the career of Ulysses Grant equalled probably those of his eminent biographers, and finally, in the belief that there were virtues in the true Grant to which full prominence had not been given, possibly because Grant himself would have regarded them as matters of course, there came the desire to write of our great commander as he seemed to one of the least of these his subalterns, and from the fulness of a store of information garnered through reading and hearing for half a century this memoir practically wrote itself. The real work came when it had to be planed and pruned to the prescribed limits.

Grant's own memoirs, the biographies of Badeau, James Grant Wilson and a score of writers, but especially the soldierly pages of Horace Porter, James Harrison Wilson and William Conant Church have been read again and again. From the lips of Sherman, Sheridan, Cullum, Crook, Augur, Pitcher, Buckner, Longstreet, Hebert, Hodges, Upton, Chetlain, Professors Davies, Mahan, Church and Kendrick, and from many an officer of the Armies of the Tennessee, Cumberland and Potomac, came in the course of years a flood of reminiscence, and from old neighbors of the dreary days of " Hardscrabble " and Jo Daviess County many a detail of pathetic interest.

To one and all these, therefore, thanks are due, and in the matter of our illustrations the worthy mayors of

PREFACE

Georgetown and Galena (Messrs. Charles B. Fee and J. W. Westwick), Lieutenant Harry L. King, U. S. Cavalry, the Chicago Historical Society, companions of the Illinois Commandery of the State of Illinois, Military Order of the Loyal Legion, Mr. Charles H. Stephens of Philadelphia, Mr. F. H. Meserve of New York who has permitted so many reproductions from his collection, Mrs. Frank H. Jones (Nellie Grant), Mr. Hamlin Garland, Mr. E. Ross Burke, the *St. Louis Post-Dispatch,* Mr. Warren Crawford of Chicago, others whose names appear in connection with the illustrations, and finally General E. A. Spencer, Mr. C. F. Blanke and Major Julius Pitzman of St. Louis—the latter intimately associated nearly sixty years ago with the fortunes and misfortunes of the Grants—are entitled to grateful acknowledgment.

And now, with full realization of the responsibilities, but without the Grant-like lack of fear, this memoir is submitted by

THE AUTHOR

MILWAUKEE, April 30, 1914

CONTENTS

CONTENTS

LIST OF ILLUSTRATIONS

The True
Ulysses S. Grant

CHAPTER I

ANCESTRY AND BIRTH

FORTY-FIVE miles from Cincinnati and a little south of east there lies a country town that should live in history. At the time of Abraham Lincoln's election to the presidency it mustered probably a thousand souls. It numbered possibly two hundred voters whose suffrages went largely with those of the Democratic party. It seems that most people of southeastern Ohio had been Southern in sentiment and pro-slavery in politics until that April morning of 1861, when the guns of Sumter, solemnly booming their parting salute to the flag they had so vehemently yet vainly defended, sounded a reveille that woke the sleeping North.

Then of a sudden an apparently passive, peace-loving nation that knew little of the use of arms, came clamoring to the recruiting offices when the President issued his call for men. Their one demand was to be led against those whose aim was the destruction of the Union and whose act had been the humbling of the Flag. The transformation was as sudden as it was surprising. The South had looked for nothing like it. Long accustomed to dominate in the affairs of the nation, having only fifteen years earlier compelled and brought about an utterly unjust war for the purpose of enlarging and extending slave territory, having long cherished the belief that the North, absorbed in commercial pursuits, would shrink from fighting even in defense of a principle, the South had now to face a war for which, like that with Mexico, it was mainly responsible, but which promised very different results. Yet the South was confident. Late as early April the greatest city of the Union, New York, had listened unremonstrant to secession speeches, and viewed without protest secession emblems flaunted in the corridors of some of its leading hotels. Ten hours and all this was changed. The news from Charleston broke the shell of tolerance, and the pent-up patriotism of the North burst forth. Its best and bravest sought instant service, and, in proportion to population and previous condition of political servitude, no community outdid that of little Georgetown, Brown County, Ohio.

Four generals and one colonel, graduates of West Point, and nine more officers of general or field rank, all reared in that peaceful township, were enrolled for defense of the Union. For the cause of the South, in spite of divided sentiment as to slavery, and even as to right of secession, it seems to have furnished none. As for individual merit or value of officers born or " raised " in Georgetown, the great cities of the North combined can lay claim to nothing to match a single record of a Georgetown boy, known to the world as Ulysses Simpson Grant.

That was not his baptismal name. Hiram Ulysses * he had been registered in babyhood, Hiram being his father's choice, Ulysses that of a grandmother who had read much of that soldier solon of the Trojan war. Nor was Georgetown his birthplace. " Ulyss," as he seems to have been hailed about the homestead, first saw the light of day at Point Pleasant on the banks of the Ohio, only a few miles away in Claremont County. But in that beautiful hill country over against the Kentucky shore he spent his boyhood, and at the age of seventeen set forth upon a career he never would have chosen, enlisted, as it were, in a service utterly repug-

---

* Grant was never formally baptized until late in life, and then, by his own choice, as Ulysses S. He would not take the full name of Simpson, which was borne by his younger brother, but elected to be baptized as he had been so long and well known to the Nation.

nant to his tastes and ambitions, became the foremost leader in a profession for which he had felt himself the least fitted, and the foremost citizen in a nation whereof he had deemed himself among the most obscure. Born but a few years before him and but a few hours' journey beyond the winding river, reared in poverty and obscurity exceeding that of the Ohio boy destined to become his right arm, Abraham Lincoln, the wisest, the gentlest, the greatest of the nation's leaders, rose, through thought and observation of men, to guide the Union through the crisis of its history. Study and statesmanship bore him on to the pinnacle of fame.

The Ohio lad who proved his main reliance was neither scholar, student, nor even sound in his knowledge of men. Our modern Ulysses won his way to eminence through sheer soldiership—about the last thing on earth he would have selected as the means. Therefore is his career the most remarkable of his day and generation if not of our national history. It has even persuaded some writers into the belief that he was what they called him—Grant, "The Man of Mystery."

Of the lives of other men who had become great it would seem that, unlike Lincoln, Grant had read but little. Speaking of this, he declared in after life that what he most wished to know of the great leaders of men was that concerning which the least was generally written: he longed to hear of the boy life, the home life, the school life, the formative period in the lives of those whom the world had declared famous. He wished to study the influences that had served to mold the character of men of eminence, of commanding powers in the affairs of peace or of surpassing generalship in the field of war. And now were he to study the pages of his own life, though he has had more biographers, apparently, than any other American, he might suffer keen disappointment, for beyond his own modest narra-

13

tive there is little if anything to draw from, so placid and uneventful were the days of his boyhood, so serene and simple the village life in which he moved and had his being.

Grant himself cared little for genealogy. Great names and lofty lineage inspired him with no especial feeling of awe, much less of reverence. In the presence of royalty he later stood quite unabashed and calmly at ease. It mattered little to him from what particular clan across the seas his sires were sprung. It was sufficient for him that because for eight generations his immediate forebears had made their way on American soil, he could claim to be thoroughly American. When in large numbers the descendants of the proud old Grant clan answered the call of their putative head, a field marshal of the British Army, our Grant courteously but firmly declined. "We have been Americans over two hundred years," said he, and he could trace his descent in unbroken line back to Matthew Grant, to Dorchester, Massachusetts, and to May, 1625. The Grants had been Americans too long, he thought, to feel sure they had ever been Scotch.

But there are those to whom family tradition means more than it did to Grant. It is for the benefit of such, therefore, that his genealogy is here given as recorded by James Grant Wilson:

1. Matthew and Priscilla (——) married 1625.
2. Samuel and Mary (Porter) married 1658.
3. Samuel and Grace (Miner) married 1688.
4. Noah and Martha (Huntington) married 1717.
5. Noah and Susannah (Delano) married 1746.
6. Noah and Rachel (Kelly) married 1791.
7. Jesse Root and Hannah (Simpson) married 1821.
8. Hiram Ulysses, later known as Ulysses Simpson, born April 27, 1822.

Of all these ancestors few achieved distinction of any kind. The first Matthew made his home at Windsor, on the banks of the Connecticut, and for no less than forty years was county surveyor. His eldest son, the first " Sam " Grant in the American line, took up lands on the opposite bank from Windsor, and to the days when one of their kith and kin sat as chief magistrate of the entire nation, those lands were occupied by descendants of the original Sam.

Troublous times came to the colonists. Quitting England in quest of the blessings of religious liberty, the Pilgrim Fathers had landed on the " stern and rock-bound coast," where they speedily showed themselves as intolerant of forms of worship other than their own as ever had been the narrowest of the church party at home. The early days were to the full as strenuous as ever had been those of their elders in Albion. Beset by savage foes, the settlers tilled the fields with their antique firearms strapped to the plough handles. They appeared even at divine worship full panoplied for fight. They took their king's shilling and " listed " for the wars against French and Indian, learning much thereby that reacted on His Majesty's loyal forces when later his recalcitrant subjects denounced in convention their monarch and his minions, fiercely as in their covenant they renounced the devil and all his works. Noah and Sol Grant, of the fifth descending generation from Matthew, fought valiantly as commissioned officers in the British ranks, and both were killed in 1756. Noah, the next, he of the sixth generation and the grandfather of the great Grant of our day, was just nine years old when his father and uncle died fighting for the king's colors, and twenty years thereafter with all his might he lived and fought against them. He " went to the wars " with the Connecticut line, served all through from Bunker Hill to Yorktown, yet in the midst of war's alarms was human enough to yield, as later did his illustrious grandson, to promptings of the tender passion. Unlike the latter, he had not to wait until the close of hostilities to claim the lady of his love.

Soon after the surrender of Cornwallis he found himself once more in Connecticut, father of two sturdy little Grants, but a widower. Leaving the elder lad with kinfolk at home, Noah took Peter, the younger, to Westmoreland County, Pennsylvania, and as "Cap" Grant, the characteristic American abbreviation of his military title, started life anew, presently marrying for the second time, and this time a name suggestive of the shamrock rather than the thistle, for the grandmother of our Ulysses was a Kelly. Later still one more move was made and this time to southern Ohio.

In this move young Peter did not participate. Peter's mother had been a Connecticut Yankee, and her boy was born with a sense of the value of money and a gift for business. Noah, the father, like many another soldier, had neither. Peter had no prejudice against his stepmother, nor the brothers and sisters who speedily came to swell the family expense account, but he saw the need of cutting loose and providing for himself. In brief, Peter moved to Maysville, Kentucky, persevered, prospered, married, raised a large family and a larger business, becoming owner of a tannery among other properties, taking to his roof and heart again the aging and impecunious father, when in 1805 Noah's second wife died, "leaving seven children," says our own Grant in his Memoirs, the two youngest going with their father to live upon the bounty of the one prosperous and thrifty member of the family. When Peter Grant was finally drowned in the Kanawha, in 1825, he was one of the wealthy men of the West, and he had been a devoted son to the Revolutionary soldier and a protector to many of his younger kinsfolk.

Of these latter, however, there were some who strove to make their own way in the world. Foremost was the eldest of Peter's half brothers, Jesse Root. Jesse, at the breakup of the family in 1805, found a home in the household of Judge Tod, of Deerfield,

Ohio. Good and charitable folk must these have been, for they took the motherless boy to their fireside and cherished him as though he had been their own. A hard-headed, argumentative citizen young Jesse grew to be, a man never conspicuous for softness of heart or sweetness of disposition, yet to his dying day Jesse Grant could never speak of Judge Tod or the judge's gentle wife without emotion. " She was the most admirable woman I ever knew," he often declared. As for the judge, there was no bound to the respect and esteem in which Jesse held him. As an inmate of their home it is presumable that Jesse must have well known the son, who, in point of public life and prominence, outranked the genial and kindly father. Governor Tod, the son, became one the nation heard of and the state admired, but in the eyes of Jesse Root the governor never stood on a plane with his father, the judge.

It was presently the lot of Jesse Grant to become identified with another famous family and world-renowned name. For a year or so he had been taken over by Peter to learn the trade of a tanner. Returning to Deerfield, Jesse found a home and employment with a family of Browns—benevolent and unpretentious people who might never have been heard of but for a son, John, a mere boy when Jesse, a well-grown youth, lived in daily association with him. They grew to know each other better, to differ widely in their views on political matters, but to remain good friends. " He was a man of great purity of character," declared Jesse, afterwards, " of high moral and physical courage," as recorded by Jesse's famous son, " but a fanatic and extremist in whatever he advocated." This was said of him who later became known to the world as " Ossawatomie " Brown. This was the Ossawatomie of whom two million or more battling men in blue were destined to sing that his body lay mouldering in the grave as his soul was marching on. This was he whose mad fanaticism led him, with a handful of followers, to attempt the invasion of a sovereign state, and to die self-martyred on the scaffold. This was he who, before surrendering to Colonel Robert E. Lee at Harper's Ferry, practically brought about the tremendous war which was to close only when his chivalric captor should in turn surrender to the chivalric son of his boy friend and house mate, Jesse Grant. Verily, it would seem that in Brown County, Ohio, were centred for the time the destinies of the surrounding nation. Verily, there is food for thought in the fact that while the fathers of John Brown and Ulysses Grant were dwelling under the same roof in southern Ohio, there were, a few years later, to be spending their boyhood in Ohio towns within a few hours' ride of one another the three embryo soldiers destined to become, in the tremendous scenes soon to follow, the foremost of the generals who fought to save the Union—Grant, Sherman and Sheridan.

For a time after launching out for himself Jesse Grant conducted a small tannery at Ravenna. Then he moved his little "plant" to Point Pleasant, a beautiful spot on the Ohio. In June, 1821, he married Hannah Simpson, then in her twenty-first year, the third child of John Simpson, of Montgomery County, Pennsylvania, a man who cared as little for genealogy as his son-in-law cared much. John Simpson could tell nothing of his line further back than his grandfather. Jesse Grant had every birth, death and date for seven generations of Grants at his fingers' ends. Jesse Grant, though engaged in a business that yielded small profits, was keen and thrifty. Jesse Grant, moreover, was a man of parts. Schooling he had had next to none, but he had learned to spell, to cipher, and he taught himself to write. A more rapacious reader than Jesse Grant was not to be found in southern Ohio. He borrowed every book he could lay hands on and laboriously mastered the contents. He pored over the papers, and

JESSE ROOT GRANT
From the collection of F. H. Meserve

HANNAH SIMPSON GRANT
From a photograph in the possession of E. Ross Burke

took part in impromptu debates innumerable. He studied politics with especial avidity, and "Harry of the West," Henry Clay of Kentucky, was Jesse's political file leader. Before he was twenty-one Jesse Grant had begun writing to the papers—a fad he clung to long years of his life, even after his soldier son besought that he stop it. There was a time, just after his marriage, when, weakened by fever and ague, Jesse became impoverished, but when able to move to Georgetown, where there were better facilities and abundant bark for his tannery, he began again to prosper. He was aided in his economies by a gentle and sympathetic wife, whom their first-born—the boy Hiram—devotedly loved. She bore quite a family and reared her birdlings as befitted folk in very moderate circumstances. Jesse was a sturdy and independent soul and had little sympathy for men who owed, and less for men who failed. The time was to come when this trait was to tell heavily on his first-born, but the boyhood years of that eldest hope were at least as free from care and hardship as they were from luxury of any kind.

Born on the 27th of April, 1822, the future foremost citizen of the United States spent his babyhood in a little frame cottage close to the banks of the Ohio. The site and scene are beautiful. The home was humble in the extreme, but it sufficed for all their needs until the baby boy was over a year old. Then Jesse Grant bundled up his few belongings and moved northeastward to Georgetown, in the adjoining county.

The business sagacity of Jesse was manifest in this move. The little tannery on the outskirts of the peaceful country village prospered from the start. Within the second year of his venture Jesse was able to build a comfortable two-story house of brick and stone. By the time the chubby-faced first-born was toddling and tumbling about the new premises, the cradle was again in requisition, and to Ulysses was born a baby brother. In the course of the eight or ten years in which he was waxing in strength and usefulness there came sisters, and yet another baby boy, until George-town could have boasted of six young Grants who, in order of rank and " entry into service," as soldiers say, are recorded as follows: 1. Hiram Ulysses. 2. Simpson. 3. Clara. 4. Virginia. 5. Orvil L., and 6. Mary Frances.

And as these little folk in turn began to talk and toddle it is something to remember that in their eyes the eldest, the big brother, was for long years decidedly a hero. The paternal given name of Hiram appears seldom to have been used. " Lys," or at most " Ulyss," the youngsters and the neighbors called him, and the father seemed eventually to have followed suit. Just why he named him Hiram, there having been no Hiram of consequence upon the family tree, the father has not taken the trouble to explain. That the boy's maternal grandmother had developed a taste for classic reading —that she was a woman of some culture—is manifest in the choice of the name she so greatly admired. The little man in whose coming and christening she took so deep an interest, lived to adorn and honor it as even his fond mother could hardly have dared to dream— Ulysses, the warrior sage of heroic days whose life has been the theme of the poets from the days of Homer, and the meditation of readers for centuries. Was there something of the Sybil in that second wife of plain John Simpson, the Pennsylvania farmer,—he who had found in southern Ohio a new home and a new mother for that silent, self-effacing, prayerful daughter? It might well be claimed for her; it might well be credited that in the choice of that name she had unerringly fore-seen the future of that baby boy; for, when all is said and done, when all his ventures as soldier and man are set over and summed up as against the puny column of his faults and foibles, lived there ever a man since

BIRTHPLACE OF ULYSSES S. GRANT,
POINT PLEASANT, OHIO

From "Ulysses S. Grant, His Life and Character," by Hamlin Garland.
By kind permission of the author and Messrs. Doubleday, Page & Co.

THE LEATHER STORE AT GALENA, ILL.

See page 136

From a photograph in the possession of Mr Warren Crawford
of Chicago

Ulysses of old, so worthy the glowing description penned by Fénélon and recalled and applied to our own Ulysses by William Conant Church? "His heart is of an unfathomable depth; his secret lies beyond the line of subtlety and fraud; he is the friend of truth, saying nothing that is false, but, when it is necessary, conceding what is true; his wisdom, as it were, a seal upon his lips, which is never broken but for an important purpose."

Study the catalogue of Christian names, study the life and character of this first-born son of Jesse Grant, and choose if possible a name that shall better fit the man.

CHAPTER II

BOYHOOD AND MOTHER

AMONG the frugal, simple folk that made up the mass of the population of our western States, most boys worked in one way or another as soon as they were big enough to work at all. The "senior subaltern" of the household in the new two-story home on the banks of the White Oak began before he was big enough to run errands. Grant, the father, divided his time between his tannery and the newly-purchased lands. Grant, the son, decided before he was five that he preferred the farm. Jesse had bought a number of acres along the wooded banks of the creek, together with a cleared patch or two closer to the household, and on one of these stood the barn. The mother hand first led the youngster to watch the workmen, and then sought to restrain him as, eagerly, the little fellow strove to reach the horses plodding home with their load of lumber. Barely three years of age was he who later was destined to ride at the head of two million of men at arms, when first he was set astride a horse, and it appeared that the youngster even at that early age had views of his own as to horsemanship. It was told of him in the family that the chubby fists instantly gathered up the reins, and that he promptly and impatiently shook off the hand that sought to aid him in his seat. Before he was four the boy had backed every horse that came to the little farm, and was spending hours each day studying the pair his father bought. His earliest ambition was to ride. From morn till night when a five-year-old he hung about the horses. If they were afield hauling wood or stone, he was perched contentedly astride the near one. By the time he was seven he was practising acro-

GRANT'S BOYHOOD HOME, GEORGETOWN, OHIO

batic feats of his own devising; nor had he yet seen a circus; that and resultant essays in equitation were yet to come. Before he was ten years of age all Brown County, however, seems to have heard of that small boy of the Grants—the little chap that could ride like a monkey, standing and balancing on one leg, running the horses up and down the soft roadway along the creek bank, " far more at home in saddle," as was presently said of him, " than he'll ever be at school."

But it was not yet time for school. Moreover, schools in those days and in Ohio were few and far between. Up to the time he was ten years old about all the schooling that came his way was at his mother's knee, and there the boy learned lessons that influenced his entire life. Home from his labor in the tannery or the field, Jesse, the father, lost himself speedily in the columns of the Cincinnati papers, in the pages of his book, in letters to the press, or in the evenings of debate on mooted questions at the town hall. The mental and moral training of the children in their tender years seems to have been left entirely to the mother, and what they owe to her no one of their number has ever adequately told. Ulysses, at least, strove hard to do so, for in letters written to her long years after, especially in those that were penned in his " plebedom " at West Point, he opened his heart, and told her how deeply her teachings had taken root—how firmly implanted were the lessons of truth, patience, self-sacrifice and of reverence for religion that he had learned from her gentle lips. A rare woman was Hannah Simpson; sweet and comely to look upon in youth, she had gained in her maturity an added dignity of bearing. A silent, observant nature was hers. Deeply religious in temperament, reared in the austere and solemn tenets of the Methodist church, she looked upon life with eyes that saw only its duties and responsibilities. She had a smile for every one, but laughter with her was as rare as wrath or anger. Soft of speech, just, gentle, yet firm and steadfast, she proved an admirable help and stay for the sometimes erratic Jesse; but for her children she was a guide and comfort unspeakable. Chiding when necessary, but "nagging" never, she watched over her little brood with the vigilance of the mother partridge. Shielding them ever from that which menaced their innocence or their wellbeing, she reared her children pure of heart and pure of speech, and the best of her, because he had the most of her, seems to have concentrated in Ulysses.

Before he was six the boy was helping her about the woodshed and kitchen. Before he was seven he could groom and harness, feed and water, ride and drive any horse about the growing farm. By the time he was eight he lived all day afield, doing the "chores" about the house, bringing in the wood and water and driving the cows to and from pasture. But his glory and his principal care were his father's horses; the tannery he could never abide. He saw nothing in the trade that did not repel him, whereas he would gravely study for hours the work of the plowmen, the woodmen, the harrowing, seeding, planting and mowing, and, as best he could, strove to imitate or improve upon their methods. But about the horses he had methods of his own. It began to dawn upon the elders and their "help" that between the lad and his big four-footed friends there lived some strange sympathy and understanding. With less trouble, with fewer words and no blows, the boy could get more out of the farm horses in the way of willing work than could any of the grown folk.

And so it resulted that in the fall of the year when the wood choppers had felled the destined trees, though small for his years and only eight that spring, it was the boy who took charge of all the hauling. The men loaded or unloaded the firewood, but no one thought of meddling with the team. Perched on top of the

24

pile, with his bright, blue-gray eyes and his sun-tanned, cheery face, the lad would cluck to his friends, the horses, and they would start for home. Almost any farm-bred boy would probably be whistling, but if ever our Ulysses hummed or whistled an air he could not for the life of him tell the name of it. All tunes were alike to him, and he had no love for any. Only once in all his career is there record of his being moved by music, martial, sacred or secular; that was when, at his signal, the stars and stripes slowly floated to the peak of the flagstaff overlooking the mighty river that from that instant flowed " unvexed to the sea," and the massed bands, and the myriad voices of a host of battle-worn men broke forth in the triumphant strains of thanks-giving and praise, and the walls of Vicksburg resounded to the solemn harmonies of " Old Hundred."

But Jesse Grant, himself unschooled, was none the less a student and a thinker; Jesse, who was self-edu-cated, believed implicitly in education for his children, and early in the boyhood of his first-born began to look about for schools. Such as they had in Brown and Claremont Counties were known as " subscription schools," and in one of these Ulysses began his lessons. He didn't like them. He much preferred the farm, and the sight of a strange horse would tempt him away from his desk and into the street, the misconduct leading to reprisals such as were practised in that day and gen-eration.

When Ulysses Grant was eleven years of age he was doing much of the plowing, planting, seeding and hoeing about his father's farm, yet, obedient to his father's wishes, never missing a day of the school term. When he was placed a quarter, and later a winter, at a time, as a boarder in a private school at Hillsboro, or over at Maysville, Kentucky, with local masters of much repute, Ulysses declared that such was his natural repugnance to school books that he believed the money spent on his education was utterly wasted. Moreover, it seems that by one of his masters, an expert in that method of imparting instruction, the future head of the nation was occasionally and soundly flogged.

It is characteristic of Grant that he should write of this teacher, Mr. J. D. White, that he was a kind-hearted, excellent man, that he did only as did almost every other pedagogue of his time,—that he, the often birched and berated pupil, bore no ill will whatever to the wielder of the rod. What we should like to know, and what he does not tell us, is just how he took it at the time. It is hazarding little to say that he bore it silently, with set teeth and perhaps tearless eyes. It is hazarding nothing to say that other future lieutenant generals of the army of the United States were learning *vis a tergo* the lessons of fortitude and self repression, for, each in his day, two of them, Sherman and Sheridan, as we have said, were reared almost within long gunshot of each other and barely one hundred miles northeast of the Georgetown home.

And yet Ulysses was anything but a vicious or heedless boy. He was as square and dependable a lad as lived in all Ohio. He was industry itself about the farm. He was gentle, docile, thoughtful about the house. He was of serious mold, little given to mirth or mischief. He says that in his home life he was never punished or scolded, for his father appreciated his usefulness and was probably proud of his horse knowledge. At an unusually early age the boy was permitted to take any of the animals, winter or summer, single or double, and go driving about the country, sometimes visiting his Simpson grandparents, frequently visiting Cincinnati; once or twice driving neighbors, where stages were not to be had, distances of seventy or eighty miles. In summer time he went swimming with other farm or village lads, in winter sledding, sleighing and skating. He had no real intimacies among his neighbors and no real enemies. He had many friends, and so far as he recalled, only one fight, and that was with a boy bigger than himself and something of a bully. "Ulyss" was slender but sinewy, small but plucky, and when tormented beyond endurance turned upon his tormentor, as the latter hoped and planned in anticipation of easy victory over the lad he envied because so many others hailed him as the best rider in southern Ohio. It may be that this happened just after "Ulyss" had won the plaudits of all Brown County and the ringmaster's five dollars by riding the trick pony when the great event of the year took place and the circus came to Georgetown. It was a battered but victorious Ulysses that went home after that memorable combat on the banks of White Oak Creek; nor was that the only adventure that befell him thereon. Once when fishing with a boy friend (the future Admiral Ammen), it fell out that the future general fell in and was for a moment or two in grievous plight. Admiral Ammen laughed throughout a lifetime over the picture presented by the bedraggled Ulysses, as he led him dripping up the bank. His blouse or "jumper" was of red and white striped Marseilles when the boys went forth together, but the stripes were merged in one limp and lurid blotch as they drew near home.

When fifteen years of age young Grant's repute as a horseman had spread to adjoining counties. He knew the points of a good roadster as well as any trader along the Ohio, but his chief delight was in a fine saddler. Over in Kentucky the fox trot and the single foot were the gaits most favored, but Ulysses had a way of teaching the pace that added to his fame and not a little to his fortune. In his Memoirs this fact finds no mention—neither does he tell about the memorable day when in the presence of all the pretty girls for miles around and hundreds of town and village folk, he circled the circus astride that plunging trick mule (neither does he men-

27

tion his later fame as by long odds the best rider of his day at West Point), but Brown and Claremont Counties knew it, and farmers far and near brought horses to the fields of Jesse Grant, there to be taught to pace by Jesse's eldest son. In this way and in "hiring out" to convey travellers long distances over the Ohio and Kentucky roads, Ulysses had earned no little money, much of which,—several hundred dollars, says one of his most conservative biographers,—he thriftily saved, for his one consuming desire as he reached his seventeenth year was to be a "travelled man."

No boy of his acquaintance had then seen as much of the world as Ulysses. He had even been as far as Louisville—a wonderful steamboat ride from Cincinnati. He began to study geography, at least, with some show of interest. He was naturally quick at figures and mastered the rudiments of mathematics with consummate ease. He believed even then in law and order as his Maysville teacher, Mr. Richardson, tells of two measures that were introduced in formal meeting of the school debating society by Ulysses Grant. They were as follows:

"*Resolved,* That it be considered out of order for any member to speak on the opposite side to that to which he belongs.
"*Resolved,* That any member who leaves his seat during debate shall be fined not less than six and a quarter cents."

But while it was admitted that Ulysses could break, train, ride and drive horses to the admiration of everybody, there was one thing he would not and could not do, and that was strive to persuade a man to sell a horse for less than the horse's worth. In the eyes of Jesse, the money-maker, this offset his virtues, and the father never ceased to look upon the son as, from a purely business point of view, rather a hopeless proposition. There was once a colt Ulysses longed to own and had not money to buy. This was when the boy was less than ten. The owner valued it at twenty-five dollars. The boy believed him fully worth it. The father long held out for twenty, but at last gave over the needed twenty-five with the parting injunction: " Offer him twenty dollars. If he won't take that, then make it twenty-two fifty, and if that won't do then let him have the twenty-five." Rejoicefully the youngster galloped away and literally did he obey his instructions. " I've come for the colt, Mr. ——," said he. " Father says I'm to offer you twenty dollars, and if you won't take that, make it twenty-two fifty, and if that won't do, to give the whole twenty-five dollars." And, as the general whimsically says in his Memoirs, " It wouldn't take a Connecticut man to guess the price immediately agreed upon."

But Ulysses got that colt and trained and rode him several years, and sold him for twenty dollars when no longer suited to his needs. Yet the Georgetown boys, envious of his horsemanship and eagerly and properly disdainful of his business methods, guyed him without mercy over that story, and so did his father. The boy might have an eye for a horse, was the verdict of Brown County, but he had no head for business.

And Brown County was prophetic. Looking far into the future was it possible that Georgetown foresaw the failure that was, in Wall Street, the sensation of the day—the peril of an honored name, the forfeit of a fortune, which in the autumn of his age well-nigh broke the stout heart of Ulysses Grant?

It was soon after this episode in his boy life that Ulysses became a sufferer from chills and fever—the scourge that for a time had broken the health and checked the fortune of his father. Then it was that again and yet again the growing lad became as a child at his mother's knee, and thus it was that even in his sturdy, self-reliant boyhood, he was thrown so much upon the care and comforting that only a mother could give. Thus perhaps it came about that just at the time when most boys seem cutting loose from the maternal apronstring, the future hero of the fiercest war of modern times, all unconscious of the momentous change so speedily to come into his life, fell more and more under the sweet and soothing influences of that mother's love—influences that abode with him for all time.

CHAPTER III

A SOLDIER IN SPITE OF HIMSELF

THE summer of the seventeenth year of Grant's life had come. His sixteenth birthday had found him just finishing the winter term at a Maysville school, and once again he was busily engaged about the farm, when his father decided the hour at hand in which to determine the boy's future vocation. Frankly, yet respectfully, the lad had declared that if he must learn and labor at the trade of a tanner he would do so only until twenty-one. Then he would shift for himself. Already the "best travelled boy" in Georgetown, he still longed to see more of the world.

By this time Jesse Grant was a man of mark and influence in the community. Possessed now of moderate means, he was bent on providing his children with the best education to be had, yet, true to his business instincts, sought to do so at the least cost to himself. One wintry evening when the son was home from the last of the local schools he ever attended—a private affair at Ripley—the father appeared with a long, official-looking envelope in hand, and very briefly announced the appointment of Ulysses to a cadetship at the National Military Academy at West Point. The rest is best told in Grant's own words, "'But I won't go,' said I. 'I think you will,' said my father, and I thought so too if he did, and the matter was settled then and there."

How it all came about is rather a curious story. The Hon. Thomas L. Hamer then represented that congressional district, and was entitled to name the lad who should fill the vacancy at West Point created by the recent failure of a Georgetown boy. That failure had stung to the quick the father of the luckless cadet in question, and the poor fellow had been sternly forbidden to show his face at home. Everybody seems to have known it, and Ulysses had been thinking much of the sorrows of his former playmate, and how strange it was that one so capable in his school work at home should have made so complete a failure of it elsewhere. Ulysses did not know that more than half the "candidates" who then entered West Point were unable to meet the requirements or stand the strain of the four long years of incessant study and discipline, and sooner or later fell by the wayside.

But that the appointment should come from Mr. Hamer was a surprise to all Brown County. Hamer and Jesse Grant had differed widely on some political matters, and Jesse, as was ever his wont, had been venting his views in the public press and saying things as to Mr. Hamer's sagacity and statesmanship that had greatly angered Mr. Hamer at the time, and the two men met as strangers when they met at all.

So Grant had written to a senatorial friend—a man who liked the outspoken tanner, and whom Hamer liked and was glad to oblige. The senator wrote to Hamer and, time being short and mail communication slow, other business and no other candidates pressing, it resulted that Mr. Hamer at once sent to the Secretary of War what he believed to be the correct name of the son of his truculent fellow citizen. The Hiram part of it he had never heard. The Ulysses part of it was on many a tongue when last the congressman was at home, and all Brown and Claremont Counties knew that the boy's mother was that gentle daughter of John Simpson. The War Department asked no questions, but promptly filled the customary blank which formally notified one Ulysses Simpson Grant, of Georgetown, Brown County, Ohio, that the President had been pleased to designate him conditionally as a cadet at the U. S. Military Academy, where he would be pleased to report himself to the superintendent thereof on or about the 1st of June for further examination. Then followed some printed instructions as to the physical and mental qualifications—the latter then little more than the " reading, writing and 'rithmetic " he had been learning at odd intervals for several years. Before Ulysses was a day older he found himself booked, as it were, for a life career which was just about the last he would ever have chosen and for which he deemed himself in the least degree fitted.

And yet it so happened that within ten years both the congressman and the cadet of his nomination were destined to meet as fellow soldiers in the field of arms, and to record each of the other high estimate of ability, energy and value. The one as a field officer of volunteers, the other as a staff officer of regulars, met and joined hands in front of Monterey. It is pleasant, too, to record that when Mr. Hamer got home from Washington in the summer of '39 his former critic and censor, Mr. Jesse Grant, lost no time in journeying to find him, and to thank him heartily for the appointment given his boy, and these two men of mark thus buried their differences and shook hands over the clouded past. Henceforth they had an interest in common.

But the object of that interest meanwhile had been by no means happy. Little as he desired to go to West Point, he less desired to return from there except victorious, with diploma and commission to crown his efforts, and now Ulysses was worrying over the possibility of failure. If some convulsion of nature had toppled the entire Academy into the Hudson that spring of '39 he could have read the news with rejoicing. Indeed he himself records that, soon after his entrance upon duty, he watched with actual hope the progress of the move in congress to abolish West Point. If

3

Congress killed the Academy, he could then return blameless and scot free to resume the farm life and the horse training he delighted in.

That spring of '39 he rode in to Cincinnati in quest of an algebra, thinking to learn a little of the first year's mathematical course. Arithmetic he knew by heart, but this strange new work, with its mystic symbols, proved, as he says, all Greek to him, and there was no one in Georgetown who could then explain its mysteries. It only served to add to his apprehensions.

The time soon came when he must set forth on what was then a journey of a week or more. There was between him and that devoted mother much planning and preparation over the modest stock of clothing to be taken, and who knows what confidences, what admonition on the one side and promise on the other, passed between these two, who, loving each other so very much, spoke of it so very little. One letter written from West Point within a few months of his entrance—one probably of many, for others are referred to—reveals unerringly the depth of the reverence in which he held his mother. Let that speak for itself.

But the note of preparation was not without its humorous or whimsical side. When the old-fashioned hair trunk, lettered with brass-headed nails, was brought forth, and on either end was disclosed the legend H. U. G., the wise Ulysses promptly rebelled. Mindful of the deviling to which the village boys had subjected him over the colt purchase, and foreseeing the fun his future comrades would have over that alphabetical combination, he insisted on another trunk and a different legend. The trunk which entered West Point with "New Cadet" Ulysses Simpson Grant was marked U. H. G., thus leading to further complications.

The Grants were given to little show of emotion at any time. The parting with mother was not for other eyes. There were Georgetown girls and boys to "see him off," even after the cheery farewell to father and the sisters at the front gate. The girls of Georgetown had ever been his friends, because no one of their number had ever known him to be guilty of a rude act or word, and now that he was going it began to be further remarked amongst the town folk, old and young, that that boy had never been guilty of a mean act or an untruthful word. There was something to him, after all, besides a gift for training and trading horses. It was recalled that when a wandering phrenologist visited the village six years earlier, the elder Grant had insisted on the boy's bumps being interpreted, and what that phrenologist told Jesse—a believer in the new cult—astonished and delighted the elder as much as it dismayed the boy. "Whatever you do, don't tell it," Ulysses had begged, when he saw how seriously his father took it, but all in vain. Somehow it leaked out that those bumps indicated that the first-born son of Jesse should one day be President of the United States, and the fun Georgetown had at the expense of the Grants lasted many a year. Very possibly that gifted practitioner had prophesied the same thing of other boys at several other " stands " along his route; in these cases, however, fond parents found no subsequent reason for mentioning the fact.

But Jesse Grant was unprepared for the first indications of a will of his own on part of the son. It seems that our Ulysses was bent on making the most of his first wanderings away from the home State. It was a three-days' run by river boat to Pittsburgh. It was a long, slow ride thence by canal packet to the base of the Alleghenies, and over their summits by wagon or stage. It was another long, slow ride down the eastern slopes and the winding Juniata. Then at Harrisburg, the State capital, the Buckeye boy bought his ticket to Philadelphia by the first railway train he had yet seen, and nearly a day was spent in trundling over the twisting road of iron at the astonishing speed of twelve or even fifteen miles an hour. Then Ulysses devoted an entire week to sight-seeing in Philadelphia. He had money of his own, his earnings and savings, and there were kinsfolk of the clan to visit. There was, moreover, abundant time, yet all this independence startled Jesse, the father, and brought from his ever ready pen a letter of rebuke, which, like many another letter received in after years, was read without resentment and pocketed without remark, left in fact to answer itself in course of time, as most letters will.

And now, oddly enough, while the home folk were fretting not a little at the deliberation with which Ulysses moved on to his destination, there was something of a show of impatience at the other end of the line—something that would have surprised no one more than Ulysses himself. West Point reception of all newcomers had sometimes exaggerated that of the colleges of all Christendom. In one and all the neophyte has had to learn that an immensity of distance lies between him and the honors and dignity of the upper classman. On this point there are none so insistent as the so-called sophomores in college or " yearlings " at the national schools. Having only just emerged from the meekness of their own year of probation, they turn with eager delight upon the " freshies " of the new class, and in the vernacular of the campus " take it out " of their successors.

West Point was and is no exception to the rule. It holds good everywhere in all trades and professions. Soldiers, sailors, students, school boys, miners, woodmen, " gangsters " generally, wherever the male animal is employed or engaged, sometimes even where two or three are gathered together in Sunday-school or theological seminary, the newcomer is the butt of the jokes or pranks, more or less malicious, of the older " hands." It is even whispered that there are colleges where co-education is unknown, and only the softer sex admitted, where " hazing " is carried on as merrily or maliciously as ever it was at the Point. In Grant's day the practice had not risen to the proportions attained when his own first-born " reported," and in turn, with cheery and uncomplaining equanimity, took his share and more of the " levelling " process devised by his elders in the craft. When still again, in the third generation, the line of U. S. Grant was enrolled in the famous gray battalion, there were disciplinarian methods and refinements of torment in practice never dreamed of in the days of Grant, the grandfather, the first Ulysses, for whose coming in June, '39, a swarm of mirthful spirits were eagerly watching.

It was all due to those magic initials U. S. In his own Memoirs General Tecumseh Sherman—he who was destined a quarter century later to be the strong right arm, and stanchest, sturdiest friend Grant found in all the army—records that when the list of new cadets was posted along in the springtime, as was ever the custom, and the youngsters swarmed about the bulletin board to study the names and speculate as to the personality of the expected class, the liveliest comment was aroused by the name of the representative of the Fifth Congressional District of Ohio. It is safe to say that when a few weeks later the neophytes began to arrive, and shyly, sullenly or stoically, as temperaments determined, submitted to the ordeal of initiation, the centre of interest for several days was that rather bucolical-looking young fellow from the Buckeye State. Then it as surely settled elsewhere. From the moment of his arrival Grant was so hopelessly good natured, so cheery and serene, so unruffled even by taunt, sneer or sarcasm, that the few malignant spirits sought other victims, while the main body, the manly and self-respecting class that have ever made up the great majority of the Corps of Cadets, soon took him into fellowship as one of the steady goers of the battalion, and left him to work out his own destiny in the most utterly democratic institution on the face of the globe. In this little community, no matter what may be the conditions as to birth, breeding, family connections or worldly goods, all who enter leave such behind, and at the outset agree to be bound by the same rigid rules as to dress, diet, deportment and duty, to eat, drink, sleep, study, drill and do as prescribed in the regulations. Thus starting on precisely the same plane, each for himself, as natural or acquired advantages, coupled with industry and energy, may best enable him, the cadet determines his own future standing in the records of the Academy.

And so started and so for four long years steadily and serenely plodded the Ohio lad known to his comrades of the Corps as Sam Grant. Only in one way was he destined to become conspicuous in the Academy. Only to one earthly being did he communicate his hopes, fears or most intimate impressions. Removed by long miles from the sweet influences that had surrounded and guarded his boyhood, entered against his will upon a career distasteful to him, circumscribed by conditions that were often repugnant, and governed by a routine he considered harsh at most times and needless in most cases, he passed through plebe camp in silent submission, and settled down to his first year's studies in the bare old barracks, with neither hope of nor desire for reward in the profession prescribed for him; with neither enthusiasm nor even respect for the soldier part of his work; with nothing but a sense of duty and a never-surrender spirit to direct his efforts. To this was added the filial obedience he owed his father and the devotion with which he regarded his mother, for here is what in 1839 he wrote to her:

"I seem alone in the world without my mother . . . You cannot tell how much I miss you. I was so often alone with you and you so frequently spoke to me in private that the solitude of my situation here at the Academy among my silent books and in my lonely room is all the more striking. It reminds me all the more forcibly of home, and most of all, dear mother, of you. Your kindly instructions and ad- monitions are ever present with me. How often do I think of them and how well they strengthen me in every good word or work."

CHAPTER IV

CADET LIFE AND COMRADES

IN those days the age limit for admission to the Academy was from sixteen to twenty, and of the number sent thither for preliminary examination in June, '39, just seventy-six were duly enrolled as new cadets. Thirteen of their number were named by the President himself, sons of prominent officials or personal or political friends. A dozen hailed from New York; nearly as many from Pennsylvania; three from Virginia; four only from Ohio; the others " scattering." Of these seventy-six only about one-half were destined to answer to the final roll-call of the class when summoned four years later to receive the prized diploma.

Nor was it a class remarkable either for scholarship or soldiership. No one of their number was graduated directly into the most scientific Corps of the Army, the Engineers. William B. Franklin, who eventually ended at the head in general standing, was gazetted to the " Topogs "—a secondary branch of the Engineers, which many years later was merged with that Corps by act of Congress. The next man, George Deshon, of Connecticut, was assigned to the Ordnance, but ere long quit the army for the priesthood, and lived and died in holy orders. For a time he and Grant were roommates, they were ever friends, the one already dreaming of the mitre and vestments of the Church of Rome, the other an unobtrusive follower of his mother's creed —that of the most earnest Methodism. Next in rank came Brereton and Grelaud, assigned respectively to the Ordnance and the Artillery. William F. Raynolds, hailing like Grant from Ohio, was graduated fifth and was at first assigned to the Infantry arm, but was able as early as the 20th of July to effect a transfer to the Topographical Corps. Sixth in order of graduation and assigned to the Artillery, was Quimby of New Jersey—the finest mathematician of the class. Excellence in mathematics was not infrequently counterbalanced by inaptitude in languages. Excellence in languages is rarely accompanied by like ability in "math." Yet Quimby was to become in Grant's eyes the most enviable man of all their number when, in 1852, he resigned from the army to take a professorship of mathematics. Of the members of this class of 1843, Franklin, Peck, J. J. Reynolds, Augur, C. S. Hamilton and Fred Steele rose with Grant to the grade of major-general in the command of volunteers during the great war of the nation. Ingalls became famous as chief quartermaster of the armies in Virginia, Clarke as a chief commissary, Reynolds and Hardie in the staff, and Potter, Dent and Judah won their stars as brigadiers.

Two of their brave young band, Chadbourne and Hazlitt, met their soldier fate when mere boys, killed in the earliest battles of the Mexican War, while George Stevens, of the Dragoons, after valiant deeds at Palo Alto and Resaca, was drowned in attempting the passage of the Rio Grande. Two, Northern born, for some strange reason forgot their duty and their flag, and tendered their swords in '61 to the States arrayed against the Union. Two fell by the wayside and left the service by sentence of court-martial. To one and to one alone it was vouchsafed, after most gallant and conspicuous services in battle while only a beardless subaltern, after trials, vicissitudes and humiliations that might well have crushed a stouter heart, to take up arms against a sea of troubles, to triumph over every adverse influence, to rise to the command in chief of the greatest army of modern times, and then, acclaimed by the entire nation, to the highest honors and rewards ever accorded by the people of the United States, and all this through the profession of all others he would never have willingly chosen—the cheery, modest, but most determined lad, Mr. Hamer's appointee from Georgetown, Ohio. West Point indeed had verified the confident prediction of Jesse Grant. It had developed the latent something that the father declared was slumbering in the son.

But life at the Military Academy in the old days had little of the life one now can see there any sunshiny day. Railways and steam ferries were only just beginning to be heard of in the beautiful Highlands of the Hudson. Perched on its rocky promontory, compassed about by its mighty barriers of wooded heights, swept by the swift tides of the noble river, the little military bailiwick in the heart of the Empire State was as isolated as though it had been walled in and the public barred out. Visitors to the Academy, who came often in the summer time, were landed at the old north dock from the dayboat plying 'twixt New York and the bustling river towns.

Even in the forties it took the better part of a long summer day to reach the Academy from any one of the river towns above and below, and as for the two hundred and fifty young soldiers in cadet gray, selected from all over the Union and secluded there to be trained for its military service, only once in two years, except in rare individual cases, did they set foot beyond its borders. They took no part in presidential inaugurations (the first time they ever appeared at Washington was when one of their number who entered in '39, hoping to learn enough to become a teacher of mathematics, was being escorted to the capitol to take oath as Chief Magistrate of the Union he had been largely instrumental in saving). They had no annual outing for the great game on Franklin Field, for Annapolis was only just evolving from a dream of George Bancroft. They had no base-ball, foot-ball, basket-ball teams, no gymnasium worth the name. They had had some rings and bars or wooden "horses" in the ground floor of the old Academic building, but just the year before Grant and his fellows were started on their slow race, these impedimenta were dragged out, the floor was carpeted with tan bark, and presently equine and ammoniac aromas ascended to the recitation rooms above. Riding at last had been added to the curriculum. A sergeant of dragoons and half a dozen troopers had been brought over from the cavalry station at Carlisle Barracks, Pennsylvania, together with a small collection of quadrupeds—animals whose pedigree and proficiency as saddlers, however, had not been subject to examination. A sorrier lot of riding-school mounts could hardly be found on the face of the globe, but they were merrily welcomed. Bad as they looked and were, they supplied a long-felt want and about the only lawful diversion known to the Corps of Cadets.

Just how young men could live through the dull, dreary monotony of the five wintry months of each of those academic years it is difficult now to see. Aroused at daybreak by the thunder of the reveille drums, hustled out to roll-call, then back to their bare and cheerless rooms, to sweep out for inspection and sit shivering through an enforced study period of an hour or two before breakfast, marched to meals three times a day (about the only out-of-door exercise they had from October to April), penned up in quarters when not at recitation or drawing, permitted no healthful sport of any kind except on a Saturday afternoon, and then provided with the means for none, the marvel is that more numerously they did not break down in health or break over the rules. Grant says he took to tobacco principally because it was forbidden. The lessons were long and hard, but study hours were longer and if anything harder, for nothing but study was prescribed.

43

The forcing house system, according to the theory of the day, would achieve the best results, and so far as rule and regulation could make it, cadet life, nearly nine months of each year, was well high monastic.

As a natural result the lads overleaped at times the barriers and set forth in search of adventure. These were the halcyon days of dear old Benny Havens, whose bones are now mouldering in the hillside graveyard a little below " the Falls," but whose soul goes marching on through song, story and tradition, and whose fame will live long as that of the brainiest of many of his patrons. To skip to Benny's of a cold December night, when the officer in charge had " doused his glim," and the stars were gleaming on the glistening breastplate of the Hudson, was a matter of but twenty minutes. Skates in hand, the daring fellows would tiptoe out of barracks, scramble down the cliff at Kosciuszko's Garden, don their steels on the icy flats beneath, and then go skimming away down stream to where, just below the foaming little cataract, a big, roomy, stout-built, wooden-shuttered, two-story house stood on a rocky ledge at the water's brink—all darkness without, all gleam and glow, warmth and welcome within. Oh, what nights of song and wassail, of cheer and laughter, of feast and fun, enlivened the dull, dead monotony of those dark and dreary months! What hours of mirth and merriment were these wrung from the bleak chronicles of barrack life! Oh, that with all the reminiscences ever written—Grant, Sherman, Sheridan, Scofield, Keyes, Howard, Hamilton, Strong, Boynton, and fondest of them all, by Morris Schaff, in whom " the Spirit of old West Point " lives sweet and incarnate—there might have been those of him we hailed long years as patron saint—genial, fatherly, blessed and benevolent old Benny Havens! His stories could have outranked them all as his song runs on forever.

But before the academic year of study had its

opening in September, there were some ten weeks of strictly soldier work in camp, to the newcomers the harshest and sternest of their career. Those were the weeks in which the raw, untutored lads from field, farm and village, had to be transformed as speedily as possible into the smartest, snappiest, most precise of soldiers, spick and span in dress, spotless in arms and equipment. These were the days of the "ramrod" tactics of Winfield Scott—the starch and stock and buckram days of the army. "Old Fuss and Feathers" his detractors called him, but with all his pomps and vanities a splendid soldier was Scott, a model either on the drill ground or in deadly battle. Ten years had rolled away since the relief of Major Worth as commandant, the idol of the Corps of Cadets, the ideal drill-master of the army, but the methods and mannerisms of that most soldierly of instructors were still followed, the snap and style of his drill (pronounced by Prof. Church, who had seen every commandant from Worth in 1822, to good old "Beau" Neill in 1878, "the most electric of them all") still lived in the cadet battalion, and our farm-bred Ulysses had the time of his life trying to "fall in" with it. There was probably no man in his class to whom it came harder.

Phlegmatic in temperament and long given to ease and deliberation in all his movements at home, this springing to attention at the tap of the drum, this snapping together of the heels at the sound of a sergeant's voice, this sudden freezing to a rigid pose without the move of a muscle, except at the word of command, was something almost beyond him. It seemed utterly unnatural, if not utterly repugnant. Accustomed to swinging along the winding banks of the White Oak, or the cow paths of the pasture lot, this moving only at a measured pace of twenty-eight inches, and one hundred and ten to the minute, and all in strict unison with the step of the guide on the marching flank or at the head of column, came ten times harder than ever did the pages of "analytical" or the calculus. Grant had no sense of rhythm. He had no joy in martial music. The thrill and inspiration of the drum and fife, or the beautiful harmonies of the old Academy band, then a famous organization, were utterly lost on Ulysses Grant. In all that class of 1843, it may well be doubted if there lived one solitary soul who found there less to like or more to shrink from than this seventeen-year-old lad who, thanks to the opportunities and to the training there given them, was in less than a quarter of a century to be hailed as the foremost soldier of more than two millions of men in the Union blue.

All the same he had silently donned the queer little bob-tailed, bell-buttoned "coatee" of the fashion of 1812, the skin-tight trousers of white drilling, the "uniform" shoes of the pattern worn by the rank and file of the army, but luckily made to measure. It wasn't hard to button that gray straight jacket about his slender waist—he was one of the slimmest of the Corps —but the high black stock at the throat was a nuisance, and the little turn-over white collar, pinned to the inner side of that rigid necklet of gray, a source of endless bother and demerit. A crease, a wrinkle or a blotch would bring the heartless report of "Grant—collar soiled at morning parade," and reports of this character, it must be owned, rained thick and fast upon his record. "Belts twisted," "Gloves torn," "Shoes not polished," "Brasses tarnished," "Not keeping dressed marching to dinner" (which did not imply that he was losing some of his apparel: It was simply the West Point way of saying that for a second or two he was out of line), and above all, "Losing step" were "skins" that are samples of those which even to the last year of the four kept the future head of the nation far, very far, from the head of his class.

And yet even that cadet "plebe" camp was not

utterly unhappy; and yet the long winter of work that followed had its hours of hope and encouragement. The drills developed healthy appetite that made even the dubious fare of the cadet mess hall, as in those days provided, nutritious and welcome. The hard day's work, followed by a swim in the Hudson, promoted sound sleep and digestion. The ordeal of camp was over at last. The snowy tents were struck at the tap of the drum. The jaunty battalion, with colors flying and heads held high, marched blithely away to winter quarters, and two days thereafter the lessons of the long academic course were begun.

Then it was that Grant made a discovery which gave him surprise and gratification. Out of place as he had felt in the serried ranks, striving awkwardly at times to keep step with some frolicsome file leader who delighted in tripping him, he found himself at ease and almost at home in the mathematical section room.

Mention has been made of his purchase of an algebra in the spring of the year, and his finding it all Greek. Now in the fall of '39 he stepped into the presence of an instructor who made its complicated pages luminous with meaning. Now the curt, sharp, stinging comments of the cadet officers gave place to clear and kindly explanation of every doubtful paragraph. Now he found himself listening absorbed to the teachings of a master who was the monarch of his art, and in less than a week that which had seemed burdened with mystery unfolded itself to his receptive mind, under the guidance of the clearest demonstrator he or West Point had ever known—the little man with the head of an intellectual giant and the heart of gold—Albert E. Church, for nearly half a century the unchallenged chief of the Department of Mathematics.

And Church was but one of a little coterie of great teachers, all of them then young, vigorous and full of enthusiasm in their work. From the thirties to the seventies, forty long years, every graduate of the Academy was made and molded by these men. They more than deserve the tribute of fervent gratitude and affection that many a pupil would gladly pen, did he believe he could do even faint justice to the subject. It was the writer's privilege to stand almost "in the presence," the day on which the general-in-chief of all the armies once again appeared within the academic halls, and with full heart and eager hands, shyly, almost faltering made his reverence to the men who it might almost be declared had made him. Beyond all question they had shaped and molded the fine and flawless clay that came to them in Ulysses Grant.

CHAPTER V

WEST POINT AND ITS PROFESSORS

From its infancy until the summer of 1866 the Military Academy remained under the guidance of the Corps of Engineers. From the days of Jonathan Williams to and including the administration of George W. Cullum, only officers of the Corps of Engineers were its superintendents, and from 1818, until July 30th, 1866, only the chief of the Corps of Engineers served as its inspector. Joseph G. Swift, its first graduate, was its first inspector. Sylvanus Thayer, who longer than any other served as superintendent, never rose to the head of the Corps, but the graduates of his quarter century administration would never admit that he had an equal. Joseph G. Totten, its inspector from the year before Grant's admission, 1838, until the year in which Grant became general-in-chief, 1864, never served as superintendent, yet had studied the Academy from "turret to foundation stone." Richard Delafield, who succeeded him as inspector, had twice served as superintendent. In January, 1861, when most of the Southern States had severed, as they thought, the ties that bound them to the Union, and war was imminent, it pleased Mr. Secretary Floyd to send Major P. G. T. Beauregard to the Point, with orders to assume command and relieve Colonel Delafield. That closed the career of Floyd, who was himself promptly relieved by Joseph Holt, and the obnoxious order as promptly revoked. Finally, last of the Engineer superintendents in the direct and unbroken line, there came to the Point in 1864, one of its most devoted and distinguished graduates in the person of George W. Cullum of the Class of 1833. It is only to be regretted that the selection had not been made years earlier, and that it could

4   49

not have held years longer. No man in or out of the Corps of Engineers better knew the Academy, better served it, loved it, than did General Cullum.

As given, not in the order of their establishment, but in the records of the days whereof we write, the Academy consisted of the Departments of Tactics, of Civil and Military Engineering, of Natural and Experimental Philosophy, of Mathematics, of Drawing, of Chemistry and Mineralogy, of Ordnance and Gunnery, of Geography, History and Ethics, and finally of French. The Department of Tactics was purely military and its head was the Commandant of Cadets, whose term of office rarely exceeded four years. The others were as entirely academic, and, with the exception of ordnance, were headed and controlled by men chosen by the Corps of Engineers and for what were then considered life positions The utmost care had ever been taken in the selection, with the result that, in 1839 when Grant and his classmates entered upon their career, the three great departments—Engineering, Philosophy, and Mathematics—were presided over by men who stood unsurpassed in their line and unchallenged in their high estate until, bowed with the weight of years, they successively retired. One and all they were there to greet their former pupil when at the close of the great war, as commanding general, he once more stood before them.

"Dean of the Faculty" was Dennis H. Mahan, Professor of Engineering. Next to him stood W. H. C. Bartlett, Professor of Natural and Experimental Philosophy. Third on the list was Alfred E. Church, Professor of Mathematics. Each in turn had been graduated at the head of his class. Each in his earliest days of service had been assigned as instructor in the scientific branches of the curriculum. Each had proved his mettle and been chosen for further advancement. It is no disparagement of their successors, or of their associates, to say that for thirty years this immortal trio stood paramount at West Point and gave the tone that made it famous. Strong and virile chiefs were they, spurring the laggards, cheering the ambitious, hewing ever close to the line and standing shoulder to shoulder against every attempt to lower the standard. Stern in their creed they may have been, but unerring in their practice. To their hands the nation had committed its chosen to be schooled for its defense and fitted for the profession that demands of its votaries the supreme measure of self-sacrifice and devotion. Men of gentler mold, but of enthusiasm like unto their own, were at the head of other departments, notably Baily in Chemistry, and later the courtly and genial soldier who had so long been his first assistant, Henry L. Kendrick,—both well worthy to sit in council with the immortal three.

In the Department of Drawing, where to his own surprise Grant was destined to do some very creditable work, the artists of America were represented by Prof. Robert W. Weir. The Department of French, wherein Grant found himself utterly at sea, was conducted by Prof. Claudius Berard. Gentlemen of the old school were these, but being chosen from civil life, they wisely left all matters of academic or military discipline to their more martial associates. The matter of military discipline, *pur et simple,* was vested in the head of the Department of Tactics and in the person of the Commandant of Cadets. This office was filled in Grant's day by Colonel Charles F. Smith, whom Grant declared his ideal of the officer and the gentleman. A more knightly, courteous and soldierly man never wore the uniform of the United States. For three of his four cadet years Grant lived under the constant supervision of this most distinguished officer and looked up to him as he did to no other. When in 1842 and the close of First Class Camp, Colonel Smith finally gave way to another, Grant and his classmates thought never to look upon his like again, and in less than five years it was Grant's lot to share with Smith the honors and plaudits of their chiefs and comrades in one of the fiercest assaults before the walls of Mexico. In less than twenty years, strangest of all, it was Grant's lot to be issuing orders in front of Donelson to his right hand man, his best and noblest division commander, his most loyal subordinate in that first fierce campaign—the commandant of his admiration in his cadet days at the Point. It reads like romance.

For the first two years of this academic career, from September 1st to June, and for six days out of every seven, the young West Pointer of the *ante bellum* period was reasonably sure of coming under the eyes of Prof. Church, and that mathematical course is the basis of West Point's educational system. At the beginning of the third year of his bondage, as Grant regarded it, Prof. Bartlett took up the reins where, at the close of the Calculus, they had been dropped by Church, and for nine months longer the pupil was driven at steady, unswerving gait through the intricacies of Mechanics and the later glories of Astronomy. In the fourth or final period, he fell under the daily comment and criticism of the Professor of Engineering, whose duty it was to impart the finishing touches. Keen, incisive, often satirical, sometimes sarcastic, his daily rasping stung the mental skin to vehement action—a recitation in Engineering or Strategy in that awesome presence was an intellectual needle bath of ice water, swift followed by swifter rub with a steel wire towel. The cadet who came before Mahan with merely a superficial knowledge of the subject inevitably found himself in pitiable plight. There never was a quicker eye or sharper tongue for shams of any kind. Unerringly and almost instantly he could discover just how much a pupil knew on any one point, and then if

MAJOR-GENERAL CHARLES F. SMITH
Grant's hero to the end

that pupil were not humility personified it was rich to hear Mahan dissect him. No cadet from the head of the class down to the foot was safe from his sarcasm or proof against his prodding. They feared even as they admired him. They gloried in his teachings as one does in a desperate battle—after it is over. There was just one quality in a pupil which he apostrophized again and again as indispensable to the would-be commander of fighting men. Without it brilliancy, knowledge, book learning, study, strategy and tactics, all combined, were of little worth. "Common sense," said Mahan, was worth them all, and was the one quality without which no man could hope to win. This he held to as a theory prior to the great war of the sixties; this he triumphantly declared, as a result of observation of all its leaders, a proved and petrified fact; and this he emphasized in his lecture room in May, 1866, to the very last class graduated under the auspices of the Corps of Engineers. As the crowning example of his theory he pointed to the career and record of the man who away back in '43 had impressed the master above all his mates, the shy, unobtrusive, somewhat unsoldierly youth whom we have seen entering in 1839, Mr. Hamer's unwilling candidate from the Buckeye State.

Here is what the great teacher said late in the sixties of his modest pupil of the early forties:

Grant is remembered at his alma mater as having a cheery and at the same time firm aspect, and a prompt, decided manner. His class standing was among that grade which has given to the line of the Army some of its most valuable officers, like Lyon, Reynolds, Sedgwick, etc. . . . He was what we termed a first section man in all his scientific studies; that is, one who accomplishes the full course. He always showed himself a thinker and a steady worker. He belonged to the class of compactly strong men who went at their task at once and kept at it until they had finished. His mental machine was of the powerful, low pressure class, which condenses its own steam and consumes its own smoke, and which pushes steadily forward and drives all obstacles before it.

But all this came as the result or end of the four years of training. We have still to speak of the means.

There were other famous teachers at the Academy in Grant's day, men who helped to shape his course in life, and some of them, later, to be closely and intimately associated with it. Chief of these was William W. S. Bliss of the Class of '33 and of the Fourth U. S. Infantry, assistant in the Department of Mathematics, he whose charm of manner and whose gifts and graces were such that he had won from his own classmates the pet name of " Perfect." When it is remembered that then and ever after, cadet nicknames were bestowed rather for some salient physical peculiarity, or in commemoration of some luckless and ludicrous slip, it is indicative of the extreme of cadet regard in the case of Bliss. The same gifts attached to him as instructor in mathematics, and later still as the brilliant and admired aide-de-camp of Zachary Taylor—the same gifts had so impressed his pupil in 1840, and his regimental comrades in the Mexican war, that the news of his lamented death, in 1854, brought grief and mourning to the man of all others to whom that death brought temporary benefit. Promoted captain Fourth Infantry, *vice* Bliss, deceased, Ulysses Grant stepped in 1853 from the quartermastership of the regiment, a position which he had occupied much of the time since the Mexican war, into the captaincy long held by Bliss, and with it into the control of adverse fate and influences. That upward step led him within the twelve-month down and out of the regiment in which he was held in honor and affection, and which, in spite of his dislike of the military service, he had yet learned to love. There were days of bitter sorrow and humiliation in store for him whose cheery manner and round, boyish face, as says Mahan, gave little evidence of the strength and purpose stored up in his character. Possibly in the Divine pity and the prescience which " shapes our ends "

54

it was deemed essential to the fruition of the future that for the time being the wanderings of Ulysses should lead him to the desert places, through penury and privation, through slight and sufferance, through the valley of the shadow that, having explored the depths he should the more vehemently strike against their more deadly miasma, that he should presently reappear, crowned with strength and energy, and then sweep onward with vision undimmed and purpose undaunted to the crowning triumph of an utterly unmatched career.

One may well be warranted in believing that there was ever present with Grant the guidance of these great teachers of his boy days, that in the hours of his humiliation and neglect the spirit of the young soldier who won such fame at Monterey, at Molino and Chapultepec, and yet so soon found it forgotten and outweighed, was sustained by the spirit of his admired predecessor, teacher and regimental comrade, " Perfect " Bliss. Be that as it may, through all the trials that were to come, this much is known from his own Memoirs and from the admiring testimony of old comrades who were occasionally thrown with him—he never lost his faith, or grit, or hope, and even for those who had most harshly judged, most despitefully used him, he never lost his own sense of justice, he never failed to exercise his charity. Whether he knew it or not, there stood ever by him " The Spirit of Old West Point."

For even in his cadet days there had come to him an odd presentiment or vision. For many a long year, remembering possibly the fun and raillery at home over his father's hapless boast concerning the phrenologist's prediction, Grant kept this to himself, but in his Memoirs he admits that the sight of the magnificent Winfield Scott, full panoplied and in the dazzling uniform of the earlier days, receiving on review the

55

salute of the rigid gray and white line, awoke in him a strange conviction that some day it should come to him, too, to stand in Scott's stead on that beautiful parade ground, to hear the cannon thunder and the glistening line crash to the " present," to see the sword blades gleaming and the silken colors drooping, all in his honor.

But enough of sentiment and dreaming. It is time to take up the practical, every day, humdrum of cadet life as Ulysses found it. To tell of that and possibly of a certain few besides, his classmates, whose association in those early days led to momentous consequences in days to come, and then to lead him to the longed-for hour of which his comrades used to sing, and he to smile in sympathy, for sing he could not:

> Hurrah, hurrah, for the merry bright month of June
>   That opens a life so new,
> When we doff the cadet and don the brevet
>   And change the gray for the blue.

CHAPTER VI

WEST POINT AND ITS CURRICULUM

THE first year's course at the Military Academy in the days of Grant was confined mainly to recitations in mathematics, in French and in what were termed English studies. The lessons were long, but abundant time was given in which to learn them, and every reasonable precaution was taken to insure the purpose of the study hours. Inspections of quarters were frequent during the day and sentries twixt seven and ten at night paced the corridors and barracks, and occasionally peered into the rooms to satisfy themselves and inquisitive officers that everything on their posts was " All right, sir." This was a comprehensive formula. It meant that every cadet in that corridor was in his own room and presumably engaged in his allotted task, that no smoking, skylarking or surreptitious enterprise of any kind was going on. At 9.30 P.M. the drums and fifes came thundering " tattoo " among the resounding walls, and then, and not till then, the cadet was free to make down his bed and turn in for the night. At ten P.M. there came three sharp staccato drum taps, at which summons the cadet inspectors of subdivisions made swift circuit of the rooms to see to it that every man was in and every light was out.

But cadet sentries were not required to see to it that the book in use was Davies' Bourdon or Church's Analytical. The library of the Academy was even then well stocked with standard fiction. Cadets were given daily access to its shelves during the brief release from quarters between four P.M. and the sunset gun. One book a week might be taken out by any cadet so minded, and it presently resulted that the reading habits of the father had in Grant's case, become fixed in the son. It was the one relaxation of that gloomy year of his " plebedom."

Finding after the first few weeks, under Prof. Church and " Perfect " Bliss, that algebra presented no difficulties, Grant proceeded to take things easily. The routine, the roll-calls, the ramrod precision in every detail, the incessant facings and marchings bored and wearied him. The studies at the start failed to arouse his energies. He had time, now that camp and its hourly drills were over, to reflect on his surroundings and his prospects. The more he saw of the former the less he liked them; the more he could hear of the latter the less they appealed to him.

But in boy days about Georgetown he had learned at his mother's knee the old, old admonition as to him who " having put his hand to the plough," there was to be neither look nor footstep backward. The die had been cast. For weal or for woe he had signed with Uncle Sam, and he was made of stuff too stern to think of falter now. Very modestly, long years later, he had disclaimed, as has been said, any right to membership among the descendants of the vehement old Clan Grant, yet, subconsciously, perhaps, and in his own simple, matter-of-fact way, the young cadet was living up to its spirited motto, " Stand fast—stand sure." He had entered for the contest, and though he cared nothing for the prize, he meant to fight on to the end. That trait proved rather a valuable asset to the nation in the by and by. We read of it at intervals in the sixties.

Meantime, to make plebe life bearable, he took to reading. The standard novelists of the day were Scott and Bulwer. The sea tales of Marryat and Cooper were fascinating. The unwritten laws of the Corps of Cadets left the Fourth classmen entirely to themselves throughout the barrack days of the initial year—the object being to level the array, to develop class feeling, and to teach them thoroughly to know one another. Outside of the few in his own corridor or section, Grant mingled very little, even among his own classmates. Kindly and good natured, he was nevertheless looked upon at the start as a trifle shy and unresponsive. They let him alone, and in his possible loneliness the authors whom he read so carefully became his friends and familiars.

And so it happened that after the January examinations and the closing of algebra, with Grant standing easily in the highest section, and the taking up of geometry and French, he had acquired the habit of only reading once through the lesson of the day, and of giving hours to the pages of romance. Moreover, he was writing much that winter to home and mother. There was rude awakening to come with the new term. Geometry was less clear to him than were the intricacies of algebra. "Shades, shadows and perspective" were a bagatelle, but "descriptive" proved a stumbling block, though there was not then enough of it to greatly lower his standing. The foe that threatened his defeat was the French language.

From start to finish Grant could never master nor abide that tongue—the language of courts and diplomacy, the language of all others that Talleyrand must have had in mind when he declared its main purpose was to conceal thought. Holding his own in mathematics during the second half, Grant found himself going down section by section in French, until there was danger of his dropping out entirely, and yet it seemed to give him no concern.

A furious debate was raging that winter in Congress. A quarter century had passed without a war, excepting the deadly encounters with our Indian wards, which always cost the army heavily. The very arguments we hear to-day and heard so very often in the fifties were being urged against all expenditure for military purposes, and it was seriously proposed to abolish West Point as a costly and unnecessary burden, even as a menace to the interests of the people. The friends of the Academy took alarm, and one cadet, at least, took comfort. So probable seemed the success of the movement that he had become almost indifferent to the weekly marks. He was too young at the time to realize that in all such anti-military demonstrations one hears mainly the orators of the antis. The wiser heads are silent until it comes to a vote. When the opposition finally ended and Grant found that the Fates were with West Point, and though he knew it not, with him, he was disturbed to see how far he had dropped in French, and how his marks even in mathematics had suffered. Moreover, by that time the spring was well advanced and there was left too short a while in which to recover the lost standing. In French he could not regain his ground, even with the encouragement of kindly old Claudius Berard. This accounts for his low grade in the Fourth class year.

Another matter that worried him awhile: he found himself registered as Ulysses Simpson Grant, and sought through proper military channels to have it changed to the Hiram Ulysses of his birth. But the initials given him by Mr. Hamer appealed to the authorities of Uncle Sam at Washington, and Sam Grant he was destined to remain.

In June the class of '43 was advanced to the dignity of "yearlings," and the delight of welcoming the new-comers—perhaps the most thrilling epoch of cadet life—and then another trait became noticeable in Grant: he would take no part in any "hazing" that inflicted humiliation or pain. He worried through the summer camp of 1840 with no more enthusiasm, but with all the serenity, displayed in that of '39. He welcomed the return to barracks and the studies of that second year, even though French continued a bugbear, because he

shone in the section room through analytical geometry
and calculus, standing in the highest grade, and finishing tenth in rank. Drawing, too, proved attractive.

Standing only " one file from foot " in French, at
the end of the plebe year, he had climbed to forty-
fourth place in that study in a class numbering fifty-
three, at the end of the second. Mathematics and drawing were far easier to him, and therein he stood far
higher. But then there was the Conduct Roll. From
first to last there never was a time when " demerit "—
the black marks given for every violation of the regulations, great or small—did not throw him back into
the lower fourth of his class. Just what made up the
bulk of the reports at his expense it is easy to conjec-
ture. He never could be " military " as it was termed,
and yet, in spite of all his distaste for soldiership, he had
found a friend and believer in the soldier of all others
whom he most admired—their model commandant and
head of the Department of Tactics, Colonel Charles F.
Smith.

For purposes of instruction the Corps was then
divided into four companies of about sixty each, making a compact little battalion which, including the cadet
officers, was about two hundred and fifty strong. As
the plebes became yearlings in June some twenty of
their number, those most soldierly in bearing, in dress
and in general conduct, were decorated with the chev-
rons of a corporal. At the end of the second year the
best of these were advanced to the grade of sergeant—
the very best becoming sergeant-major and first (or
" orderly ") sergeant. At the end of the third year,
and just before they entered on the glories of First Class
camp, the highest prizes of the military course were
meted out—the model soldier officer of the class becoming the cadet adjutant, four of their number being appointed cadet captains, and twelve were named lieutenants. In the wildest dreams of his plebe days, if

ever so matter-of-fact a fellow had any, Grant never beheld himself in any higher rôle than that of a cadet private—the grade with which all start alike and all but a chosen few retain to the end. But something in that unobstrusive, uncomplaining youth from southern Ohio appealed to the soldier sense of Colonel Smith. At all events, some two or three of the class fell short of the commandant's expectations and, to Grant's utter amaze, his name was read out before the battalion the night they returned from " furlough " late in August— Sam Grant was made sergeant.

It was told at the time that the wit of the class explained it by saying " the Commandant had to get ' Sam ' out of sight and into the line of file closers where his being out of step was less apt to be noticed. The only way he could fix it was to make Sam a sergeant." Color was given to this half malicious explanation by the fact that when the First Class officers were " made," the following June, Sergeant Sam was incontinently dropped. With unruffled composure he laid aside the sword and stepped back into the ranks, a First Class private, and the real explanation was that Grant didn't seek the office and didn't want it, because it involved certain duties and responsibilities from which he shrank—those of reporting minor errors, neglects and misdeeds of fellow cadets.

Certain it is that Grant got more demerit as a sergeant than he ever did when a plebe and in any one of the years in which he served as private, and yet the commandant would have it there was soldier stuff in " that young fellow with the old head," and, as has been said, Smith lived to prove he was right—lived on to see his would-not-be sergeant win the highest honors accorded a subaltern in the Mexican war, lived to be his pupil's most loyal and devoted subordinate at Donelson, and died but a few weeks later up the Tennessee at Savannah, his most distinguished and lamented associate. Even Sherman had not then reached in Grant's affection and gratitude the place held by Charles F. Smith.

"Entirely cool and without emotion," says an old friend and neighbor, when he drove him from the end of the stage route to the waiting family at Georgetown, was "Lys" when he came home on furlough. It seems that something of warmth and sentiment was looked for, but that wasn't the way of the Grants. Hearty "How are yous?" passed between father, son and brothers, but the meeting between the mother and her first-born, now in his twentieth year, was not for even neighbors' eyes to see, nor for Grant to speak of then or thereafter. Frank as are his Memoirs, there are some matters he leaves to the imagination. For instance, there was one matter greatly to his young renown which he does not mention at all.

Perhaps it is because there was no need, for all West Point was telling of it at the time, and it was not long in spreading throughout the army. In his cadet days there was one accomplishment in which he outclassed the entire Corps. He was but a tolerable fencer, he was no dancer, but even the riding master himself was no match for him in horsemanship. Sam Grant's riding was the envy of every man who saw it.

Only in 1839 had riding become a part of the instruction at the Point, the first teacher being James McAuley, who is said to have had a fair knowledge of the old-time cavalry seat and not much else. Nevertheless, it was he who schooled the Class of '43 until within six months of their graduation, when he resigned and his place was promptly filled by a gruff and martial dragoon of the German type—one Henry R. Hershberger, who lasted six years, and saw Grant's, and five other classes through their graduation ride.

Mention has been made of the queer lot of horses at the Point in 1840. Few of them were good, some were positively bad, and one or two well nigh intractable. Of the last was a big, raw-boned sorrel, named York. He had a trick of rearing and tumbling over backwards that was disconcerting to most riders. McAuley could do nothing with him, but young Grant quietly said he thought the horse could be ridden, and proceeded to show how. No matter what the brute could do, except lie down and roll, Grant seemed to stick to him like a burr. He broke him of rearing and tumbling by a well-directed tap or two of the butt of the pistol, between the ears. Then with patience inexhaustible he began to teach that horse better manners. " He'll kill you some day, Sam," said a classmate. " I can die but once," is said to have been Grant's answer, though it sounds unlike him. York became known as Grant's horse, and when pompous old Hershberger took up the reins in January, '43, he speedily saw in Grant the most accomplished rider and trainer in the class, and wisely left him to his own devices. The result is an old story, best told, probably, by General James B. Fry in his Reminiscences. Grant in his Memoirs never so much as refers to it.

As General Fry says:

" The class, still mounted, was formed in line through the centre of the hall. The riding master placed the leaping bar higher than a man's head and called out ' Cadet Grant.' A clean-faced, slender, blue-eyed young fellow, weighing about one hundred and twenty pounds, dashed from the ranks on a powerfully built chestnut-sorrel horse, and galloped down the opposite side of the hall. As he turned at the farther end and came into the stretch at which the bar was placed, the horse increased his pace and measuring his stride for the great leap before him, bounded into the air and cleared the bar, carrying his rider as if man and beast had been welded together. The spectators were breathless."

Prof. Coppee's description of York and his method of leaping adds to the fame of Grant's horsemanship. It would seem that York in taking a high bar never did so from the stride, but rather as the cat leaps, crouching first and then bounding upward—the most difficult of all leaps for the rider to sit either gracefully or securely.

Moreover, Coppee's description of Grant, the cadet rider, goes more into detail. The picture he draws of the quiet young horseman is typical of the times. The Corps had no riding dress in '43. The designated platoon donned its oldest coat and trousers, held the latter down over the shoe by the strap of the uncouth spurs then issued to our dragoons; the cadets went through their hour in the dust and dirt and semi-darkness, with little thought of appearances. Neither then nor for fifty years thereafter did the cadets learn very much of the finesse of equitation. The methods were as crude as the mounts, but in most cases a good military seat was acquired and many a dashing cavalry rider was developed. For many a long year the record of Sam Grant and York stood unmatched, and the methods of the riding hall unchanged.

Riding and reading seem to have been Grant's only recreation during the few years of his cadet life. There was one diversion or distraction, however, that is significant. Although he did not dance it seems that even in undergraduate days he was susceptible to feminine influence, and to one of his most loyal friends and faithful biographers Grant himself told the story. The last two years of his academic life were quite filled with romantic dreamings in which a certain fair daughter of the Jerseys was the central figure. Always courteous and gentle to women, Grant found pleasure in their society. He was a good talker, too, and a cheery companion. One who knew and admired him, wrote of his sunny manner, and his trim, slender, soldierly form. West Point had taken the farm boy stoop out of his back and shoulders, even though it returned with the weight of cares and the farm days that followed his

5   65

resignation from the army in '54. Though never attaining the cadet standard of soldierly smartness, Grant seemed martial enough, no doubt, in the eyes of girl friends at home and at the Point. In one of these latter he became sentimentally interested, yet won his wager that she would marry before he would be free to wed. It was fortunate for his peace of mind, perhaps, that he saw the inevitable in abundant time.

And as it drew toward its close Grant's cadet life proved after all not so wearisome. He had acquired a fine education in science, a fair one in history and in the essentials,—a mental discipline given probably in those days in no other school in the United States, and he had blossomed out, as it were, during the last two years,—mingled more with his kind and become known to and appreciated by his fellows in the Corps. That cheery manner had gained him the good will of men in the upper classes, even while it endeared him to so many of his own. As for the juniors, as they entered year by year, his simple kindliness, his utter lack of pretense, speedily won him their liking, and as they grew to observe him and better to know him, that liking became solid respect. In his own class he had little by little come to be looked upon as one of the soundest, surest men, "Not brilliant," said they, "but shrewd, square and full of common sense."

Even in " plebe " days there had been First Classmen who had a pleasant word for Grant. There was his " statesman," Sherman, from up Lancaster way, a quick, nervous, energetic, talkative fellow. There was the grave, dignified Virginian Thomas, there were Van-Vliet and Getty and that farsighted Southerner Ewell, who at the outbreak of the war in '61 was heard to say: " There's one man I hope the North won't find out in time. He's quick and resolute and daring," and he was speaking of Grant. In the class next Sherman's were Lyon, Garesché and John F. Reynolds, all gallant soldiers, all destined to be shot dead in battle for the Union. There were the two Garnetts, Bob and Dick, both to die fighting for the other side. There was Levi Gantt, who was to head the stormers at Chapultepec, and fall " shot to flinders," yet urging on his men. There was Richardson, who was to meet his soldier fate at Antietam, and Don Carlos Buell, destined to command the Army of the Ohio side by side with him, Grant, of the Army of the Tennessee. In the class just ahead of Grant was another of his statesmen—Rosecrans, whom he was to relieve at Chattanooga. There were George Mason and Henry Stanton, whom he envied, because they entered the dragoons on graduation, both doomed to die in battle. There was Williamson, whom in '51 he envied even more, because he had become professor of mathematics at the Kentucky Military Institute. There was the tall Southerner, Longstreet, who was to stand up as one of his supporters at his wedding, and stand up against him in many a hard-fought field, and, later still, by him and because of him, to be drawn again into the fold of the Union.

Then entering the year after him were men whose friendship he valued. Buckner, of Kentucky, who "staked" him when his fortunes were at lowest ebb, whose sword he received in unconditional surrender at Donelson, and whose purse he replenished on the spot. There were Burwell, Woods, and J. P. Smith, who battled side by side with him at Molino, Monterey and Chapultepec, each dying on the field, while he, fighting as fearlessly, went on without a scar to the achievement of his higher destiny. There was Hancock, superb on many a field and unrivalled as a corps commander. There was Aleck Hayes who, brave as Cæsar and beloved among his generals, was to die under him in the Wilderness. There was Reed, another object of his envy, because in 1850 he, too, had been summoned to the Kentucky institution as professor. There was still another class, that of 1845, in which he had friends and followers—yearlings who looked up to him as a First Classman, and were close to him in days to come—Davy Russell, of his own Fourth Infantry, who was to fall " beneath a soldier's blow " in battle in the Shenandoah, Perry, who was to die fighting at Molino. There were " Baldy " Smith and Thomas J. Wood, who were to win the double stars under his command. There was Thomas G. Pitcher, who, in 1861, mustered into the military service of the United States the Twenty-first Illinois Infantry Volunteers, with their colonel U. S. Grant—Pitcher whom in time it was to be Grant's lot as acting Secretary of War to select for the superintendency of West Point, a jump at once from the highest corps to what was held to be the lowest, when in 1866 the congress took the Academy from the control of the Engineers and threw it open to the line.

There were even plebes who looked up to him, as plebes ever will to First Classmen, lads who entering in '42 spent one year with him in the battalion. Of these were George B. McClellan and Thomas J. Jackson, names destined to become famous but a few years later, to be linked with his own in Mexico, as was that of gallant " Sandy " Rodgers, who, joining Grant's regiment after Monterey, died fighting among the foremost at Chapultepec. In this class, too, were Stoneman, Wilkins, Wilcox and Thomas McConnell, who was to be adjutant of the Fourth Infantry and Grant's fellow staff officer, and finally, at the foot of the class, George E. Pickett, of whom hereafter.

Chosen friends he had in his own class. There were a dozen of them who formed a little circle within the class, the T. I. O. (twelve in one), the dozen who wore a ring with a mystic symbol, and swore eternal friendship, as boys will, and kept it, as boys seldom do. Then as graduation drew nigh, and the class were bidden to set down their preferences for future employment in the army, Grant promptly declared himself for the Dragoons.

Great was his disappointment, though not his surprise, when a few weeks later there reached him at the old home in Ohio the brief official announcement that, as brevet second lieutenant he had been assigned to the Fourth Regiment of Infantry and ordered at the expiration of his graduation leave to report at Jefferson Barracks. There was just one consolation, that was closeness to the home of his chum, classmate and, toward the last, his roommate at the Point—Frederick T. Dent, of Missouri. That he should some day be general-in-chief was already one of Grant's beliefs or fancies, as he has frankly told us. That he should find his own domestic commander-in-chief in the sister of his former chum and in the suburbs of St. Louis he does not seem to have anticipated.

CHAPTER VII

FIRST IMPRESSIONS OF ARMY LIFE

IT cannot be said that Grant's entry into the military service was auspicious. There were several reasons for this. First was the old antipathy to the career of a soldier—he much preferred the arts of peace, the associations of the home, the farm, the fireside. His tastes were domestic, and his belief at the time of graduation was that the United States would have little need of soldiers. In the second place his health had begun to suffer. The fever and ague of his boyhood had left him keenly sensitive to colds, and about Christmas time he had contracted a cough which refused to yield to the treatment in vogue at the Point, which increased as June drew nigh, and which sent him home reduced in flesh and looking and feeling far from well. There had been consumption in the family, and both his father and mother became alarmed. Let it be recorded at once, however, that fears of consumption were banished and the cough gradually routed by the best and most rational treatment yet devised—abundance of open air, sunshine and healthful exercise. As when on cadet furlough, Grant found an excellent roadster all ready for his use, in the old barn, and he spent many hours of every day in saddle, and sometimes in driving, with mother, sister, or possibly some Georgetown girl as a companion, and long before his leave expired he was well on the way to robust health. Yet he was not happy. It has pleased some of his biographers to speak of his class standing as rather low. This is unjust. In all the really difficult branches, those which call for mathematical ability, his standing was high. Moreover, we know that his professors considered him one of the brainiest men of his class. Hardie, his classmate, has gone on record as having said in the spring of 1843: " If ever the country is confronted by a great emergency Sam Grant will be the man to meet it." Prof. Davies declared at Columbia College in New York City, the winter of 1861–62, that he had predicted Grant's generalship as far back as the month of his graduation, and was confident that Prof. Church had equal confidence in him. That Church had that confidence as far back as 1843 is obvious from the fact that he assured Grant of a detail as instructor in the Department of Mathematics.

As summed up in June, 1843, Grant came out sixteenth in engineering and seventeenth in chemistry. He had stood sixteenth in mathematics the first year and tenth the second. He was well up in mechanics and in astronomy. It was in French, in ethics, and in the drill books, that he fell below twenty. In artillery, for instance, he stood as near the foot as he did in French, and in the matter of demerit for minor breaches of the regulations he was, as has been said, among the " lower fourth." His general standing at graduation (twenty-one out of thirty-nine) was lowered, therefore, by these lapses in branches he looked upon with rather good-natured indifference.

But if a military career after all was to be his, a commission in the Dragoons would suit him better than any other branch. He knew and loved horses, knew how to train, care for and humor them. He felt that he would be a capable and useful cavalry officer, and therefore sought the mounted service. In those days we had two regiments of Dragoons and one of Mounted Rifles. Grant had asked for the Dragoons. Now if he had asked for the Rifles, he might have had his wish. The War Department for some reason refused at first to commission any of the Class of '43 in the Dragoons. It assigned George Stevens, Lewis Neill, Rufus Ingalls and Cave J. Couts to the Rifles, and later transferred them to the Dragoons. Grant, too, might have succeeded had he availed himself of this roundabout method, but his application was uncompromising: "Dragoons or Fourth Infantry"—and infantry it proved to be.

Along late in August the new uniform came—the severe, single-breasted, dark-blue frock coat of the existing regulations, absolutely clerical in cut and plainness, its only ornament the row of brass buttons, a pair of shoulder-straps to be worn for "undress," and a pair of gilt epaulets for parade. With this were prescribed sky-blue trousers with a white stripe down the outer seam, a plain black leather sword belt, a sash of crimson silk net, and a flat "Palmetto" cap. There was little to attract the eye in the dress of a soldier of these United States in 1843. There was even less in '61, and Grant's first public appearance in the garb of a subaltern of infantry, as indicative of the respect in which it was held by the proletariat, disgusted him to the extent of wishing he might never have to wear it again. Although in saddle, where he appeared to best advantage, and in the everyday uniform, without sash, belt or epaulets, he was greeted with derisive grins and gibes by youthful fellow citizens, and on his return from a ride to Cincinnati, found that magnate the village blacksmith swaggering ostentatiously about with a pair of broad white stripes of cotton pinned to his trouser seams in obvious and satirical imitation. It is comfort to scores of his brother officers of every grade who on many an occasion have had to suffer like indignities, sometimes at the hands of men who knew better, that they had this at least in common with Grant.

The incidents recorded here added not a little to Grant's aversion to the service. There were times when Grant looked at his father's busy tannery, and asked himself whether it might not have been better to graduate even there; but, once again the old lesson came up before him: he had put his hand to the plough, he had agreed to serve four years as an officer in return for his four years as a cadet, and those four years, at least must be paid in full. If they could be spent teaching mathematics under Prof. Church at the Point, it might not be so bad. While thus detailed he could be on look-out for a professorship in some college, university or academy, and with Prof. Church's recommendation and influence there was little doubt that he could secure a position as many another had done before him.

Another matter deserving serious thought was that of pay. The generally accepted idea concerning a West Pointer was that of a young man who had been boarded, lodged, clothed, coddled and exhaustively educated, all at the expense of the nation, and in addition had been paid nearly a dollar a day—" big wages " at that time. It is true that the cadet was paid twenty-four dollars a month; but not until he left the Point on leave or furlough did he ever see a cent of it. It is true that he was given lodging in barracks, and medical attendance when ill or injured, and a most thorough schooling in science and in discipline, but there the beneficence ended. Out of his eighty cents a day the cadet had to pay for every item of his uniform and clothing, for every morsel that he ate or microbe that he drank, for his barber, his baths, for even the band, in part at least, for blacking and varnishing, for his blankets, mattress, pillow, his every text book, his drawing materials, his shoes, gloves, belts, buckles, brasses, shako, sash and plume, if a cadet officer (and costly items were they, for in the sixties it took much more than a month's pay to buy the sash itself). In fact, if it were not for the monthly stoppage of two dollars to provide for " equipment " on graduation hardly a man could hope to emerge with a cent to his credit, and in the days of Grant the graduate would begin life in the line with the munificent pay of about fifty dollars per mensem, added to which were four rations per diem, valued at forty cents, and the cost of one soldier servant, estimated at eleven dollars a month, plus a ration a day. The total amount of his stipend was less than one hundred dollars a month out of which to defray every expense except those of a living room, a doctor, and wood sufficient to warm him. Furthermore it was expected and required of him that on this sum he should maintain the dignity and station of a gentleman, and be ready to entertain hospitably such fellow citizens as came his way—and many did.

And yet, fortunately for the United States, one may hazard, there were officers and gentlemen who in spite of these and other considerations, found pleasure in army life and association, or else they were gifted with a sense of duty that held them wedded to the task in hand.

In his Memoirs Grant says very little of his home life during those three months of rest and recuperation. Late in August, however, much restored in health, he bade the household adieu, drove to Cincinnati and there took steamer down stream and, in good season, reached what was then one of the largest and most populous of the military posts of the United States. Headquarters and eight of the ten companies of the Fourth Infantry, with as many from the Third, made up the garrison of Jefferson Barracks, only ten miles below St. Louis. A fine old soldier, Colonel Stephen W. Kearny, was the commanding officer. Another and already famous officer was Lieutenant Colonel Ethan Allen Hitchcock, commanding the Third Infantry, and the very centre of garrison talk and interest because of his having for the second or third time braved the displeasure of our magnificent General Scott. Hitchcock was a monarch among army men as a scholar, a tactician, a student of

74

law and regulations. Lieutenant Don Carlos Buell had just been tried by court-martial for striking a soldier. The evidence was conclusive that the soldier had attacked the lieutenant, who struck only in self-defense. Scott had demanded that the court reassemble and explain why it had not found him guilty. Hitchcock wrote the reasons why the court could not be compelled to alter its findings, and the President sustained the court. It was only one of several occasions on which Hitchcock's letters or opinions defeated the will of the imperious general, who eventually learned to lean upon the advice of the man he almost detested, and at the outset of his famous campaign in Mexico he wisely attached Hitchcock to his staff. In years to come this same gifted soldier was to throw his stalwart influence in support of the commanding general of an infinitely greater army, and his regard for the general in question began in the autumn of 1843 when, as Brevet Second Lieutenant Grant, he served under Hitchcock's daily observation at Jefferson Barracks.

And there were others. The quarters were crowded, several of the junior officers living two in a room. The barracks could not begin to accommodate all the troops. Some of the companies were under canvas. Some of the officers were permitted to find quarters among the hospitable homes of residents in the immediate neighborhood. The city was near enough to enable them to drive thither for social enjoyment, but most of the entertaining took place at the garrison. The barracks were a famous resort for the beaux and belles of the neighborhood. Music and dancing, or riding and driving parties, filled up the leisure hours. Drills and duties except the daily dress parade were usually completed in the morning, and the first winter of Grant's garrison life moved swiftly and not unpleasantly away.

Mindful of Prof. Church's promise to apply for him as assistant in the Department of Mathematics, the young officer was studiously going over the two years' course, from algebra to calculus, by way of preparation. Not being a dancing man himself, he stood his share of the expenses, but took little part in the enjoyment. He might have escaped social entanglements of any kind but for the riding parties in which he was so much at home. The best horseman in the garrison could hardly be expected to mount and ride always alone, and among the kindly, hospitable households within easy ride of the barracks was that of the Dents, at White Haven, the home of his chum and roommate, Brevet Second Lieutenant Frederick T. Dent, now of the old Sixth Infantry, and many a mile away. Here the name of Ulysses Grant soon became familiar as household words. It seems that Grant was very much in evidence when there returned to the fireside a member of the family who had been away "finishing" at school, then visiting relatives at other points—a seventeen-year-old girl, eldest of the daughters and one possessing many an attraction. Letters from home had told her much of Fred's classmate, Lieutenant Grant. Home chat had told him much of the absent sister. Though they had never met before, they met by no means as strangers when for the first time these young people looked into each other's eyes and began a comradeship that was destined to become a permanent alliance. Julia Dent had not been home a month before her friends began the inevitable teasing and chaffing, and the man in the case was "the little lieutenant in the big epaulets"—Ulysses Simpson Grant.

It seems furthermore that the odds at first were not on the side of the young subaltern. There were these points in his favor: He had been Fred's roommate through the last year of their cadet life. They were fellow members of that little "wheel within a wheel," the T. I. O. Brother Fred's letters from the

"WHITE HAVEN"

The old home of the Dent family near St. Louis. From the original in possession of Mrs. Frank H. Jones, of Chicago (Nellie Grant). On the back of the original, in the handwriting of Mrs. Grant, is the inscription:

"Your mama's old playground."

"JULIA D. GRANT"

Point had had much to say in praise of his chum, and
the girls especially were prepared to like him. Then
it was an odd coincidence that just when the brother
had gone to join the Sixth Infantry at a distant station,
his chosen friend should arrive at the barracks, and
speedily take the brother's place at the fireside.

All over the broad United States, in every household
from which a son has been sent through West Point
or Annapolis to distant lands or seas, no visitor is so
eagerly welcomed as he who comes as classmate, comrade or intimate of the absent one. In the case of
Brother Fred's own "Sam" Grant, every member of
the family circle was eager to make him at home.
Simple, straightforward, cheery and kindly in manner,
gifted with innate courtesy toward all women and
schooled by love for his own mother to constant thought
for and deference to other mothers, it resulted that
even before the return of the eldest daughter he had
won the hearty friendship of Mrs. Dent. A more
potent ally than the prospective mother-in-law no suitor
needs. Moreover, the elder Dent, independently of his
son's biased estimate, had taken a fancy to the level-
headed youth in the queer, straight-cut, regimental
frock. A limited few of our young graduates in those
days had quit the army for a higher service and taken
holy orders. All they had to do in changing coats was
to strip the gilt buttons from the uniform, dip it in the
dyer's vat, and lo, the garb of the soldier of his country
had changed to that of the soldier of the cross. Mr.
Dent—Colonel Dent, as hailed in the American fashion
of that and many another day—was a fairly well-to-do
merchant in St. Louis, with a country home and planta-
tion some miles southwest of town and to the west of
Jefferson Barracks. The Dents were slave-holders, as
were many Missouri folk, even as far north as the Iowa
line, and "de Cunnel" as his "darkies" called the
master, had an eye for a good horse and for a horse-

man. The "cunnel" speedily discovered that in his unassuming way young Grant was a wonderful manager of horse flesh, and this in itself was much to command the elder's liking. One and all, therefore, they had grown to greatly fancy Fred's chum, when along in the winter Miss Julia came home, and then speedily it began to dawn upon the family that further possibilities were looming before them.

The young people seemed to fall in with each other's ways from the start. Duties at barracks were light in mid-winter. Grant found it possible to spend hours away from his books. For him in those days " the mess " room had no fascinations. He took no part in the six penny game of " Brag "—the southwestern prelude to poker. He took no comfort in the so-called pleasures of the table, for he never ate more than enough to sustain life, and he had not then begun to know either the stimulus or the sting that lives and lures in the bottle. He frankly disliked the dancing parties and he as little cared for the pomp and ceremony of parade. Battalion and company drill, as required by Colonel Kearny, he conscientiously took part in, but most of his afternoons he later spent in saddle and his evenings in study, having that instructorship ever in view. And when he began to appear at garrison parties that winter it was to stand and watch Julia Dent dancing with men whose feet could move in rhythm with the witching strains of Julien's waltzes (for this was before the days of Gungl, Strauss and Keler Bela), and were at home in the nimble caperings demanded by the polka or the schottische then in vogue. The concerts of the regimental band had been neglected functions so far as Grant was concerned, until some little time after Miss Dent's return. Then he began to take his place as one of the audience, although the only music that appealed to him was that of the young girl's joyous voice.

But if in concert hall, on ballroom floor, or at the

banquet board her admirer appeared to little advantage, there was none to match him when they went afield. The Dent girls rode, and rode well, as did many of the daughters of our Southern planters, and Grant rode as though he had spent his life in saddle. Long hours in the crisp sunshine of the Missouri winter they galloped through the wood paths and along the beautiful bluffs of the Father of Waters. Then as the spring came on and the young girl could indulge in her favorite study, botany, Grant was her constant escort. Of farm lore and maxims he had a head full. Of oats, barley, wheat and hay, corn and potatoes he had had practical knowledge, but in Nature's flower garden he was a novice and she was at home, and took delight in teaching, and the young student of science and mathematics who longed to quit soldiering, found that with one girl looking on even soldier life had taken on a charm, found that even the dreary hour of drill or parade had become gifted with a glamour never known to him before. And then one soft spring morning, venturing too far from the beaten track, her young and skittish mount, floundering and plunging in suddenly-discovered quicksand, well nigh hurled Miss Dent from saddle into the muddy waters. It took all her slender, sinewy young escort's skill and horsemanship to save her, and as they rode homeward that evening it became revealed to him at least that any injury to her would mean misery to him. What the incident had revealed to her he dared not at the moment inquire. What on earth could warrant a girl's leaving a home of ease, almost of luxury, to share the one room and a kitchen, then the legal lot, and something like eight hundred a year, the sum total of the pay and emoluments of a second lieutenant of infantry in the regular army?

No wonder Colonel Dent of a sudden took alarm!

CHAPTER VIII

AN INTERRUPTED COURTSHIP

But graver matters than even paternal objections had come to put an end to botanizing and to postpone for a time at least the telling of the old, old story. Troublous days were in store, especially for the South, which section had encouraged the separation of Texas from the Republic of Mexico, and was now fathering a scheme to annex the great territory to the United States. It would mean vast gain to Southern representation and influence in Congress, and vastly greater extension to the area of slavery. It is not the purpose of this volume to dissect the political questions leading to the two wars in which Ulysses Grant took part, but rather to attempt to describe the characteristics which made him a most distinguished soldier in both. Once upon a time, discussing the career of the great captains of history, a close student ventured on the assertion that no great general had failed to show in youth the qualities that made him famous. Instantly came the query: "How about Grant—who ever heard of him before Belmont?" The answer was courteous, confident and instant: "Grant is a case in point. Of all the lieutenants of the Army in Mexico Grant was perhaps the most conspicuous for soldiership, for daring and ability." For the moment it was thought that the speaker was utterly in error, but to the minds of all who heard he presently proved his case. As to this the reader may form independent opinion later on.

In the spring of 1844 relations between the United States and Mexico had become so strained that the " First Military Department " which bordered on the then independent State of Texas, was ordered reinforced. General Zachary Taylor, old "Rough and Ready," was its commanding officer and headquarters were at Fort Jesup, a few miles southward from Grand Ecore on the Red River. The South was vehemently cheering the Texans and championing the proposed annexation. The North was less vehemently opposed. Fair-minded statesmen saw in the move a wrong to a sister republic, hitherto courteous and friendly. The Grant household at Georgetown, in spite of the strong Southern and pro-slavery sentiments of Brown County, was divided in spirit. Right or wrong the administration had determined on a show of force along the border. Grant saw and heard it coming, knew that the Fourth Infantry doubtless would be among the first ordered to the front, and sought a twenty days' leave in which to visit home and see the family. There were serious matters concerning his future and he wished to consult his father.

And so it happened he was away from Jefferson Barracks when marching orders came, and the gallant Fourth was distributed among several of the old-time, high pressure, "passenger packets" plying between St. Louis, Memphis, Vicksburg, Natchez and New Orleans, and paddled away over the June rise of the mighty river, destined to see many a stirring day of battle and many a mile of marching ere ever it should again breast the tawny waters of the Mississippi.

The news reached the young officer too late to enable him to catch his regiment. The same message told him that his field kit had been boxed up and taken along by a thoughtful comrade. There was really nothing professional to demand his return to Jefferson Barracks. The shortest road to the regiment and to duty was down stream past Cairo and Columbus,—where less than twenty years thereafter he was destined to be the centre of national attention—past Memphis and Vicksburg, where later he was not to be journeying

6   81

solitary and unnoted. Yet it seems from his own Memoirs that instead of at once following on after the colors of the Fourth, he fled back to his haunts at Jefferson Barracks, deserted now by all save a mournful lot of wives, children, laundresses and "hospital" soldiers, all temporarily in charge of a certain lieutenant of dragoons, one Benjamin S. Ewell, an upper class cadet when Grant was a plebe. The garrison had dwindled from sixteen companies of foot to a handful of non-combatants, and the command from a colonel to a cornet. Ewell, with Sherman and Thomas, had taken note of Grant, as first classmen "size up" a plebe, and Ewell was unfeignedly glad to see his young friend again, glad to bid him share his quarters during his stay, glad to take the responsibility as post commander of adding a few days to his brief leave of absence, for it speedily dawned upon Ewell that there was a lady in the case.

Out toward the old Gravois road galloped Grant the very day of his arrival, through the scenes made sweet and sacred by the presence and companionship of the girl whom now he was seeking with well-defined purpose; and, barely half-way to the Dent homestead, he found the "branch," usually a placid and unpretentious creek, well nigh boiling over its banks. The ford was six feet deep in a turbid flood. Bridge there was none. There was nothing for it but turn back and wait for the waters to recede, or to spur in and swim. It was a superstition of his, says Grant, in his Memoirs, never to turn back when once he had set forth to do a thing. It was the same old lesson of the plough that he had learned long years before, the lesson that was to hold him steadfast in the snows about Donelson, stern set in the siege of Vicksburg, and indomitable even against the fearful pounding from the Rapidan to the James— the never look back, never turn back spirit that swept him onward to final victory. It was a drenched and bedraggled Leander that reached the astonished and welcoming Hero of that Missouri Hellespont. Brother Fred's cast-off "cits" had to be levied on, and the new arrival dried out, before he could take his accustomed place at the family board, but even such a drenching could not chill the ardor of so determined a wooer.

Before they parted Julia Dent had given her word to that "little lieutenant in the big epaulets," but in plighting her troth she had secured to herself the life-long devotion of a man as steadfast in love as ever he stood in war. From the day of their engagement in the early summer of 1844, the fiercest critic, the bitterest foe, of Grant's fortunes and fame could never find the shadow of a story on which to found a whisper of scandal. To his dying day the woman never lived who could win from Grant one look, word or thought that of right belonged to Julia Dent.

Alexander the Great was cold to women. Cæsar was not above suspicion, whatever he demanded of his wife. Marlborough, Napoleon, Nelson and many among their predecessors in martial renown, and many among their train, however constant to their war goddess, Bellona, have succumbed to the smiles and wiles of women other than the lawful partner of their joys and sorrows. But for this Ulysses there never lived a Circe. The drums and fifes of the Fourth were playing "The Girl I Left Behind Me" the day "Sam" Grant rejoined the colors at Fort Jesup (possibly their adjutant was responsible for that), and there was a new light in the blue-gray eyes, and a fine blush on the fair skin and clean-cut face of this old-headed youngster of the regiment as "the mess" gathered about him with their laughing greetings, but that suspected engagement, as yet a secret between him and the lady of his love, was no laughing matter to Lieutenant Grant. It was to influence, indeed to dominate, his entire life. The star of his destiny might lead him on to the highest honors that in peace or in war the nation ever yet had bestowed upon a son, but the centre of his universe was the fireside where dwelt this daughter of the West. Rewards such as no man ever yet had been accorded by the people of the United States were to him as little worth except as valued and shared by Julia Dent.

And now there came a year of watchfulness and anxiety. Mexico had not yet taken open offense at the open hostility of the southern half of the bigger and stronger republic, but there were reasons innumerable for knowing that war must come. Meantime our little army had to be put in at least partial readiness.

So much of it as was camped in the charming glade country southwest of Natchitoches—Camp Salubrity, they called it—was living in clover. The climate, the country, the country folk were all charming and hospitable. The troops drilled and lived and throve in the open air. In their leisure hours and on rainy days the officers sometimes took to cards, and Longstreet tells us that they occasionally quit the game—poker as then practised—quite concerned over the loss of seventy-five cents, as well they might be when it represented so large a fraction of the subaltern's daily stipend. They started dances and dinners by way of return for the hospitalities of neighboring planters. They essayed private theatricals, and there is regimental tradition that because of his slender, supple form and fair, smooth complexion and regular features, they once cast young Grant for the part of Desdemona, before they realized that histrionics formed no part whatsoever of his make-up. Grant, it is remembered, paid his appropriate share in all expenses for entertainment, but otherwise had little interest in them. It seems that the winter of 44–5 was to him one of serious thought and reflection. He spent long hours in saddle and alone, living in the sunshine and the open air, banishing thoroughly the last vestige of that semi-consumptive cough that had worried his mother the year before. He wrote long letters, he listened with attentive ears to all the debates, sometimes heated and acrimonious, as to the rights and wrongs of the questions at issue between the United States of America and the neighboring republic of Mexico. The more he heard the more he became convinced that Mexico was being drawn into a war with a stronger nation, without a vestige of right on the stronger side—the side which, by his oath of office taken on receipt of his commission, he was sworn to maintain against all enemies or opposers whomsoever.

Consider now the painful position in which this officer in particular was placed. The profession itself was not of his choosing. He had never liked "soldiering," as it was called. He mastered with ease the scientific part of his military education but had never become even a moderately good drill officer. Guard duty, and the minor and manifold duties of a subaltern in garrison such as supervising issue of clothing, attending roll-calls, writing up records of garrison courts, boards of survey, etc., he had conscientiously attended to, but his captain probably did most of the drilling; Grant never considered that his strong suit. He had won the name of being a thoroughly dutiful subordinate but by no means enthusiastic officer. The story told by one of his biographers of his having with drawn sword threatened a lieutenant-colonel of his regiment sounds almost incredible, even though, as told, the colonel had said, " That isn't so," in reply to a statement of Grant that all the men of his company were present except those properly excused. It is most improbable that a young lieutenant should turn upon his superior and threaten to run him through unless instant retraction were made. The articles of war prescribed that any officer who dared to lift a weapon against a superior in the discharge of his duty, should suffer death or such other punishment as a court-martial should direct, and Grant was the last man to resort to violence, regulations or no regulations.

He even had the courage to stand up against the "code duello," then dominant in the army. He utterly disapproved of the duel, and he didn't care who knew it. He held it to be the duty of an officer and the custom of a gentleman to govern his tongue and temper, and if offense were given, wittingly or unwittingly, then to settle the question by lawful and temperate means. He was anything but a soldier of the swash-buckling type. He was simply a straightforward, unpretentious, duty-doing subaltern, neither brilliant, military nor showy, a man who would hardly be chosen for the position of adjutant, who could never shine on parade, but, said the regiment, a man sure to come out strong on campaign or in administration, a man who would obey orders and do his level best.

And in this they were right. Utterly disapproving the causes leading up to the war, he had determined to stand by his colors and his oath of office at least until the stipulated four years had expired. Until that time, like Decatur, he would say "My country, right or wrong."

That matter settled, Grant went serenely on with his preparations. He obtained in the late spring of '45 another leave to enable him to visit the Dent homestead, and to secure the until-then withheld consent of Dent, the father. In this he was ably seconded by the arguments of Dent the son, and still more ably by the appeals of the wife and mother. It was hardly the match the old planter and slave-owner would have made for the eldest daughter of his house and name, but if the wife said so and the daughter would have it so, and the young man, though poor, was sound and square, why, there seemed no help for it. Meantime, however, Mr. Dent was mightily interested in the pending

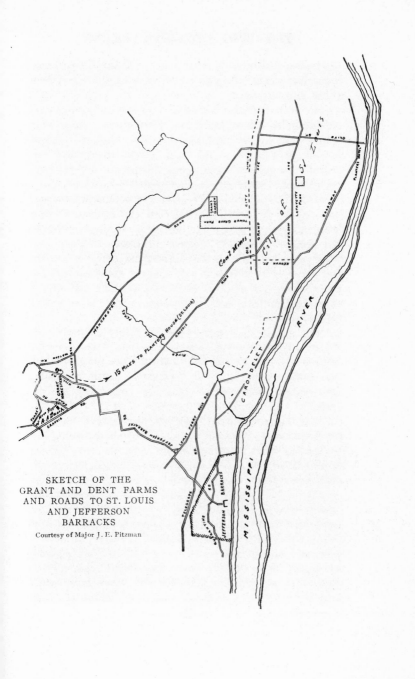

SKETCH OF THE
GRANT AND DENT FARMS
AND ROADS TO ST. LOUIS
AND JEFFERSON
BARRACKS

Courtesy of Major J. E. Pitzman

questions, in Southern and slave-holding supremacy, and in the success of the scheme to acquire Texas, no matter what Mexico might think or do. He and his prospective son-in-law were not much in accord on that matter. Possibly that had something to do with the elder's objections, but when a year or so later the little commands of Scott and Taylor had won, through sheer skill and valor against desperate odds, an astonishing series of victories, the nation forgot for the time the inciting cause—forgot for the time, perhaps forgot entirely, the fearful cost in young and gallant lives, and went wild over the heroism and daring displayed by the nation's sons. To the Dent household there came for a time anxieties innumerable, as the despatches told the tale of killed and wounded, of the Third and Fourth Infantry in the thick of every fight and suffering heaviest losses, of the gallant fellows with whom the girls had danced and dined again and again, so many of whom had died at the head of the stormers or " in the lead of the rushing charge," of their own son and brother, after manful share in the fortunes of his new regiment up to the very walls of Mexico, falling painfully wounded in the assault on the Molino; and then, but never in word or letter of his own, of the daring exploits, the consummate skill and judgment that had distinguished the young suitor soldier who was presently to return to them with honors unexcelled by any other of his grade, a record won without a scratch and yet without a stain. Verily, thought the elder Dent, if Grant can do all this in a profession he hates, what cannot he do in one that he loves?

There was no longer obstacle to naming the day. As lover, as husband and as father we are to see him through many a year. Let us see him through the first of his many campaigns.

CHAPTER IX

THE WAR WITH MEXICO

By joint resolution the Houses of Congress, in March, 1845, decreed the annexation of Texas, and the President lost little time in ordering an " Army of Occupation " to the newly acquired territory. The fighting land force of the nation at the moment consisted of perhaps eight thousand soldiers, divided into eight regiments of infantry, two of dragoons, one of rifles and four of artillery, a certain few selected companies of the latter being equipped for field service, among them the famous batteries of Bragg, Duncan and Frank Taylor, while the rest were armed and used as infantry. In point of numbers it was pitifully small, but in point of officers, especially in captains and lieutenants, no army in the world could match it. For thirty years the graduates of West Point had been coming annually into the line in little groups of two or three to each regiment, until in '45 almost every company, troop or battery took the field, officered by highly trained and most efficient men.

Except for the brief and bitter struggle with the Seminoles of Florida, and the Creeks and kindred tribes of Alabama, there had been no war since the memorable conflict of 1812, wherein our land forces, at least, had suffered many a defeat. Now the puny army of regulars, aided by such volunteers as could be hurriedly organized, was to be pitted against the armed forces of Mexico—numerous if not otherwise formidable. It was practically to be West Point's first essay in battle against a civilized foe, and as all the army knew, West Point was on its mettle.

The senior officers—the generals, colonels and even

88

many lieutenant-colonels and majors—were of the " old régime," commissioned originally long before the Military Academy was old enough to graduate more than half a dozen cadets a year. As a rule they were stanch and battle-tried. Famous names were among them, notably those of Winfield Scott, Zachary Taylor, and the colonel of the Eighth Infantry, the " electric " commandant of twenty years before, William J. Worth. Oddly enough, the President and his cabinet would gladly have had all of them " shelved " and out of the way, for though Scott and Taylor were of Southern birth, neither was believed to be in sympathy with this exclusively Southern enterprise. It is a matter of history that the President strove hard to supersede them by a general of his own creation and from civil life. If President Polk could have induced Congress to sustain him, Thomas H. Benton, of Missouri, would have been sent to the Rio Grande, with the commission of a lieutenant-general, and orders to take supreme command. But the scheme fell through of its own weight; old " Rough and Ready " had " taken hold " as it were, in a way that electrified even the reluctant North, and after the brilliant little victories of Palo Alto and Resaca de la Palma, any attempt to overslaugh Taylor would have stirred the people and swamped the administration.

Shrewdly advised, the President left to General Scott, a natural rival, the effort to clip the wings of Taylor's popularity; but, in this effort to put a damper on the national proclivity for choosing a military hero for the presidency, the administration that strove to block the candidacy of one general succeeded only in securing it to two.

To return to the Army of Occupation. Among the regimental commanders, it must be said that there were several who were unequal to the task before them, notably the colonel of Grant's own regiment, who had long contented himself with looking on at the evolutions of the battalion, and not until it was learned at Jackson Barracks that they were actually destined for service, did the old gentleman buckle on his sword and attempt in person to command at drill. The effort was too much for him—he turned and dropped dead as he left the parade ground. This was not the only tragedy that befell the Fourth before the campaign began. Two of its promising young officers, " graduates " both and senior to Grant by two or three years, were instantly killed by the explosion of the boiler of the steamer *Dayton* in Aransas Bay. One other, senior to both of these, had fallen by the wayside at Camp Salubrity, and after a fair trial by his brother officers had been summarily dismissed. The Fourth took the field with the shadow of these regimental sorrows still overhanging, but they had long months in which to recuperate, a fine, healthful sea front on which to camp, with abundant room for even brigade evolutions, with a capital beach, surf-bathing and fishing. The Fourth had, moreover, a commander in whom they felt confidence, and a new adjutant by whom they swore, " Charley " Hoskins, of the Class of '36—one of the most gifted and soldierly of their number. They had many a distinguished West Pointer among their captains—McCall, of the Class of '22, Bliss, Alvord and Scott, of the Class of '33 (Bliss and Scott serving as aides-de-camp to Taylor and Scott respectively) and Henry Prince, of '35. Among their junior officers were Dick Graham, of '38, Warren of '40, Hill and Norton of '42, though the latter was away at West Point as instructor of tactics, Beaman and Perry, of the same class, Augur, Grant, Judah and Hazlitt, of '43, Woods and Alexander Hayes, of '44, Lincoln, Montgomery, Richey and D. A. Russell, of '45. Later in the fall of '46 they were joined by Wilkins and Rodgers.

It was a gallant array, horse, foot and dragoons, that set forth under Zachary Taylor early in March,

'46, and took the road from Corpus Christi southward along the sandy coast to the mouth of the Rio Grande. It was known that a Mexican force, at least double theirs in number, interposed between them and Mata-moras, when in May the little army turned confidently northward, old "Rough and Ready" leading on. He had but six regiments, and a squadron or two of dragoons, but his guns and gunners were not to be excelled, and the martial spirit of that model command was hardly to be equalled. The fire and fury of their attack, the impetuous rush of their charge, amazed and confounded the slow-moving brigades of the Mexican line, and settled for all time the Mexican question on Texas soil.

Fought on May 8th and 9th respectively, the little battles of Palo Alto and Resaca sent the enemy scatter-ing back across the Rio Grande in utter bewilderment and dismay. They had swept the level fields with con-centrated fire from their many guns. They had poured swift volleys from musket and *escopeta* into the charg-ing, cheering ranks of blue without stopping them at a single point. They never knew until long afterward how severe a loss they really had inflicted.

In those spirited affairs our friends of the Fourth bore their share and received their due meed of credit. Palo Alto was mainly an artillery fight, and the Fourth, though itching to get at the enemy's guns, were com-pelled to wait until the following day. There is noth-ing that tries more severely the mettle and discipline of infantry or cavalry than this duty of "supporting" artillery, of sitting in saddle or standing in ranks in readiness to repel a dash at the guns, receiving heavy fire, yet unable to reply. From his station as file closer to Captain McCall's Company, it was the lot of Lieu-tenant Grant to see more than one huge gap torn through the line as the round shot came screaming from the smoke clouds a few hundred yards away. One in particular struck off the head of a soldier only a few paces away, stretched Captain Page mortally wounded, and blinded Lieutenant Wallen with their blood. Palo Alto tried the nerve of the Fourth and found it tense and true, but it was Resaca that gave the regiment the chance it longed for.

Here Captain McCall was detailed to conduct the skirmish line in the opening attack, and it fell to the lot of our second lieutenant to step to the front and command the company. Quiet and unassuming as ever but, as the veteran soldiers did not fail to note, absolutely calm and collected, their junior subaltern stood before them as their commander. In his own Memoirs he says the experience was anything but enjoyable. He gives the reader to understand that he would rather not have been there, yet it transpired that he led his men that day with consummate ease and nonchalance, even though he had to see a cherished comrade shot dead in the thick of the fray. How often, how very often, that experience was to be his. How fiercely the lightning strokes of battle were to play about his head, blasting many a brave young life, yet as God willed, doubtless for a mighty purpose, sparing Grant. Omitting all mention of their seniors or of the members of other classes than the seven with which Grant wore the West Point gray, there is no better illustration of the desperate fighting, of the reckless daring and devoted leadership of the young graduates of the Academy than is found in the solemn roster of those who died in battle for the honor of Alma Mater and The Flag.

Of the Class of 1840, Irwin, Adjutant of the Third Infantry (as Hoskins was Adjutant of the Fourth), was killed among the foremost at Monterey. Bacon, foot of the class, died of the wounds received at the head of his company at Churubusco. Of this class, too, was James G. Martin, who wore an empty sleeve from the day of Molino. Of the Class of '41, Irons, Burbank, Ernst and Morris died of their wounds, Irons at

Churubusco, the other three at Molino. Berry, of the Fourth Infantry, was one of the victims of the *Dayton's* explosion. Gantt, gallant fellow, was shot dead foremost among the stormers at Chapultepec. Of the Class of '42, Benjamin died at the Belen Gate (Mansfield Lovell, his file leader in class standing, barely escaping with his life), Mason and Hammond of the Dragoons were killed, one at La Rosia, the other at San Pasqual, while Longstreet carried to Grant's wedding, two years later, the grim scars of Chapultepec.

Of their own little band, graduated in '43, Chadbourne was shot dead in the charge of the Fourth at Resaca. Stevens, of the Dragoons, but a few days later, met his fate at the crossing of the Rio Grande. Hazlitt was killed at Monterey, and Johnstone, serving his guns at Contreras, was struck by the shot of an eighteen-pounder and never knew what hit him. Neill, as adjutant of the Second Dragoons, and Dent, the brother-in-law elect, were severely wounded and for a time incapacitated.

Of their immediate followers, the men of '44, Dilworth, like Johnstone, was swept off by a cannon shot. Strong and Burwell died at Molino, and Wainwright from the wounds there received. Woods was killed at Monterey and Smith (J. P.) at Chapultepec. Of the Class of '45, well known to the seniors in '43, Farry and Richey, mere boys of twenty-two, were shot dead, one at Monterey, the other bearing despatches. Merrill met his death by accident on shipboard in Aransas Bay, and Snelling all but died from the wounds of Molino. Then came the boys who were plebes when Grant and his fellows were First Classmen, and among these there were two bearers of illustrious names, Alex. Rodgers, son of Captain George Rodgers of the navy, and nephew of Commodore Oliver H. Perry, and his next number in the class, Oliver H. P. Taylor. There was bitter sorrow the woeful evening of Chapultepec. The stars and stripes were floating in triumph over the battered walls, but the dead lay thick below, and among them "Sandy" Rodgers, only twenty-one, he who but a few days before grieved so sadly over Eastley's death at Churubusco. Taylor lived, unscathed by Mexican blade or bullet, only to die leading his Dragoons in Indian battle long years later.

These, be it remembered, are but the fatalities among Grant's intimates and contemporaries. The list of those of other classes who fell in that fateful war far exceeds in number those mentioned here. And there were others, too, commissioned from civil life, yet close to Grant—Captains Page and Hanson, of the Fourth Infantry, Sydney Smith, the wit of the regiment, whose merry sayings made joyous many an hour for Grant, and whose lamented death within the walls of Mexico made him a first lieutenant.

It has been pointed out by military historians that in no previous war was the loss of officers, in proportion to the numbers engaged, ever so great.

The casualties in Scott's column alone, from Cerro Gordo to Chapultepec speak eloquently as to this. Thirty-three officers had been killed and one hundred and seventy-nine wounded. Three hundred and fifty men had been killed and two thousand one hundred and seventy-two wounded, and all this out of a force at no time exceeding eight thousand men.

And yet, it has pleased a prominent captain of industry, in his address to the Peace Societies of St. Louis in April, 1913, to refer to these engagements as a series of mere skirmishes. It is recorded of the same speaker that he further declared the profession of the officer of the army and navy of the United States to be about the least hazardous occupation within the scope of his knowledge. The records of the great Civil War, the list of our fallen in Indian battle in the ten years of profound peace that followed, the number of our dead in Cuba and the Philippines must therefore have been unworthy the financier's notice.

CHAPTER X

A FIGHTING QUARTERMASTER

ON the road to Monterey Grant found himself again in saddle, and for the first time detached from his company in the responsible position of regimental quartermaster. In these days only captains, men of several years of experience, are selected for such duty, but in '46 a colonel could pitch upon any one of his subalterns for staff service. The two coveted offices were those of adjutant and quartermaster, and as a rule they fell to senior lieutenants. Charles Hoskins, of the class of '36, as has been said, now held the adjutancy, but there was no surprise in the Fourth when it was announced that " Sam " Grant was slated for the quartermastership.

There were reasons why the detail should have been a source of satisfaction. He was only three years out of West Point, therefore it was an unusual compliment. He was one of the outspoken opponents of the war itself, and therefore might have welcomed a berth which promised to keep him well to the rear, and out of the hard knocks and fighting at the front. Moreover, his well-known gift for managing horses, it presently transpired, extended also to mules and even to men. The hired teamsters were a quarrelsome, turbulent lot; the mules lost nothing of their native propensities through daily association with such characters. Those were the days of the knock-down-and-drag-out methods of discipline. The little army of old " Rough and Ready " had about as many hard characters among its camp followers as any that ever took the field. That oft-mentioned array of military experts, " Our Army in Flanders," had no such mules as these of our Army

95

in Mexico, and the rank profanity that prevailed in both became something more than famous in the latter. The roads and the language alike were something infamous. It had been a creed in the quartermaster's department that no mule could be induced to throw his heart into the work except under the influence of lurid and resonant blasphemy. It became noised abroad by the time they cut loose from Camargo that the Fourth Foot had a new quartermaster who could "snatch a six-mule team out of the worst kind of a slough without so much as a swear word." The thing was incredible, yet it was true. The mild-mannered, taciturn young man who rode a Texas pony with such negligent ease, proved able to deal with hitherto intractable mule teams in a way no veteran could fathom. By the time that compact little column of regulars was trudging into sight of Monterey, Garland's brigade was bragging about the way " Sam " Grant had straightened out every mule and man in the train of the Fourth. His wagons were never stalled or sidetracked. Grant had a way of his own of putting them through, a way that lasted him throughout other years of campaigning in days that were to come. "He was the most popular quartermaster in Taylor's whole column," said an appreciative officer of the envious Fifth, a few years later. All this therefore should have made Grant reasonably content with his new lot.

But Monterey and other battles proved that he was not, and "the most efficient quartermaster in the column" was begging to be relieved from a duty that kept him from sharing the fortunes of his company. The man who hated soldiering and detested war in general, and this one in particular, was demanding that he be allowed to quit his trains in order to take his part in the fight.

Monterey brought matters to a climax. The story of the spirited battling about its walls has been told ten thousand times over, and we have to deal only with Grant and his part therein. Three miles to the rear the trains had been parked while the battalions went striding into action, and presently the thunder of the cannon told the story of sharp and fierce encounter. It was too much for the quartermaster of the Fourth. His own regiment, beloved by this time in spite of his pacific tendencies, was supporting those guns somewhere among the outlying farm enclosures toward Fort Teneria. Putting spurs to his horse, Grant left his wagons and property to the care of the teamsters and galloped in pursuit, joining just in time for their daring charge.

Hard by the roadside and among the groups of wounded on the following day he found his senior staff officer, unhorsed and in sore trouble. Orders to be carried at once and not a mount to be had. "Take mine," said Grant, springing from saddle, "I'll find another," and away went Hoskins in the wake of the smoke-shrouded line, the last Grant ever saw of him alive. Hoskins fell, shot dead among the stormers. "You'll have to act as adjutant, too, Grant," sadly said their chief that night, but by that time "Sam" Grant was something more than a double staff officer in the eyes of Garland's brigade. With another day the whole division was telling or hearing the story. After hours of hard fighting, the Third and Fourth were close under walls that were lined with the enemy. They could go no further, for cartridge boxes were almost empty. They could not go back even if go they would, for the open ground was swept by the enemy's fire and it was death to attempt it, yet Garland called for a volunteer. Some one had to make the hazardous essay —the trip to the ammunition wagons—and that some one was Grant. Somehow, somewhere he had picked up another mount and speedily made himself master. Somehow he had managed to bring that horse along and had him screened behind a shoulder of wall. There was no question in Grant's mind as to the need of cartridges or the method of getting them. Silently he tightened the girth, quickly he mounted, headed the excited beast for the rear, gave him rein, lash and spur, and as he darted away for the white wagon tops, Grant flung himself out of saddle, crooking a leg about the cantle and clasping an arm over the neck, and thus, Indian fashion, at full tilt, with his horse as a shield, he drove through the sputter of musketry and safely reached the train. Within the hour Garland's brigade was resupplied, thanks to the daring and skill of their quartermaster. Within the week the story of that exploit had gone throughout the little army, and when " Sam " Grant penned his appeal for permission to rejoin his company, Lieutenant-Colonel Garland saw fit to reply that his services on the staff were too valuable to be spared. It led to Grant's writing about the nearest approach to insubordination that ever flowed from his pen—" I must and will accompany my company in battle," and followed the words with the information that if not permitted to do so he would quit the service entirely.

That exploit of Grant's should have brought him his first brevet, but the army had just emerged from an absurd squabble growing out of claims for precedence because of brevet rank—claims so inimical to the views of most of the officers of Taylor's command, that no less than one hundred and thirty signatures were attached to the appeal, written by Colonel Hitchcock and sent direct to the Senate.

Loyally did his officers, West Pointers and all, stand by old " Rough and Ready " in this his first clash with his senior, Scott, and great was the wrath of the latter when for the second time within three years he found his rulings attacked by an officer so many years his junior. It was gall and wormwood to one of Scott's imperious nature to be opposed by his subordinate, but "that pestilent penman," as the big, brave, but self-opinionated chief referred to Hitchcock, won out for the second time, and Taylor was sustained.

Naturally now there was some reluctance on Taylor's part to suggest brevet rank as a reward for the exploits of his officers. Scott had "overworked the brevet business" in the past and was destined in the near future to overwork it again. Many an act of daring and devotion therefore went utterly unrewarded in Taylor's little army. Among the most gallant and distinguished of his volunteers, by the way, was no less a personage than Lieutenant-Colonel Hamer, Grant's former congressman.

Meantime, however, even the Northwest went wild over the tidings of Taylor's victory, and even in its hour of congratulation the administration at Washington took alarm. A Whig general was winning the laurels of the war devised by and for the opposite political party. The joy bells were ringing all over the land. The name of old "Rough and Ready" was on every lip. The stirring, soldierly, yet modest and model report of the battle, signed Z. Taylor, was in every paper and on every tongue. Every word of it, of course, was penned by Bliss. North and South the bluff frontier leader had become the personal hero and political probability. Something had to be done to check his onward sweep to undesired victories, and then it was that Scott received his orders to proceed in person to the seat of war.

And presently he came. It was mid December when Scott left New Orleans for Brazos Santiago, and one of the first things he did—for he was fully conscious of enmity and intrigue at Washington—was to strengthen his position with the army itself by summoning to his staff some of its ablest officers. Scott's sagacity was never more apparent than when, to the amaze of Colonel Hitchcock, he sent for that "pestilent penman," loaded him with compliments and made him inspector-general at headquarters in the field.

About the next thing done was to issue orders checking Taylor's onward move from Monterey and taking from him the very flower of his regulars. Unwillingly they marched away, our friends of the Third and Fourth still in Garland's brigade, and with no little anxiety (for Santa Ana, with over twenty-five thousand men, was reported advancing on Taylor by way of Saltillo) they left old "Rough and Ready" to what many feared might be his fate.

And their fears were prophetic, though not exactly as they feared. Shorn of his right arm, Worth's regulars, and having with him only the batteries of Bragg, Sherman and Washington, the Dragoons, and then the gallant regiments of volunteers, Taylor had dared to face the overwhelming force of the Mexican leader and to overthrow and soundly thrash him at Buena Vista. That magnetic triumph, with its catch words of "A little more grape, Captain Bragg" (which probably were never spoken) and "Tell him to go to hell: put that in Spanish, Bliss" (which undoubtedly were), made Zachary Taylor at the very next election President of the United States.

Scott, sailing for Vera Cruz and San Juan de Ulloa, received the news of this astonishing victory and realized that now the race was won. Yet a brilliant campaign, and a series of brilliant and stirring battles were destined to be his own. The siege of the old Mexican seaport and the reduction of its famous castle were swiftly followed by a successful march with barely eight thousand men into the very heart of the enemy's country. Cerro Gordo, fought in the thick of the mountains on the way, was a finely planned tactical battle, a success accomplished without storming walls or tragic loss of life. The Third and Fourth Infantry were still sore hearted over the heavy toll taken from their commissioned list at Monterey, and Scott nursed his regulars along to the beautiful valley beyond the old Orizaba range, and here finally, on the high and health-ful tableland about Puebla, with the grand mountain chains to east and west in full view, with pure air and water and unclouded skies, he placed his little army in camp, awaiting the arrival from the States of the needed reinforcements. It was a long wait. It might have been a most dangerous wait, had there been unity in Mexico, but the populace and the army were broken by cliques and dissensions. They were quarrelling among them-selves and Scott took advantage of the situation to set his army to serious work in brigade and battalion drills. Week after week he had them out long hours each day, drilling, drilling, hardening and steadying, until as the summer waned, and the new levies finally came, he found himself again at the head of eight thousand men, most of them seasoned, disciplined, splendidly officered, and in spite of the few recruits and the many hard characters among them, ready to follow him and to fight like game cocks wherever he should lead. Then once more he launched them forward, now destined for " the halls of the Montezumas."

In four fine divisions and in capital fettle, Scott's army resumed its march on Mexico, leaving the snow-capped height of Orizaba far to the rear, and the glistening cone of Popocatapetl to the south—the left flank of the column. The landscape was beautiful, the weather was fine, the enemy were everywhere about them, but nowhere too near; there was promise of stir-ring adventure ahead, so in buoyant spirits our friends, still with Worth's famous division, trudged away, " Sam " Grant disgustedly bringing up the rear and the train of the Fourth Foot. With a battery of what was then poetically referred to as " flying artillery " attached to each brigade, Duncan's renowned gunners grinning in the dust of Garland's, with the Engineer officers and the Dragoons far in the lead, and the divisions in easy supporting distance in case of attack, the little army pressed forward through the range, and presently debouched upon the plain of Mexico. Far to the front, across long sweeps of lowland dotted with glistening lakes, could be dimly seen the towers of the capital city, the centre of an encircling frame of rolling hills. Approaching it as they did from the southeast, until the head of column halted near the hamlet of Ayotla, the Engineers could see that the direct road was borne onward to the gates only along a narrow causeway flanked by marsh, wet meadow and then by lakes; guarded, too, and squarely in their front by the rocky height of El Peñon, strongly fortified and bristling with guns. Cortez and his mailed horsemen had fought their way against throngs of hapless natives who were armed only with bow and spear, but now the causeways were commanded by heavy cannon. Passage from the southeast was impossible, and the skilled and gifted guides of the army turned their eyes westward to where Lake Chalco lapped the foothills of the southward range. The tall, courtly, dark-eyed Virginian, bred to the purple, Scott's right arm among the brilliant group of star graduates of the Academy, riding back from the Ayotla front to reconnoitre the southern shores of Chalco, stopped to bait his horse among the wagons of Garland's brigade, and to exchange greeting with the slender, blue-eyed, plain-spoken son of the people there in charge. Fourteen years lay between them in date of graduation—the former was by that time a senior captain in the Corps of Engineers, the latter a junior subaltern in the marching line, yet as the two sat in saddle a moment later, and parted at the roadside, two finer horsemen were hardly to be found in all that array. Grant, as we know, has owned that in West Point days he dreamed he might succeed to the rank

and title of General Scott. Did he dream that August
morning as he gazed after the cavalier knight of the
army—the honored and envied engineer to whom,
more than to any other (bar only himself), Scott attributed the victory of Vera Cruz, the triumph of
Cerro Gordo—that the day was to come at the close
of four years of tremendous battling when he who
bore so gracefully the high honors of the Mexican campaign should ride again into his presence, superb even
in utter defeat, to tender to him, the farm boy of Ohio,
the surrender of all that was left of the proudest,
bravest, most devoted army that ever yielded to fate and
to superior numbers?

CHAPTER XI

THE SOLDIER OF SAN COSME

WITHIN that week, leaving but a puny force on the Puebla road, Scott's army was skirting the lower shores of Chalco, bent on forcing a way through the open fields, the outlying villages, farms and haciendas that lay to the southwest and west of the capital city. Again the Engineers and the escorting Dragoons were out in the lead. Again gallant Captain Thornton, commanding here as on the Rio Grande the foremost troop, was reported killed, and this time unhappily it was true. He fell, first victim of the guns of San Antonio.

And foremost of the divisions marched the famous regulars. The Third and Fourth Infantry, long partners in camp and garrison, in march and battle, had suffered divorce, the former having been transferred to Persifer Smith's brigade of Twiggs' division, the latter, brigaded with the Second and Third Artillery, was still under its old chief, Garland. In the Second Brigade, Colonel Clarke's, were the Fifth, Sixth and Eighth Infantry, all of Worth's division. One division, the Third, under Major General Pillow, of the Volunteers, was made up of what might be termed untried men, even though heralded as "regulars"—the Voltigeurs, the Ninth, Eleventh, Twelfth, Fourteenth and Fifteenth Infantry, only just organized and destined to exist only to the end of the war. Quitman's, the Fourth Division, except for the detachment of Marines, was composed entirely of New York, Pennsylvania and South Carolina Volunteers, brigaded under Shields and Watson.

It was on the 7th of August that the little army began its march from Puebla. It was the 10th of August when it crossed the divide, eleven thousand feet above the sea, and began its swoop upon the capital. It was a week thereafter before the actual battling occurred to the south and west of Chalco. But now the armed forces of Mexico were treated to some astonishing moves and methods.

They had strongly fortified the roads and approaches between Chalco and the westward hills. They had loop-holed and sandbagged the walls of San Antonio, as well as strengthened the rocky fortress of Contreras to the southwest. In the natural order of things the invaders should first assault the foremost line, leaving Contreras to be cared for later. Scott did just the opposite. Directing Worth's division to threaten San Antonio from the front, he slipped half his force under the cover of darkness through a new, night-built road his Engineers had traced around the southern flank of the Mexican line, and just at dawn of the 20th, in twenty minutes of furious fighting, they had swept over Contreras and were bearing down from the heights upon the approaches to the strongest position of all— Churubusco on the southern causeway—the key to the city gates.

And here followed almost at once the headiest, heaviest battle on the plains of Mexico, and the sorest of the blows received by the Mexican arms—the general action of Churubusco. So dazed and disorganized were the enemy as a result of their overthrow at this point, that Scott's victorious columns could have chased on at their heels into the heart of the capital city.

But here again occurs a curious illustration of the American method of waging war under civil supervision. The administration had sent to join Scott's army a " Commissioner," Mr. Nicholas P. Trist, a worthy and amiable gentleman, yet an embarrassing adjunct to a conquering army. He and Scott had begun by misunderstanding each other at Vera Cruz, and misunderstanding had led Mr. Trist to misrepresentation. The administration at Washington grieved not at all over the prospect of a rupture between Scott and Trist; very possibly it was with this hope that the commissioner had been sent to Mexico. Oddly enough the plans of the Polk cabinet miscarried here, even as they had in case of old " Rough and Ready." Ruptures came thick and fast, soon after Churubusco, and Scott was the vortex of the storm, but the trouble was not with Mr. Trist.

Both Scott and Trist had reason to believe the Mexican government so rent and torn that if driven from its capital there would be left no recognized authority with which to settle the terms of peace. As these included the yielding up of every claim to Texas and the sale of New Mexico and California, the Mexicans speedily broke over the traces and violated the armistice agreed upon, and less than three weeks after Churubusco, the war, with new and unequalled fury, was on again.

But meantime Scott had been writing despatches. Scott had confidence in his pen equal only to that in which he held his sword. Certain of his subordinates, too, had been writing. Scott's reports were for the War Department. Scott's subordinates' letters were for the press and personal glorification. Scott's prominent political division commander was General Gideon E. Pillow, and while Scott was penning pages of official detail as to the recent battles, Pillow was publishing long columns claiming to himself the honors of the move to the south of Chalco, and for himself and Worth the salvation of Scott's army.

Nowhere near as desperate or deadly as either Monterey or Buena Vista, Scott had crowned Contreras and Churubusco with a halo of martial glory, and whole sheafs and paleways of brevets. Gallant and meritorious indeed were the services of his officers in these two stirring affairs, but Contreras, with a total loss of only sixty, was won in a single whirlwind charge, and the Churubusco battle was a series of attacks along the hostile front, while with one brigade he took the enemy in flank. Resistance seemed vain, and with fewer casualties among his officers, as compared with those of Taylor in his two great battles, Scott had rushed the enemy off their feet. Then, exulting in such success, he sought to lavish reward and honor on the gallant men who had led his battalions and companies. Of Taylor's West Pointers brevetted, there were twenty-five for Palo Alto and Resaca, forty for Monterey, and thirty for Buena Vista—many of these, like Charles F. Smith, McCall, Duncan, Bragg, J. F. Reynolds, George H. Thomas, coming in for two apiece. No man could say that Taylor's recommendations were not in any case deserved, but when Scott's list for Contreras and Churubusco burst upon the army comments were, to say the least, satirical. The forty odd West Pointers named for Cerro Gordo had been accepted in all good faith. In nearly every instance, said their fellows of the staff and line, the recommendation was well merited.

But when on top of this there came a roster of no less than one hundred and twenty West Pointers brevetted for gallant and meritorious conduct at Contreras and Churubusco—fights in which but seven of their number had been killed (Bacon, Burke, Capron, Anderson, Irons, Johnstone and Easley)—the graduates took alarm. It was a case of " running the thing into the ground." Phelps of the Class of '36, and Hawes of '45, begged to be excused and respectfully declined, while Grant of '43, on being told that he, in connection with a certain other subaltern, had been recommended in the same letter of a regimental commander, very promptly and indignantly protested: " If that man's entitled to a brevet I am not," is the way one of his biographers tells it.

And yet, for the desperate assaults so soon to follow at Molino and Chapultepec, Scott's lists were reduced by much more than half, while his casualty lists were very much more than doubled, so far at least as his West Pointers were concerned. It is melancholy to think that, when showered so liberally on the just and the unjust, there were yet heroic souls that took their flight, after noble leadership on many a field, unhonored by a single brevet. Of such were J. W. Anderson, Dunn, McKavett, Martin Burke and Capron; of such were the first William Montrose Graham, of the old Fourth Infantry, dying at Molino commanding the Eleventh Infantry, and Merrill heading the stormers of the Fifth; of such were Bacon, Burbank, Burwell, Daniels, Easley, Ernst, Farry, Gantt, R. H. Graham, and so on down a list that, coupled with the names of those who died brevetted, might well challenge the statements of the gentlemen who so lately spoke in sneering terms of the trivial skirmishes of our war with Mexico, and of the profession of arms as practised by officers of the United States.

Long before the Churubusco shower reached Washington, however, there had been fighting such as Mexico had never seen or heard of, and deeds of daring that thrilled even our surfeited press. Yet so many a glad young life was snuffed out, so many a brilliant name was stricken from the rolls, that mourning was as widespread as triumph over the tidings of Molino, Chapultepec and the gates of Mexico.

In these assaults it transpired that our young quartermaster again left his legitimate duties, with his wagons, far in rear, and turned up just as far in front, bearing a manful hand at Molino and covering himself with credit as an amateur artillerist at the San Cosme gate. And yet, as he declares in his Memoirs, Molino was a sad mistake, a totally unnecessary battle, and he who clambered to the low roof of one of the outbuildings, and secured as prisoners a Mexican officer of rank, with a dozen followers at his back (winning thereby a brevet he would not decline), insisted always that Molino could have been " turned " instead of taken at fearful cost, and that Chapultepec need never have been stormed at all.

Scott in his autobiography asserts that from the walls of Tacubaya, looking northeastward, they saw before the armistice was closed, strong columns of the enemy taking up position at the old " King's Mills "— *los Molinos del Rey,* where a long, low, foundry-like building had been heavily fortified, where its neighbor, the Casa Mata, was reported crammed with ammunition, and whither the very church bells were being carted to be cast into cannon to replace the many captured by the hated Yankees. Scott's line by this time, too, included Tacubaya, four miles out, and when sudden end came to the armistice of nearly eighteen days, Worth's division was nearest Molino, and to Worth, with only three thousand two hundred and fifty men, was intrusted the reduction of that improvised fortress.

The guns of the citadel at Chapultepec to the northeast had a plunging fire upon the approaches to the old mills; the walls and buildings were crammed with infantry, far outnumbering the assaulting column, but Worth sent them in, and for hours the battle raged, hand to hand, as did the savage fighting of the Guardsmen of England and the flower of the French Infantry about the walls of Hougomont. Here died Ransom, colonel of the Ninth; here died Graham, commanding the Eleventh; here fell Kirby Smith, Shackelford, Daniels, Armstrong, Ayers, Burbank, Ernst, Morris, Strong, Burwell and Farry, shot dead or speedily dying of their wounds. Here was freely shed the blood of many another of the gallant band of graduates, George

Wright and Francis Lee (major commanding Grant's regiment), Anderson and Montgomery, Cady, Talcott and Price, Larkin Smith, Mason, Walker, Ruff and Henry J. Hunt (he who was to be our great chief artillerist at Gettysburg), C. S. Hamilton and " Ruddy " Clarke, Grant's classmates, George Andrews, Lincoln, Foster and Snelling, young and enthusiastic subalterns they, and all these, be it remembered, out of only three thousand men engaged—all these being but the larger portion of the killed and wounded among the officers, for only the West Pointers here are named. Molino, in proportion to the numbers engaged, was the deadliest battle of the Mexican war. Chapultepec, carried by storm only two days later (and celebrated to this day as a glorious victory by many a credulous Mexican), was far less costly in life and limb, though it was there young Gantt and " Sandy " Rodgers laid down their lives, and Lee, Longstreet, Mackall, Tower, Page and Innis Palmer were stung by hostile lead.

It was on the San Cosme road and causeway that " Sam " Grant, of the Fourth, reached the height of his early fame. Along the two causeways now the Americans were fighting their way to the city walls, Worth's division heading the advance on the San Cosme and Quitman on the Belen gate. With the very foremost of Worth's pioneers went the quartermaster, who officially belonged to the hindmost. The arches of the aqueduct gave partial shelter until they reached the junction with the east and west road, and here the aqueduct turned; here cannon and musketry both blocked the way, and here the common sense of the quartermaster came into play. A walled enclosure abutted on both roads in the southeast angle. Grant managed to reach it, and presently had led a little detachment under shelter of the walls to a point on the eastward causeway, beyond the guns and the main body of the defense, a piece of Yankee enterprise and effrontery that proved too much for Mexican nerve, and opened the onward way to the gates.

And here again was a stiff and stubborn fight, and here again common sense and the quartermaster became prominent factors in the victory that followed. The Mexican guns at the gateway and musketry on the walls swept the causeway far out to the west. To right and left of it were wet ditches, marshy ponds and but little solid ground, yet on such ground there was to the south of the road a stone church and convent, and thither Grant managed to make his way, clambered to the belfry, and there under his eyes and but a few hundred yards distant, were the guns of the San Cosme and their defenders. Sheltered from the direct aim of his comrades along the causeway and sweeping it with every discharge, the Mexican defenders were exposed to a raking gunfire—if only he had the gun.

As luck would have it, a mountain howitzer had been brought along by the Voltigeurs, and it was somewhere back among the archways of the aqueduct. Hastening thither and asking no authority, Grant pointed out the church to the gunners, told them of the splendid chance it gave and offered to lead them on, and on they went, over hedges and ditches, dragging their little "boomer" with them. Then up the steep and tortuous stairway, with prodigious energy they boosted their gun and hoisted shell and cartridges, and then suddenly from that isolated belfry there burst a challenge of flash and flame and the loud bellow of the howitzer, and all Worth's division saw with delight that some one had had the "horse sense" to reach out and seize that commanding perch, and was pouring death and destruction among the defenders at San Cosme Gate. Rejoicefully Worth sent his aide-de-camp, Pemberton, to find the officer who headed that enterprise and fetch him to the presence of the division commander, and so the future defender of Vicksburg poked his head up into the fire-spitting, smoke-shrouded, ecclesiastical gun platform and asked who was doing all this, and his future conqueror, all dust and grime, had no time to answer questions until told the general wished to see him and personally thank him. Bloody fighting they were having over at the Belen Gate, as many a gallant officer had found to his cost. There Drum and Benjamin lay dead, and Beauregard, Brannan, Lyon, Lovell, Van Dorn and Fitz John Porter were bleeding from their wounds; but here at San Cosme Sam Grant's sacerdotal howitzer had blazed the way for his war-worn comrades, and, sweeping the defenders from the guns, had enabled the storming column to reach the walls.

"Splendidly done, sir!" was the compliment he received from his division general, and no less than three commanders by name referred to him in their official reports. Frank Lee, major commanding the Fourth, wrote of Lieutenant Grant that he had borne himself with "distinguished gallantry," while his old chief, Garland, still heading the brigade, recommended him for official notice and reward for "acquitting himself most nobly on several occasions." No subaltern in all the line had won higher praise or more of it. His brevet of captain, while still a second lieutenant, dates from this 13th of September, "for gallant conduct at Chapultepec," as the general engagement was named.

In two years now, so swiftly came the casualties of the Mexican war, he had risen from the foot to the head of the list of second lieutenants of the Fourth Infantry, and here and within the compass of another day came still further advancement. Such determined valor as shown by the storming columns had proved too much for the Mexican chieftain, Santa Ana. With the "Gringos" thundering at both the Belen and San Cosme Gates, he that night turned loose the convicts and desperadoes in the city prisons, left them arms and ammunition with which to pour desultory fire from house-tops and windows when the invaders burst their inevitable way, and, gathering his chosen about him, slipped northward out of the city. Next morning when the leaders of the Fourth Infantry broke cheering through the portal of San Cosme and swarmed into the city streets, one of the first to fall, stricken down by the bullet of a felon, was Sydney Smith, who, dying, made his mourning and admiring friend a first lieutenant.

It was Grant's last battle for many a day.

That winter was spent in and about the city of Mexico, recuperating, making themselves acquainted with the country, and reading the tremendous tales in the papers of their prowess in the field; but the tales told of and by General Pillow and certain of his followers eclipsed all others. They ignored the commanding general; they exalted beyond all measure the services of Pillow's division; and they brought about a lamentable breach between brave and brilliant Scott and two of the bravest and most brilliant of his subordinates, erstwhile devoted followers and friends—Worth, commander of the famous and hard-fighting First Division, and Duncan, the "lightning" commander of their famous battery. It was something Grant never forgot. It was something he had in mind when, after his own brilliant campaign in central Mississippi, one of his corps commanders took to publishing, even as had Pillow in '47, and it led to prompt and summary action, as will later be seen. But Scott in '47 had no friendly and grateful administration behind him as had Grant in '63.

Worth had been Scott's aide-de-camp in days gone by, and loved him. Worth had at first been Scott's most admired division commander. Even at Churubusco he had praised him as daring and skilful, and at Molino had given him the post of honor; but an envious soul had sought to break up that time-tried comradeship, and had succeeded. Scott had become suspicious and Worth estranged. Duncan had sided with his division chief, and the army looked sorrowfully on as the breach widened and the war of words and recrimination waged. Exasperated at length, Scott had ordered Worth, Pillow and Duncan in arrest, and the answer of the administration was the promotion of Duncan to be colonel and inspector general of the army; and, with the order for a court in the case of the accused officers, there came from Washington as the final reward of his brilliant services, the order for a court of inquiry on Scott himself.

But before this melancholy close had come to his brilliant campaign and career in Mexico, Scott had figured in many a dramatic scene—his spectacular entry into the capital city was one; his memorable dinner in honor of General Twiggs was another. Twiggs was to take command at Vera Cruz, and on the eve of his departure Scott feasted him at a banquet attended by Commissioner Trist, by several prominent civilian residents, British and others, and by Generals Twiggs, Persifer Smith, Franklin Pierce and Caleb Cushing, and by half a dozen officers of high rank, of whom only two were graduates of West Point. Scott wished to spare their blushes, he said, for it was on this occasion he toasted the Military Academy of the nation and paid to its *élèves* a remarkable tribute: " But for the science of West Point," said he, " this army, multiplied by four, could not have entered the capital of Mexico."

Still later, testifying before a congressional committee, Scott said as follows:

" I give it as my fixed opinion that but for our graduated cadets, the war between the United States and Mexico would have lasted four or five years, with, in its first half, more defeats than victories falling to our share, whereas, in less than two campaigns we conquered a great country and a peace without the loss of a single battle or a skirmish."

THE SOLDIER OF SAN COSME

And of these graduated cadets, as the winter wore on, by common consent among the survivors, there was no junior in the entire array who had acquitted himself with higher credit, or had rendered more valiant or valuable services, than the very modest and mild-mannered young quartermaster of the Fourth Infantry, not yet four years out of the leading strings of West Point, and yet widely known among the little army of exiles at the capital city as " Old Sam Grant." And all of this was soon to be forgotten, and in spite of all this it is often declared that Grant had never been heard of before the war for the preservation of the Union.

CHAPTER XII

PEACE—THE PACIFIC COAST AND TROUBLE

THE T. I. O. of cadet days had by this time become widely scattered. But presently there grew up within the walls of Mexico an association of officers that lived long famous in the annals of the army. Created by graduates of West Point, it was planned to include in its membership many a gallant and worthy officer of volunteers, and the very first president elected by the " Aztecs " was the commanding general of the Second Brigade of the Third, Pillow's, Division, Franklin Pierce, of New Hampshire—he who was to defeat Scott for the presidency in the fall of 1854, and to be lampooned from one end of the Union to the other, after the manner of our press and politicians, as a contemptible coward. That he should have been chosen by the almost unanimous vote of his brother officers, most of them regulars, to be the first president of that exclusive body, the " Aztecs," is sufficient in itself to refute the charge that he was hiding in the ditches at the rear while his men were fighting at the front. The few months that elapsed before the recall of General Scott had given the little army opportunity to sift the truth out of most of the stories in circulation, and the difference between the accounts brought home by the earliest returning warriors, and those which became the standard versions among the " Aztecs," the stay-it-through soldiers, was a curious and interesting study. Many a reputation that went up like a rocket in the fall of '47, came down like a stick with the final returns. But one thing the campaign had proved beyond peradventure, and that was the fighting power of the young West Pointers, fifty of whom had been killed and eighty-seven wounded in battle, the classes nearest Grant being by far the heaviest losers.

And while studying these statistics of that unrighteous war with Mexico, it may be well to record this fact: In point of numbers actually engaged there was never a fight of any consequence in which the Mexican force did not far outnumber the Americans, usually three or four to one, but Mexican leadership from first to last was wretched. They lost to a fighting force that at no time exceeded eight thousand men, no less than forty thousand taken prisoners, a thousand cannon, and ten fortified positions carried by siege or assault. As the entire army of the United States contained at that time no more than five hundred graduates of West Point, it may reasonably be conceded that there was glory enough to go round and leave abundance to be shared by their comrades the volunteers. Surely Baker's men at Cerro Gordo, under the lead of that heroic figure, the earlier friend and " statesman " of Abraham Lincon, the later gifted orator of the Pacific coast and of the Senate of the United States, the soldier sacrifice of Ball's Bluff, had won a place in history. Surely the flank attack of Shields, another famous volunteer from Illinois, had vastly helped to turn the tide at Churubusco. Surely the Mississippians at Buena Vista had won old Rough and Ready's hearty praise, and more than that, his final forgiveness of that undesired, but most gallant, son-in-law, their wounded West Point colonel, Jefferson Davis. Surely the Kentuckians at Buena Vista, after losing in succession their heroic leaders, McKee and Henry Clay, colonel and lieutenant-colonel respectively, and West Pointers both of high renown—surely these had won a name the nation never yet has forgotten and never will forget, so long as men read, and hearts thrill over the glowing words of Theodore O'Hara:

THE TRUE ULYSSES S. GRANT

Sons of the Dark and Bloody Ground,
    Ye must not slumber there,
Where stranger steps and tongues resound
    Along the heedless air.
Your own proud land's heroic soil
    Shall be your fitter grave.
She claims from war his richest spoil—
    The ashes of her brave.

But after all the fighting came the lull of inaction
and the letters and papers from home, and then dissensions among the chiefs and discussions among the
juniors, the wiser heads avoiding both. During the fall
and winter months that followed the final victory many
and various were the methods resorted to for killing
time. Cards, drills, dances and dinners were the main
devices, though we hear of an occasional cock fight and
even a semi-occasional bull fight gotten up by the natives
for the lucre, not the love, of the hated invader. For
none of these had " Sam " Grant any liking whatever.
The cock and the bull fights he would not attend. Many
of the officers took to learning Spanish. The methods
were alluring and many of the teachers charming, but
for Spanish Grant felt as much aversion as he earlier
had for French, and as for the teachers, they lured
him not at all.

In those months of rest and relaxation there was
active employment for the staff, and Grant had his
hands full. His duty it was to provide for the needs
of the inner as well as the outer man. There were no
regimental commissaries in those days; this function
devolved upon the quartermaster, and in the performance of these duties Grant very successfully ran a
military bakery which produced bread of excellent
quality at moderate price, and declared a dividend in
favor of the Fourth. He made peaceful forays into
the interior, and brought home food, fruits, forage, all
much appreciated, both by man and beast. He had few

ULYSSES S. GRANT
While Lieutenant 4th Infantry

The photograph from which this was taken distinctly shows captain shoulder straps under the epaulettes. It must have been taken just after the Mexican War, at the time of his marriage in 1848— when he was brevet captain.

From "Grant's Life in the West and his Mississippi Campaign," by Col. John W. Emerson, published in the *Midland Monthly.* By kindness of G. P. Putnam's Sons

books to read, but there were frequent letters now, long ones, that seemed to give him infinite satisfaction, and to require long hours of semi-seclusion for absorption and for reply.

And yet his old comrades tell of him that he was far from being reserved or solitary then. He seemed to enjoy the fun and chaff and chatter after mess, only it was his way to listen rather than to talk. His keen eyes, twinkling with fun and appreciation, would glance from speaker to speaker, " taking them all in and sizing them up," as once said a veteran of the " Aztecs," to the end that as the springtime came on, and the treaty of peace at Guadalupe Hidalgo, it would seem that Grant had made a rather accurate mental estimate of the character and capacity of most of his messmates and many a man in other commands. There was to come a time when such knowledge would prove of infinite value to him and, through him, to the nation.

They made an excursion to Popocatapetl, too, and had a trying experience, with no little temporary suffering, but after all they were glad, without exception, when the *dolce far niente* days about the capital were ended and the army on the march for home. Grant had saved a little money from his salary, for expenses were not high in the land of mañana. Peace with honor had come, and he was being hailed by the Fourth as Captain Grant, in spite of the fact that the Senate was unaccountably " holding up " some brevet nominations, even while lavishly confirming others. The home folk were all eager to see and welcome him at Georgetown, but out at White Haven, on the Gravois road southwest of St. Louis, there was waiting a girl who was prouder of that Monterey-Molino and San Cosme record, and of those two brevets, than were even the gentle mother and sisters at home. Julia Dent had a brother in the army and knew something about such things, but Grant, the father, Jesse Root of Brown

County, looked only with pragmatical eyes upon the reward for services rendered. What were brevets of first lieutenant and captain if they brought with them no extra pay with which to purchase captains' shoulder-straps and epaulets—the only tangible tokens of the honors the son had received?

But meantime, on the homeward way, misfortune had come to Grant.

Just before the march began, while still at Tacubaya, our quartermaster found himself with something over a thousand dollars of government funds which had to be taken along and for which he had no safe. Exactly one thousand dollars, therefore, was placed in the trunk of Captain Gore, as secure a receptacle as any one could suggest, and ten nights thereafter that trunk was skilfully taken from the little tent in which Captain Gore and his young lieutenant, John de Russy, were soundly sleeping. A board of officers convened at Jalapa and exonerated Grant of all blame or responsibility, but Uncle Sam is a relentless creditor in such matters. The Treasury Department held it up against the helpless officer, pending the remote passage of an act of Congress for his relief, and for years that possible stoppage against his pitiably small stipend hung ever above him. That, too, was to augment his worries in the near future, but for the time being, supposing official exoneration all sufficient, he lived in roseate hope and anticipation.

A luckier regiment was sent to occupy the Fourth's old quarters at Jefferson Barracks; but, along in the early summer, looking somewhat tanned and a trifle older, the young soldier suitor reappeared at White Haven, and a quiet little ceremony was presently enacted, attended by several cherished comrades of the war days, notably Cadmus Wilcox and that tall Eighth Infantryman Longstreet. There was a brief and modest honeymoon, and then along in the autumn the young couple journeyed to Sackett Harbor, New York, and regimental duty was resumed. The old Fourth by that time was scattered among the few stations along the great lakes—mainly at Fort Wayne, just below Detroit, at Sackett Harbor and Mackinac.

But the Fourth was changing. Major Lee was no longer in command, and presently, in May, '49, Lieutenant-Colonel Bonneville, a comparative stranger to them and to their traditions, joined and assumed command. The quartermastership had been resigned about the time of the marriage, and Grant did company duty for a while, cheerily enough, for the young bride was there to tie his sash and buckle the belt more trimly, and persuade him, long accustomed to the laxities of bearing and dress permitted in storeroom and corral, to pay more attention to his military appearance. Though neat as a new pin, Grant hated the black stock and snugly buttoned frock. It was not long, however, before the quartermaster *pro tem* found other and more attractive duty, and regimental sentiment recalled "Sam" Grant. Colonel Bonneville, already aging (graduate of the Class of 1815), was twenty-eight years Grant's senior in the service. He had other views as to that vacancy, but so strong was regimental feeling in the matter that he decided it unwise to oppose it. Grant was again, in September, '49, called to the office, and for four more years uninterruptedly and most creditably performed its manifold duties, but during those four years marked and memorable events occurred, and the high content with which he resumed duty as quartermaster, and the happiness the army home life now afforded him, were destined to suffer serious relapse.

The Mexican war ended, and all hope of promotion blocked by the opening of the year 1850, a period of semi-stagnation fell upon the service, in the midst of which, in '52, the government decided on sending more troops to the recently acquired territory on the Pacific coast. The gold excitement in California had led to rapid increase of population there. The Indians in Oregon were giving trouble, and, as luck would have it, the old Fourth were ordered to leave their cosy, homelike stations along the lakes, bid farewell to civilization, and prepare for duty in an untrodden wilderness. The blow came upon the Grants when their first-born, named for his gallant Uncle Fred (Frederick Dent), was just beginning to toddle about and tumble into mischief. There were now other reasons why it would have been a grievous hardship for that young wife and mother to attempt the long, trying trip by sea, to the far-away shores of the Pacific. There was again aroused in Grant the desire to quit the army as so many of his West Point comrades were doing, most of them for fairly lucrative positions in civil life. Barely four years after their happy wedding Grant bowed to what he considered the inevitable, and decided to leave his wife and son to the care of the Dents at St. Louis, to accompany his regiment and see the marvellous new El Dorado within the Golden Gate, when possibly at San Francisco he might find the very opportunity he sought, but if not, surely where so many others had succeeded in obtaining professorships or engineering work in " the States," the chances were that he, too, could do so. The mails were burdened with his letters to all manner of men who had quit soldiering for civil pursuits. There were Gilham and Johnson, of the Class of 1840, both established as professors, the one at the Virginia Military Institute, the other in that of West Kentucky. There were Whiting and Tilden, of the same class, both teaching for a living. There was Sears of '41, already professor of mathematics at the University of Louisiana. There were Stewart, of '42, professor of mathematics at Cumberland University, Tennessee; Hill at Washington College, Lexington, Virginia, and Williamson at the Kentucky Military Institute. Quinby of his own class, their crack mathematician, had just resigned and taken a professorship at Rochester University, New York, and there were Curd and Read of '44, both professors of mathematics or science. There were a dozen others, Fahnestock, Hammond, Darne, Johnstone, Robertson, Story and Hebert, all reported doing well as planters or farmers. There were McCalmont and Collins in the law; Gill and Thomas in railway engineering. There was that odd genius of the plebe class when Grant was a senior, Thomas J. Jackson, of Virginia; he, too, had just taken a professorship at the Virginia Military Institute. Then Deshon, his roommate at one time, had resigned after eight years of ordnance duty, and was seeking holy orders. Then there was Couts, after years in the dragoons and Lower California, who resigned to become a ranchero. If all these men whom he well knew, and so many more of whom he had only heard, could so readily establish themselves in civil pursuits, surely he, too, could find something better for himself, for his young wife and that burly baby boy than the one-room-and-a-kitchen-with-less-than-a-thousand-a-year, which was the best the Army could promise him for a decade or more to come.

It would seem that right here and now the prospering father might have borne a hand. The best, however, that Jesse had to offer, if anything, was the tannery again, and it all ended as it had in '45, with Grant's going with his regiment, and for a second time, and under far more trying and touching circumstances, with his heart yearning over " the girl I left behind me." For once in his life, if not oftener, he thanked his stars he could not tell one tune from another, or in spite of his manhood his eyes might well have brimmed over when the fifes and drums of the Fourth struck up the soldier lay to which for half a century, at least, wherever " England's martial drumbeat, companion of the hours" had girdled the globe, her men-at-arms and those of her independent daughter Columbia, had marched away to other fields, leaving weeping wives and maids at home.

A solemn journey was that to the Pacific. A crowded, side-wheel steamer took the eight companies, men, women and children, in the very season of all others when they should not have been sent there, mid-summer, to the Isthmus of Panama. From Aspinwall they could be trundled on the new railway as far as the banks of the Chagres River; then they had to be poled or pulled in small boats up stream to Gorgona; then came twenty-five miles "mule back or marching" across the range to Panama and the Pacific.

Bonneville and the troops marched away from Gorgona in comparative comfort, leaving the quarter-master to look after the many wives and children of the soldiery, all the regimental baggage, the sick and broken down, the skulkers and stragglers. It is no trick to ride away at the head of a regular regiment for a march of twenty or thirty miles, but the labors of Hercules were light in comparison with the burden of respon-sibility and care the colonel shunted on the shoulders of Grant. It was that summer they began to stoop.

They were all to follow "by contract" from Cruces, but the contractor could not begin to fill the bill, he had not mules enough by half. They were marooned, a colony of fretful women and crying children, in the pestilential thickets of the Chagres fully a week, wait-ing for the new contractor Grant had found, and in the midst of it all and of their enforced camp, there came that dreaded foe, the cholera.

One company had been left to guard them from marauders or plunderers, but the coming of the plague, from which no human force could then defend them, made other guards unnecessary. Grant ordered that company forthwith to rejoin the regiment. Then with his little band of helpers reduced to the married soldiers, he gathered up his stricken caravan and started on the slow and mournful march to the coast. Barely twenty miles had he to cover, but by the time he turned over his charge to the officials at Panama, one-third of his number had succumbed to cholera and had been buried either at Cruces or along the way. No wonder " Old Sam " Grant seemed aging more rapidly than his fellows.

When at last the voyage to San Francisco could be resumed, some three weeks later, Grant was looking ten years older. The regiment was rallying about him more cordially than ever; company officers and men all seemed to swear by him, but Major Lee, his stanch friend, had been promoted out to the lieutenant-colonelcy of the Sixth. The new major fell in with the lieutenant-colonel commanding, and with a captain or two, men who had served with other commands at Vera Cruz and the march to Mexico; and so it happened that officers who had borne the heat and burden of the day and had fought and bled and shared every peril with the Fourth, although largely in the majority, were not the men in authority—the men in highest rank and in control. These were considerations destined deeply to affect the fortunes of the man the regiment all the more stoutly supported in the quartermastership, and, unconsciously, perhaps, added to the latent antagonism existing in the mind of the lieutenant-colonel commanding, and by him (is it an unfair inference?) communicated to his own especial associates, the major, and a senior captain destined presently to be detailed to important and significant commands.

A brief while the regiment tarried at Benicia, and then was shipped up the coast to the Columbia, where headquarters were established at Columbia Barracks, now Fort Vancouver, with two companies detached to a lonely station at Humboldt Bay to the south. The command of the district of Northern California was presently given to the major, George Wright. The command of the little isolated post of Fort Humboldt had fallen to that senior captain and veteran soldier, Robert C. Buchanan. Meantime for a year Grant continued his duties as regimental quartermaster at Columbia Barracks, a year filled with cares, anxieties and yearnings that no one fully understood, since he so rarely spoke of them, and that withdrew him little by little from the cheery companionship of his fellows.

To begin with, there had come, even as he was fighting cholera on the Isthmus, a second baby boy, and the reason why so devoted a husband as Grant could leave his wife behind was more easily understood. But these hostages to fortune involved care and cost and responsibility in proportion to the numbers, and Grant had other cares. That confounded thousand-dollar loss at Puebla had been a sore distress. There were men at Sackett Harbor with whom he had business relations in bygone days, who owed him money in considerable sums but, now that he was long months and miles away, ignored his claims. He had embarked in some little enterprises about Vancouver which he hoped might add a few dollars to his pay, and they were doing just the reverse. He was becoming more and more silent and obviously sad, and presently it became known to many an officer that " Sam " Grant was beginning to drink more than was good for him.

He who had been so free from vice of any and every kind, was yielding to a not uncommon weakness, probably because in his loneliness and longing it seemed to bring him temporary surcease from pain. As regimental quartermaster, and temporarily on a bachelor status, he had more room in his quarters than other comrades, and visiting officers, as a consequence, became his charge and guests. Coming and going all the time these were many. Coming and staying for several weeks was George B. McClellan, of the Engineers, with whom Grant had served in happier days in Mexico, and McClellan noted with concern the occasional over-indulgence of his host—the First Classman who had been so cheery and kind to him when he was a " plebe." All this was to have its weight in days to come.

It was not that Grant drank much, as explained by his most devoted friends. The trouble was that a very little would flush that fair complexion of his and thicken his never glib or lively tongue. On far less liquor than many a comrade carried without a sign, Grant would appear half stupefied. At Columbia Barracks, with no guard, drills or parade duties to attend, with practically no one to supervise (for the quartermaster had scant occasion to appear before the colonel), the matter attracted no official notice. Then one day came the news that " Perfect " Bliss had passed away, and that his company, long commanded by its first lieutenant, and now stationed at Fort Humboldt, would have a new captain and commander—that after years of service as quartermaster, and away from all the starch and buckram, pomp and circumstance, fuss and feathers of military life, Captain Grant was to step at once into the presence of a soldier of the old school—a commander in every sense of the word, " the martinet of the army " some went so far as to call one of the most thorough gentlemen and admirable officers that ever wore our uniform—Brevet Lieutenant-Colonel Robert C. Buchanan, then Captain Fourth Infantry, commanding the little post at Humboldt Bay.

There are three versions of the trouble that speedily followed. In order to reach the new post Grant had first to go away down the coast to San Francisco, and there take a coastwise vessel north again. His new commission was dated July 5th, but it was September before he could transfer all funds, papers and property to his successor, John Withers, of Mississippi. It was later when he reached San Francisco, and as coasters were few, and dependent on wind and tide, it was much later when he finally reached Fort Humboldt, and Buchanan took umbrage at that to begin with. Then Buchanan was a man who in every look and step and gesture was the precise and punctilious soldier. His uniform fitted him like a glove; his equipments were always spick and span. When he spoke to a senior in rank, his heels clicked together and he stood at salute, and so he expected the juniors should stand before him. It was the writer's privilege to serve in subaltern days under that gifted soldier's command, to hold him in admiration and esteem unbounded. The daily "matinee" at which Buchanan, then Colonel of the First Infantry, assembled all the officers in garrison, and the prompt dressing down he administered to any officer who presumed to pick up a newspaper, who dared to yawn, or who had the hardihood to glance out of the nearest window, were admirable in their effect upon the laggard or the slouchy among his subordinates. And all these traits he had as commander at Fort Humboldt, and this was the man whom Grant had now to serve. Between two soldiers of such variant types there was no possibility of sympathy. Buchanan had no tolerance for weakness of any kind. The deeds of daring, devotion and soldiership of the highest order that had made Grant famous in the Fourth were all apparently forgotten. The story told the writer by one of the oldest in the old Fourth, and one of the fondest friends Grant ever had —and he had them then by dozens and later by tens of thousands—was to the effect that after a warning on one occasion, Buchanan had, on a second, called upon the captain to place in his, the post commander's hands, his written resignation, with the understanding that should there be another lapse, that paper would inevitably go forward "Approved."

"Grant was well nigh sick of it all, anyhow," as his fellows said. That winter of loneliness at Humboldt, with the home letters full of love and yearning from his fair, young wife, and the prattle of his baby boy of which she told him, seem to have determined and decided him. The captaincy was worth just then about thirteen hundred a year. If he could not make at least two thousand farming, engineering or teaching mathematics, he was better under the sod. There came a day when Buchanan saw reason to forward that resignation, dated July 31st, 1854, and to the sorrow of many a fellow who had learned to love his simple nature and straightforward ways, "Old Sam" Grant bade adieu to Humboldt, went direct to San Francisco and, eager to rejoin the dear ones at St. Louis, took the first steamer he could catch for home. To him and to the men who best knew him he was quitting the service because the life and isolation away from family and fireside had become insupportable. To many a senior, to many a soldier, and to heaven only knows how many a citizen thereafter, it was given out and understood that he left the army because he had to. Of the former were such sturdy Fourth Infantrymen as C. C. Augur, a Christian gentleman and soldier, Henry M. Judah, who stood by him in his sorrows at Humboldt, "Davy" Russell, of the Class of '45, Macfeely, of the Class of '50, Henry C. Hodges, of '51, one of the most soldierly men of his day, who still lives to tell of Grant as the most truthful man he ever knew. There were Kautz, of his old Georgetown home, who served with him at Vancouver, and George Crook, who lived with him awhile at Humboldt, both of '52, and then just after he left there came to join that array of Grant's friends and backers, the little giant of the Class of '53, with his snapping black eyes and quick, abrupt manner—like Kautz and Crook and Grant, a Buckeye to the core—Phil Sheridan by name. It was never safe to say in presence of such as these that "Sam" Grant *had* to quit the army. There were those among them who could not forgive it in Bonneville and Buchanan that he had been permited to go at all.

On the other hand, there were men of rank and distinction in and about San Francisco at the time, some of whom accepted the official side of the story and would seek no other explanation, nor for years would accept any other estimate of the humbled and sad-faced officer who for a few days hovered about the city. Of such was Halleck, the prosperous and successful lawyer, of such was *not* the recently resigned Tecumseh Sherman, just then trying banking as a starter, the man to whom Grant might readily have appealed for aid had he not been too sensitive and proud.

There were two men in San Francisco, as one of his biographers declares, who owed him a little money, and both of them were penniless when he applied to them for payment. Almost every dollar he could hope to get, therefore, was in an order for extra pay for court-martial services, and, because of some little technical flaw, the paymaster refused to cash it.

To a clerk in the depot quartermaster's office, who well knew Grant as regimental quartermaster, he was indebted for the only aid that came to him in all that crowded city. It was he who cashed the draft, he who secured a suitable stateroom in the returning side-wheeler bound for Panama, and who sympathetically bade Grant farewell. To the few of the Fourth whom he had seen ere leaving Humboldt Grant had said, " If you hear from me again it will probably be as a well-to-do farmer." To this humble friend in the department he said at parting: " I could not have hoped for such comfort as this stateroom, nor do I know how I can ever repay your kindness, *but* strange things have happened and may again."

Strange things did happen. Simon Bolivar Buckner,

of the Class of '44, who fought almost side by side with him at Molino, and who, like him, would not touch a brevet that told of Contreras, had been made captain and commissary and stationed in New York, and there he was when Grant arrived, practically penniless, and Buckner it was whose purse was placed at Grant's disposal to take him to that distant home, Buckner it was to whom Grant had to dictate unconditional surrender in less than ten years thereafter, and then to tender every dollar in his well-filled wallet to his prisoner and friend and former benefactor.

CHAPTER XIII

THE USES OF ADVERSITY

Nor were the stories accepted at home, either at Georgetown or at White Haven, that Grant's "habits" had been at the bottom of his worries and troubles in the army. In point of fact, those were days in which the use of alcoholic liquor was by no means a custom honored in the breach rather than in the observance. Whiskey of excellent quality was part of the prescribed stores of the military service, was sold to officers and through them even to the men, at a very moderate price; something under twenty-five cents would buy a gallon. Whiskey was habitually served at many a leading western hotel, a little glassful as an appetizer appearing beside each plate at dinner time. Wine flowed freely at every public function, and whiskey, rum and brandy had been served in tubs at certain presidential fêtes on the White House lawn. There were strong advocates of total abstinence in the line of the army, as General Hitchcock records of the Third Infantry, just before the Mexican war; but in civil life, in the learned professions, and notably the law, in statecraft, politics and even the halls of congress, the total abstainer was a *rara avis*—the occasional over-indulgence by no means rare. In the service the story was still told of that most gallant colonel whom Hitchcock found, on his homeward way from Mexico, dying in New Orleans, the man who defended Fort Sandusky with such furious personal vim and fiery example as to enable him with one gun and a handful of men to thrash a force ten times his own in numbers. Long years thereafter when complaint was made to the President and Commander-in-chief of the major's intemperance, "Old Hickory"

"HARDSCRABBLE" AS AT PRESENT

With General Frederick Dent Grant

Courtesy of Mr. C. F. Blanke, St. Louis

turned upon the complainants with indignant protest: "That man has done enough to entitle him to get drunk every day of his life if he wants to, and," with a bang of his fist on the table, "by the Eternal, the United States shall pay for his whiskey!" Long years later still, the gentlest, most patient, yet withal the wisest of our presidents was moved to endorse, upon a somewhat similar complaint against the man upon whom he leaned in prayerful hope: "I cannot spare this man—he fights."

The homecoming was sweet and hope was still high when Grant rejoined the household in Missouri. Colonel Dent had never fancied for his daughter a life in the army, and the year just gone by, '53, had seen many resignations from the service of men confident of success in other fields. Brother Fred had recently written that their classmate, C. S. Hamilton, had tired of the service and gone to farming in Wisconsin, and Hamilton had never had Grant's practical experience in planting, ploughing and caring for the stock. Only a dozen miles out from St. Louis lay an unbroken tract of woodland which had been given to Julia Dent, and the very autumn of his return Grant himself set sturdily to work to fell the timber, clear the land, build a little log homestead for the wife and babies, and with the spring of '55 was almost happily, as in boy days, holding the plough and putting in long hours seeding and planting. He wrote hopeful letters to the father and mother and sisters at home. He worked as hard as any of the hands he was able to hire. He had to have a little help from father, and probably father-in-law, for the purchase or hire of horses, mules and implements, but if his crops turned out as his father's always had in Georgetown, it would be but a matter of three years when he could be free from debt and doing well.

In those days he was far happier than he had been in California. During the winter he drove his cord wood into town and sold it in open market, and then drove cheerily back to the little homestead and the growing family. On one of these occasions, in the rough garb of the farmer, whip in hand, he met his friend and classmate, J. J. Reynolds, another of the recently resigned, and the possessor of a professorship, and Reynolds and a little bevy of army men joyously welcomed " Old Sam " to the Planters Hotel, and, as was so many a year the custom, clinked their glasses in cordial greeting, but Grant declined. During those few years from '54 to '57, while still strong and hopeful, he found his comfort in his home, poor and crude though it was, and could not be induced, it was claimed for him, even on these week-day excursions to St. Louis, to tamper with drink.

But the crops never rewarded the labor given to them, and still he struggled on, growing a little grim now and more stoop-shouldered from much bending over farm work. He leased " Hardscrabble " in the winter of '57 and 8, and took the old Dent farm, where in March he worked three darkies, and had one hundred and forty acres planted with corn and wheat, oats and potatoes, and again there came promise of success. And then, as fate would have it, the old enemy of his boy days, fever and ague, came and laid him by the heels, and with that blow went out the last hope he had of making even a living at the farm.

They sold the stock, implements and supplies for what they could get, and the following spring moved to a very humble roof in town, and once again Grant strove to find a new way of providing for the wife and little ones. And now times became hard indeed, and the sharp, stern lesson of adversity was being forced upon him with every succeeding day. He entered into partnership with a relation of the Dents. Real estate and collections was the new venture. Grant was no failure as a farmer, but as a collector he was simply a " flat."

COLONEL DENT'S HOUSE WHERE GRANT WAS
MARRIED, 1848
Southwest corner Fourth and Cerre Streets, St. Louis

From photographs made in 1903   By courtesy of the *Post Dispatch*, St. Louis

WHERE GRANT LIVED IN ST. LOUIS IN 1859
1008 Barton Street

FIRST HOUSE AT GALENA, ILL., OCCUPIED BY GRANT AND HIS FAMILY IN 1860-61.

As it now looks after many repairs

From a photograph especially taken, March, 1914. Courtesy of Major J. W. Westwick

volunteers of his adopted State was sufficient to stagger his faith in the possibility of an early end to the rebellion. Officers and men alike were ablaze with patriotism, but ignorant of the first principles of military instruction. Regimental camps were huge town meetings. There was splendid material for the work before them, but no master hand to mould, to train, to discipline. The Governor presently sent Grant to muster into the State service the new regiments in southern Illinois, and what he saw in their camps convinced him that under such colonels, no matter how brave and willing, no real soldier work could be accomplished. He presently had opportunity to revisit St. Louis, and, together with him who was his senior in " plebe " days, and who was destined to become the greatest and nearest of his subordinates within another year—with Tecumseh Sherman, fresh from his parting with pupils and faculty of the Louisiana University, Grant witnessed, on the 10th of May, the first clash between the Union and Secession forces in the city streets. That served further to convince him that time would be required. Late in May, being utterly opposed to the methods of electing or selecting field officers in vogue in Illinois, and being fully determined to tender his services, he forwarded the then ignored, but now famous letter which is given here in full:

GALENA, ILL., May 24, 1861.

SIR:

Having served for fifteen years in the regular army, including four years at West Point, and feeling it the duty of every one who has been educated at the government expense to offer their services for the support of the government, I have the honor very respectfully to tender my services until the close of the war, in such capacity as may be offered.

I would say in view of my present age and length of service, I feel myself competent to command a regiment, if the President in his judgment should see fit to intrust one to me. Since the first call of the President I have been serving on the staff of the Governor of this state, rendering such aid as I could in the organization of our state militia, and I am still engaged in that capacity. A letter addressed to me at Springfield, Illinois, will reach me.

I am very respectfully, your obedient servant,

U. S. GRANT.

By this time, too, Captain John Pope, of the United States Engineers, had been sent to Springfield, had seen Grant and urged him to seek a command. Meantime, also, there were new regiments coming to Springfield, among them the Twenty-first, organized at Mattoon on the 9th of May. On the 15th it had been mustered into the State service for one month by Captain Grant. A lively, hilarious thousand they were, and a hopeless task it was to keep them either in camp or order. Grant found opportunity just then to visit his father at Covington, and talk over the situation. He had another object in going thither: his comrade of the Mexican war days, his guest for some weeks at Fort Vancouver, George B. McClellan, had been called from the presidency of the Ohio and Mississippi Railway, to the command of the Ohio militia, with the State rank of major-general, followed by his being commissioned almost immediately by the President as a major-general in the army of the United States—a sudden and most unlooked-for elevation. Orders from Washington assigned McClellan to the head of a military district including the States of Ohio, Indiana, Illinois, Missouri and certain adjacent territory, and the young officer, only thirty-five years of age, was busily engaged in the duties of this new and important command when Grant sought an interview, spent the greater part of two days in vain endeavor to see his former comrade, sitting the while humble and unnoticed in the hallway, and finally left disappointed. He says that he would ask nothing of McClellan, but owns that he hoped McClellan would tender him an appointment on his staff.

Fortune had reserved him for a far better fate. The Twenty-first Illinois had proved much too tough a proposition for any of the officers appointed over it. They were said to be in almost mutinous condition when Governor Yates was seized with an inspiration. If any man could do anything with them it was probably Captain Grant, and a telegram went forthwith to Covington tendering him the colonelcy of the recalcitrant regiment. Back came the answer: "I accept the regiment and will start immediately," and on Monday afternoon, June 17th, he reached Springfield and went at once to camp to assume command.

It had been planned to start proceedings with an appeal to their patriotism, and that great leader and orator, John A. Logan, was asked by the Governor to open the ball. Beside the swarthy, black-moustached, martial-looking speaker stood the new colonel, silent, travel-stained, with only a red bandana by way of a sash bound loosely about the waist of his worn, civilian sackcoat, and with a stick in lieu of a sword. Logan finished in a glowing apostrophe, and then, after the manner of the sovereign citizen of the boundless and unterrified West, the men of the Twenty-first began to shout for Grant. "Grant!" "Grant!" "Colonel Grant!" "Speech!" And the Colonel stepped quietly forward, waited for the tumult to subside, and in precisely four words made the demanded, but by no means the expected, address: "Go to your quarters!" he said, and, too much astonished for further words, the men obeyed.

Eleven days later, a silent and reasonably subordinate regiment by that time, the Twenty-first Illinois, Colonel Ulysses S. Grant, was formally mustered into service by Captain Thomas G. Pitcher, U. S. Army. Five years later, when at last the supervision of the United States Military Academy was taken from the Engineers and thrown open to the entire army, the first "general" of our service, being called upon to designate the first superintendent under the new dispensation, laid before the President the name of Thomas G. Pitcher, brevet brigadier-general U. S. Army.

The stories of Grant's brief and memorable service with the Twenty-first are innumerable. Several of them seem to be true. He was the first man to open their eyes as to the meaning of military duty and discipline—perhaps the only man then at or near Springfield who was capable of doing it. In the ten days that elapsed between his taking command, and their getting marching orders, a remarkable change had come over the Twenty-first. The bully of the regiment had come back from town one evening drunk, defiant, mutinous, daring everybody or anybody to lay a hand on him. His company officers and sergeants strove to soothe him, to mollify and persuade, which made him only more insolent and defiant. Grant saw the trouble from afar, strolled calmly over to the company street, made his way through the crowd, and with one well-delivered blow and without a word stretched the bully on his back, called for a bayonet and, after the methods of the Mexican war days, deftly proceeded to gag the rioter. A more penitent bully Camp Dick Yates never saw than the tough of the Twenty-first when finally released. Nor were those days in which he could find sympathy or support in charging his colonel with brutal methods. Even the rank and file of the regiment said, " served him right."

The next lesson was less personal in its application. The Twenty-first, it seems, took kindly to whiskey, and the Colonel one day got wind of the fact that many a canteen was "loaded." Halt, was the word, and then calmly the Colonel proceeded to have the contents of every canteen poured out into the thirsty soil of Sangamon County. The chaplain tells us all this, so it must be true.

The regiment was ordered to be in readiness to march at 6 A.M., and the Twenty-first, as had been their habit, took their own time. Those men not ready were compelled to " fall in " just as they stood or sat, and, some without shoes, some without caps or coats, were put through an hour's work before being allowed to fall out and get their entire equipment. In a week, though the drill was by no means good, the discipline was something the volunteers of Illinois, since the days of Baker's brigade, at least, had never seen or dreamed of. Other colonels came to watch the methods of this calm, resolute Mexican war man who never found it necessary to get excited or to swear.

Up at the capitol Governor Yates was rejoicing over the success of his appointee, and laughing at the croakers, including the former colonel, who had predicted the Twenty-first would prove too tough for even a veteran regular to tackle. There was another man among men, Elihu B. Washburne, of Galena, who was watching all this with keen interest and satisfaction. Both Yates and Washburne were beginning to " get his measure," as they expressed it, when sudden orders came from Major-General John C. Fremont, then commanding at St. Louis, to send the Twenty-first to the Mississippi. The order was duly transmitted to Grant as colonel commanding, and the agent of the railway presently came in to the capitol to say in effect that he had been insulted. " I went out and asked that colonel how many passenger and box cars he wanted for the regiment, and he says he don't want *any*."

The adjutant-general of the State, therefore, thought it incumbent on him to go out to the camp and remonstrate with the regular who wouldn't have dealings with a railway man.

" Will there be any railway after I get to the Mississippi? " asked Grant, and the adjutant-general replied there would not. " Then, as my men must march after they get there, I mean to teach them how *before* we get there. We march to Quincy. That's why we need no cars."

And march they did, only five miles or so a day at first, so as to gradually harden and accustom the men, teach them how to pack wagons, pitch and strike camp, etc. He had ten days in which to make the trip, and every mile was a lesson. Once a dozen of the men got drunk at a country tavern, and the Colonel, imperturbable as ever, never addressed a word of rebuke to the offenders, but ordered them "tied up" behind the wagons all the next day's march. It was hard to say which officer by this time most admired the Colonel— the worthy chaplain who tells of these effective methods, "regular," yet irregular, or Lieutenant-Colonel Alexander, whom Grant had superseded in command. Both these men were devoted Christians; Alexander died at the head of the regiment at Chickamauga, and neither of them for a moment would have dared to do what Grant's common sense dictated as the only way to speedily reduce that complex command to discipline and subordination. Strange as it may seem, the men themselves, almost as speedily, began to admire and swear by the man who never swore at them, yet made them obey.

A brisk month of marching had the Twenty-first, and for many a day they followed in the lead of that sunburned, bearded, stoop-shouldered, shabbily-dressed, but inflexible master—shabbily dressed because for a time he could get no uniform, nor suitable mount. No less an authority than General Chetlain, first captain of the Galena company, tells us that when named colonel of the Twenty-first, Grant asked his well-to-do father and brothers to advance him four hundred dollars with which to purchase the necessary outfit. On his colonel's pay he could readily return it all within a few months, but both father and brothers declined. It was the junior partner of the firm of Jesse R. Grant & Company,

148

Mr. E. A. Collins, who had taken a liking to the elder brother, in spite of his business disqualifications, who quietly mailed to Colonel Grant the draft for the much-needed money, and Grant never forgot it.

Not until they had been some days in Missouri, marching hither and yon, did the uniform come, and the Colonel was able to exchange the rusty cavalry sabre he had picked up somewhere about Springfield for the regulation sword of a field officer of Foot. That uniform had hardly been worn a week before there came news that it would speedily have to be shed in favor of another.

Meantime at Washington the President had been busy with his cabinet, his new military associates, and a countless array of self-constituted advisers, in the selection of the generals destined to lead the grand army of volunteers now called into service.

On April 15th seventy-five thousand militia, as has been said, had been hurriedly summoned, and in mid July their time would expire. On May 3rd five hundred thousand volunteers had been summoned to arms, and much more than five hundred thousand promptly responded.

Empowered to name certain new major-generals in the regular army, Mr. Lincoln had at once gone outside of the line of promotion therein, and made his principal selections elsewhere. In April, '61, the army knew but one major-general, the veteran Scott. Of brigadier-generals it had John E. Wool, W. S. Harney, and Edwin V. Summer. Dating their commissions May 14th, the President added to the major-generals of the army, George B. McClellan, from the Ohio militia and formerly of the United States Engineers, and John C. Fremont, formerly a lieutenant-colonel in the regular service, an explorer and frontiersman, whose chief claim to recognition in the eyes of the administration was that he had been the first Republican candidate for the presidency.

Later, to date from August 19th, the President named Henry W. Halleck, also an Engineer-graduate of West Point, who resigned from the army the very day after Grant, but had been a deep student and a voluminous writer in military strategy as well as in the law.

To the brigadier-generals of the army, with date from May 14th, the President added Colonel Joseph K. F. Mansfield, Inspector-General, and Major Irvin McDowell, of the Adjutant-General's Department. Dating from May 15th were appointed as brigadiers, Major Robert Anderson, the defender of Sumter, and on the same date, as quartermaster-general, Colonel Montgomery C. Meigs, also William S. Rosecrans of Ohio, another Engineer-graduate who had resigned just before Grant, and then embarked in business in Cincinnati.

These were the general officers of the regular service at the orders of the government as the summer of '61 wore on. Scott was still on duty as general-in-chief at Washington; McClellan was at Cincinnati, Fremont at St. Louis. Halleck, at the outbreak of the war, was in California, a man of weath and distinction, and major-general of the California militia. It was not until late in the fall of 1861 that he was assigned to a command in the East. In addition to these appointments in the permanent establishment, the great army of volunteers had to be provided with generals of division and brigade, and thereby hangs a tale that demands a chapter of its own.

CHAPTER XV

"THE STARS OF SIXTY-ONE"

FROM the day that Grant took command of the Twenty-first he began, in the language of Governor Yates, to "do things." His regiment progressed rapidly in discipline and efficiency. His officers and men had found their master. His early teachings had made them prompt at all duties and steady on the march. Once over in Missouri, sent hither and yon at first under the orders of Fremont, striking at reported camps of "rebel troops and sympathizers," then set to guarding the Hannibal and St. Joseph Railway, they were rapidly hardening into soldier swing, when they presently found themselves assembled with half a dozen other regiments to meet a Confederate force alleged to be in the neighborhood of Mexico, a little town some fifty miles north of the Missouri.

Here it was promptly noted that, though Grant was junior in date of appointment to all the other regimental commanders, he was, nevertheless, the only educated soldier in the lot. As though by common consent he therefore was made commander of the improvised brigade. He owns in his Memoirs to a feeling of uneasiness on the march upon the town of Florida, Missouri, to the attack of a force under one, Tom Harris, a local colonel and Confederate of much repute. When they reached Florida, however, Harris and his men were nowhere to be found, and then, said Grant, "it occurred to me that Harris had been as much afraid of me as I had been of him. This was a view of the question I had never taken before, but it was one that I never forgot afterward." It was the last time Grant felt "trepidation" in close contact with the enemy, and it is well that he learned the lesson so early in the war.

On July 31st his headquarters as commander of the forces in that disturbed district were still at Mexico. Then came orders to shift the regiment to Ironton, Missouri, via St. Louis, and it was in St. Louis, on the 7th of August, that to Grant there came tremendous news. Two years before he was walking those streets friendless, penniless and seeking vainly for employment. This day brought the tidings that he had been named by the President one of the foremost of the brigadier-generals of volunteers.

It had all come about in the most natural way, yet the writer can well remember the surprise, the comments, and in one case at least, the rejoicing among regular officers in and about Washington at the time. To many of these latter he was still " Old Sam Grant " of the Fourth Foot, who went to seed somewhere out on the Pacific coast after the Mexican war. They could hardly be expected to know what Governor Yates knew, and Elihu Washburne, and John Pope of the Topographical Engineers, and through them the Illinois delegation in Congress, that of all the colonels Illinois had put into the field this man Grant had by long odds shown the highest ability and soldiership. He had taken that " Mattoon mob," as the Twenty-first had been described after they unhorsed their first colonel, had marched it, mastered it, and withal had been so prompt, efficient and useful in northern Missouri that even Fremont had been able to see it. For three weeks or more, Grant, in fact, had been exercising the functions of a brigade commander, and was even then under orders for an important command to the southward.

And so it had happened that when the President asked the Governor, and the Illinois delegation in Congress, to recommend half a dozen of the Illinois colonels for appointment as brigadiers, head of their list went the name of Ulysses S. Grant, and presently, seventeenth

U. S. GRANT AS A BRIGADIER-GENERAL,
NOVEMBER, 1861

mandant, the model soldier who had tried to make him a sergeant, and his other old-time senior of the Class of 1840, now by the most extraordinary turn in the affairs of men, assigned as brigadier-generals of volunteers in western Kentucky, and actually serving under the orders of the cheery-faced " plebe " who entered from Ohio in 1839. Charles F. Smith and William Tecumseh Sherman, who had had so much to do with licking into soldier shape the fledgling cadet from Brown County, Ohio, began their career in the volunteer army under the command of their modest pupil of the long ago.

Twenty thousand men, there or thereabouts, had Grant assembled about Paducah, Cairo and Bird's Point, just as well prepared, said he, to take the field as were the sons of the South assembled about Columbus, and not only did he write and urge that he be permitted to advance and strike, but he went and urged, believing Fremont could be induced to consent. But he little knew Fremont, and he came back rebuked. Later on he ventured to impress his views on Halleck, and frigid and impassive silence was his reward. He who would not even defend himself in the public press, was being dragged into a newspaper warfare, and thereby hangs another tale.

CHAPTER XVI

SOLDIER IN SPITE OF STAFF AND KINDRED

WHEN the war broke out in '61 and an army of 500,000 men was called into the field, no difficulty was experienced in getting the *men*—what we needed was officers. Staff officers were few, and staff schools we had none. Officers appointed to brigade and division rank from the line of the army had been prompt to select for their aides and adjutants the brightest and brainiest young soldiers in the service. Officers entering from civil life upon such high and important commands, were compelled to look elsewhere. No division and few brigade commanders in the army about Washington failed to have a " regular " or two in the official family. Few division and no brigade commanders in Kentucky and Missouri had anything but untried volunteers. When Grant became a brigadier he was empowered to name an adjutant-general with the rank of captain, and two aides-de-camp with the rank of first lieutenant. For adjutant-general he wrote at once to a Galena lawyer, Mr. John A. Rawlins, a young, able and energetic writer and speaker whom the silent soldier held in much esteem. It can hardly be said they were friends or intimates. Rawlins had charge of the legal business of Jesse Grant, the father, and much, therefore, to do with the affairs of Orvil & Company. He had been a frequent visitor to the store, and had become interested in the self-effacing elder brother who seemed to shrink into the background when customers or business came. Mr. Rawlins had a near neighbor in a half sister of Grant's beloved mother, a Mrs. Lee, and Mrs. Lee would have it that in spite of appearances, adversity, and tales at his expense, " Ulysses " was

BRIG.-GEN. AUGUSTUS L. CHETLAIN

MAJOR WILLIAM R. ROWLEY

BRIG.-GEN. JOHN A. RAWLINS

CAPTAIN ELY S. PARKER

GRANT'S GALENA COMRADES-IN-ARMS

far the superior of "the rest of the Grants." It was not until the organization of the Jo Daviess Guards in April that Mr. Rawlins could see why. Then on a sudden, as it were, Ulysses abandoned the stoop-shouldered, slouchy gait he had acquired about the farm and shop, pulled his hat from the back of his head and placed it, West Point fashion, well forward, and "braced" generally. Rawlins knew of Grant's modest efforts and later tender of service and application for a regiment, and noted Grant's grim endurance of the slights that attended his appeal to the War Department. Rawlins had decided to enter the army himself, and was counting on the appointment to the majority of one of the new Illinois regiments when suddenly halted by a letter from Grant tendering him the position of captain and assistant adjutant-general. Rawlins gave up the majority and joined his fortunes with those of the shabby clerk. It fell to Grant's lot to name many another staff officer in the next three years. It is doubtful if even in all the array of brilliant minds and brainy men with whom he was later surrounded—men like McPherson, Wilson, Comstock, Rufus Ingalls and Horace Porter, all West Pointers, all loyal, devoted and almost invaluable aids—Grant ever attached to his person a stancher staff officer, or in every sense a truer friend, than that Galena lawyer, John A. Rawlins. Our best friends, as has been wisely said, are those who fear not to tell us the truth about ourselves, and from that day in August, '61, with rare fidelity and judgment, Rawlins served his kindly chief, rising with him, step by step, from the bars of a captain to the portfolio of Secretary of War, the most fearless and independent of all their number, because, perhaps, he had known and befriended his leader when most he stood in need—the one who dared admonish when symptoms of that much-talked-of-but-little-known weakness returned, the most valuable because he knew what the others lacked—how to deal with civil and political influences, and withal, not far the inferior professionally of any one of their number, because he had finally mastered in the school of actual war the principles which they had gathered at West Point. It was a red letter day for Grant when John A. Rawlins became his chief-of-staff.

Writers have referred to this selection of Rawlins as clinching proof of Grant's knowledge of men. The selection of his first aides-de-camp and of later associates, however, seems to disprove the proposition. Believing it due his original regiment to name one of its officers as one of his aides, Grant chose a lieutenant from that organization, and then, feeling free to look somewhere else, he harked back to St. Louis days, and lifted, from the law and collection office in which he had tried to work, a young man whose alert and cheery ways had much impressed the struggling, would-be collector. Then, Grantlike, having made his choice, he stood by it, keeping these two close to him through the first year of the war in spite of the fact that neither proved of military use and both of embarrassment. Then one became convinced that soldier life was not his proper sphere, and quit the staff and service by voluntary resignation. The other lasted until the 'ate fall of '63, when " relieved " by order.

But for months Grant was practically his own quartermaster, commissary, ordnance officer, inspector-general and, indeed, aide-de-camp. Rawlins speedily learned the routine of the adjutant-general's desk, but for many long weeks the general did his own writing, recording, endorsing, making out returns, requisitions, permits, passes and orders, as Rawlins discovered, when first he joined him at Cairo, and was amazed at the volume of business the unbusinesslike ex-captain of Galena days could now accomplish.

The new uniform of the generalship had not reached the brigadier when he and his chief-of-staff settled down to work at Cairo. Grant had considered uniforms as of secondary importance, even when he stopped at St. Louis to confer with his senior Fremont, who had arrayed himself in all the splendor regulations would permit, and more, and surrounded himself with a pomp, style and ceremony utterly unprovided for in those military scriptures. Grant sent in his name and rank, as required, took a seat in the hall, as he had in McClellan's ante-room in Cincinnati, and waited the convenience of the chief—waited hours in vain, an object of some curiosity, but no courtesy, to a half score of foreign-born and bred staff officials in gorgeous array—the soldiers of fortune with whom Fremont loved to surround himself. Not until a St. Louis quartermaster, an old army associate, happened in had so much as a friendly glance come his way. Startled into sudden familiarity at the sight of the best brigadier in the district sitting solitary in the semi-darkness of the hall, Major McKinstry exclaimed, " Sam, what are you doing here? " and then, bristling with indignation, went himself to apprise Fremont of the presence in waiting of one of the senior generals of his command. It appears that on this occasion Fremont received the travel-stained, unmilitary-looking westerner with some show of civility, though he could not forbear remark upon the absence of uniform, and was not too well satisfied with Grant's simple explanation that he had given away his regimentals when he ceased to be a colonel and had not yet received the more elaborate frock coat, and could not even buy in the West the starred shoulder-straps of a brigadier.

The uniform, it may be said, came safely to Cairo, and he was quite human enough to sit for a photograph or two. There was a large one representing him in the full uniform of a brigadier-general, minus the epaulettes and chapeau, but with sword, sash, belt and the black-plumed Kossuth hat prescribed in '61. It represented him as wearing a full, long beard, something he never did thereafter, for the hirsute crop during the winter at Donelson was short and almost stubby. That photograph was copied, presently, in full-page pictures by *Harper's Weekly,* and studied with infinite interest all over the land, for hope and faith, in spite of newspaper sneers as to Belmont, were settling upon him. But it looked so little like the Grant of Donelson and Shiloh of February and April, '62, that many a new arrival in the Army of the Tennessee failed to recognize the commanding general as he was.

Another photograph, a group picture, was taken about the time, which seems of late years to have disappeared entirely. He refers to it in a letter to his sister, to whom he sends a copy and a list of the officers portrayed, and it seems further that he ordered too few to supply the family demand, for there had come over the Grants a sudden and marked interest in that much-discussed topic, " the fortunes of Ulysses." From having been the humblest and least considered in the lot, the eldest son and brother was now the object of no little comment and correspondence. The family had gained an access of importance in the eyes of Illinois and Ohio friends and neighbors, and presently the letters to the district commander became freighted with all manner of requests for all manner of favors. The number of enterprising folk " with axes to grind," with fuel, forage, flour, horses, mules, beef cattle, with shoes, saddles and harness which they were eager to sell the government on Grant's recommendation was almost incredible. The family had always relied on the easy good nature of " Ulyss " in the past, and now sought to avail themselves of the relationship in the furtherance of their schemes. Now they wrote as confidently in the interest of some dealer, contractor or purveyor, nominated new staff officers, urged commissions or appointments for dozens of aspiring fellow citizens,

and asked for passes or permits for peddlers and sales-
men to pervade his camps and turn, presumably, many
an honest penny.

And now the son and brother appeared in a new and
surprising light. Ulysses, the gentle, if not the wise,
who had ever been yielding at the beck of his kith and
kin, and who was ever a willing vassal to the will of
his wife, developed an utterly unlooked for ability to
say no. Whatsoever he had been wont to yield in matters personal to himself, he would now most doggedly
deny if it affected Uncle Sam. It is noteworthy that
among all these suggestions and requests that came
from father, sisters, brothers and brother-in-law, there
was never one from that gentle mother. Between her
and her first-born there had ever been a wordless sympathy and understanding. She would not now enter
into the family schemes. As for Julia Dent, her letters
to him and his to her were ever too sacred for other
eyes. Those written to other members of the family
have been edited and published, and it is through them
there are revealed these matters on which he and his
staff would have been silent, especially that episode in
which the son, now general commanding an army in
the field, was compelled at last to rebuke and silence
the father.

Mention has earlier been made of Jesse Grant's
propensity for writing to the papers, and when these
journals began to fill up with the stories of the Prentiss
and McClernand sympathizers, Jesse, as was to be
expected, flew to pen in rebuttal and refutation. In
vain the son counselled patience and silence; the elder
loved that sort of battle and wrote again and yet again,
and was published, quoted, copied and reassailed until
Grant, the son, at last could stand it no longer and
demanded that it cease.

"My worst enemy," he wrote, "could do me no
more injury than you are doing." It seems that Jesse

had been indulging in comments of his own at the expense of other generals, " and these," said Grant, the son, " are unquestionably regarded as reflecting my views." In positive and not too filial terms he had to forbid his father's writing further for publication, and Jesse wonderingly asked himself:

> "Upon what meat doth this our Cæsar feed
> That he is grown so great?——"

But, for a time the papers had fattened on the factional strife waged in their columns. It gave to Grant his strong dislike for newspaper notoriety of any kind, and his distrust of newspaper men and mention. It led to his habit of utter silence except in presence of his trusted friends. With them he could talk and did talk fluently and well.

Whatever lingering doubt the family may have had as to the mastership of Ulysses was ended by the great victory of Donelson, and theirs were not the only eyes that were not too willingly opened. "To err is human, to forgive divine," and to forgive instant and overwhelming success in those whom we have long looked upon as flat failures is super-human. All things considered, it is almost marvellous that Grant should have won at Donelson at all.

To begin with, Halleck had reached St. Louis two days after Belmont, had taken over the command as left by Fremont and had been digesting all the newspaper misrepresentations of Grant ever since. Coupled with these were his recollections of the Humboldt stories in '54, and added to these were the tales of hangers-on about headquarters who are ever ready to undermine a rival or overthrow a coming man who has once been " going." Halleck wished to make haste slowly, as was the method of the Engineer. Grant, who had studied the field, the forces on both sides, and who knew, as Halleck did not, the generals confronting him in Kentucky, was chafing with eagerness and confident of success. Along his front were Polk and Buckner, for whom personally he felt respect and regard. With them were Floyd and Pillow, one of whom he held in aversion, the other in contempt.

Writing to Halleck proved fruitless. Grant had been urging attack on Polk at Columbus, claiming that every day was adding to the strength of its force and fortifications, but Halleck refused. Three months were well nigh frittered away, just as was the case with McClellan in the east, only there that great organizer had at his back three times the number of the enemy in his front, and vastly better drill, discipline and equipment. For weeks Grant had been begging permission to seize Fort Henry on the Tennessee, and hold the position in force. It would pierce at the centre the Confederate line. Not until January 12th could Halleck be induced to order Grant forward as a means of preventing the reinforcement of Buckner at Bowling Green. With McClernand and C. S. Smith for division commanders, in spite of roads rendered abominable by wintry rains, Grant took the field the instant Halleck would let him go, McClernand directed on Mayfield, Kentucky, midway between Columbus and the Tennessee, Smith straight at Fort Henry. Grant with Admiral Foote, steamed up the river, "sampled" the fort with a few shells and settled in their minds that it could easily be reduced and taken. But as soon as the scheme of reinforcing Buckner was fully blocked the troops were recalled to the Ohio, and Grant, without invitation, hastened to St. Louis to beg of Halleck permission to readvance and take the fort. He came back rebuffed and refused. Then Foote tried his persuasive powers, and still Halleck hung back. Twice again, on the 28th and 29th of January, Grant renewed his appeal, but never a word would Halleck vouchsafe in reply. Matters might have gone on indefinitely had not George H. Thomas whipped the Confederates at Mill Springs, far to the east of them, and as General Zollicoffer was among the Confederate dead, and the North frantically rejoiced over the little victory, the first it had unquestionably scored, Halleck decided that he would have to do something. On February 1st, therefore, he gave to Grant the long-withheld instructions, and on February 6th Grant telegraphed " Fort Henry is ours." He could as readily have done so if permitted three months before.

Then he turned on Donelson, only a short day's march away and on the west bank of the Cumberland, but now the floods came, the winds blew and all nature took a hand in favor of the South. Only six thousand men garrisoned Donelson when Henry was captured, but by the 12th, when the frost and ice and snow replaced the rains, Grant's old benefactor, Buckner, was there, one of the twenty thousand assembled under two as useless generals as ever wore the Southern uniform— John B. Floyd and Gideon J. Pillow. Donelson was an admirable position for defense. The gunboats could approach it only under raking fire. It had to be invested on the land side by Grant's three divisions. The gallant admiral, hoping to use his Dahlgrens as effectively as at Henry, ordered an independent naval attack, and in one hour's heavy battling had every boat disabled and driven out of action. Ten of his men were killed, many were wounded, he himself among the latter, and thus ended the navy's opportunity for the time being.

A dismal Valentine's Day was that of February 14, '62. The mercury went to ten below. Scores of men were frozen, but all the same McClernand, Lew Wallace and C. F. Smith had strung their lines about Donelson, almost around to the upper river. The investment was practically complete. Grant had trotted down stream in answer to appeal from Foote, who lay disabled now beyond long gunshot, and who proposed taking all the boats at once to St. Louis for repairs, the army meantime remaining in investment about the beleaguered stronghold. Grant had no objection whatever to the gunboats going for repairs—they were of no further use in their present plight—but he had other views as to what the army should do in their absence.

And in the midst of the conference came tidings of battle, and Grant, galloping back, biting hard at the end of a cigar there had been no time to light, found lively eruption along his whole line, especially at the far right flank.

It seems that Floyd had been urged to follow up the advantage gained in beating off the navy by impetuous attack on the encircling line. Grant had only a few field batteries, and the plan promised well. Floyd's men were hurled in force on McClernand's right, and drove it back, reopening the river road, but there the attack seemed to spend itself. By one o'clock Grant had rejoined, and without a moment's delay ordered a strong counter assault, beginning with his old commandant and his sturdy division on the extreme northern flank, and right loyally did that gallant soldier and gentleman respond.

Straight through the wintry woods they drove, the long, irregular lines in the light blue overcoats, the heroic figure of their tall, slender and chivalric division commander, sword in hand, towering in their midst. Grant's eyes kindled at the sight. It brought back old days on the drill ground at the Point. It recalled that famous onset at Chapultepec, and those who saw him said that gallant " Charley " Smith was never a more superb picture of the knightly soldier than when he led his wild westerners into this, his first and, as God willed, his last battle in the Civil War. Stern was their reception when they reached the Southern works, but furious their onward sweep, and as Grant galloped on through the murky woods to urge the prompt co-operation of Wallace and McClernand, the ringing cheer of the charging lines told him that even stubborn resistance had not stayed the rush of his left wing; and now his every effort was needed at the right. Heartily the men of Wallace's division had taken up their share of the fight, but McClernand had been hard-pounded early in the day, and here it required some time and urging to accomplish the desired result. Yet when the evening shadows fell upon the smoke-shrouded forest, once again McClernand occupied the lines from which he had been driven in the morning, Wallace had carried the outer line in his front, and Smith, leaping the intrenchments before him, had huddled the bewildered defenders close under the guns of Donelson itself. " Only in more compact formation for to-morrow's fight," said a croaker or two in the Union lines. But Grant had called for the haversack of a prisoner and examined the contents. Two days' cooked rations, such as they were, still remained. That meant, said he, that they had been trying to fight their way out; that meant, as the soldiers said, that " we had them going."

And so it proved. The Southern leaders met in council after dark at Dover. Floyd had had enough, and, moreover, entertained misgivings as to what might be his fate if captured, for as War Secretary of the United States under James Buchanan he had done all that lay within him to strip the Union and supply the South. Pillow, known to Grant of old in Mexico, weakened just as Grant predicted. Forrest, mettlesome trooper that he ever was, marshalled his four hundred Horse about him, slipped away under cover of darkness, and went on to a three years' career of daring deeds and desperate battle, while Buckner, soldier and gentleman, was left to make the best terms he could for himself and his beleaguered thousands of Foot and Artillery. Not only Fort Henry was won, but Donelson,

part of Halleck almost to the last, although it is admitted that, when finally committed to the move, Halleck did what he could to reinforce his field captain; but neither was needed—Grant "won out" without a hand from Buell or a man from Halleck—the hand and the man came only after Donelson was ours.

It is true that when the magnitude of the achievement dawned upon Halleck and he realized how very much greater was Grant in the public eye than any other man at the front, or even himself at St. Louis, he then had the sense to second the overwhelming nomination of the people and suggest the promotion of Grant. But even then he could not single him out as he should have done. "Make Buell, Grant and Pope major-generals of volunteers," he wired to the War Department. Mark the order in which they are named; consider what each had thus far accomplished, and defend it if it can be defended. Buell had been drilling and organizing in Kentucky, and with abundant men holding a line in front of Louisville. Pope had been commanding a district in Missouri, both doing loyal, valuable, but comparatively passive service. Grant had been active as a terrier from the very start, a leader in aggressive moves against the hostile forces in the field, personally commanding in two spirited battles, Donelson resulting in the utter demolition of the enemy's stronghold, in piercing the enemy's centre, and in widespread consternation and dismay in the South, in opening the two great rivers leading into the heart of Tennessee, in compelling the evacuation of Bowling Green to the east, and Columbus to the west, both of them "turned," and all of this brought about by sheer fighting against entrenched and equal foes. There had been absolutely nothing to match, nothing to approximate it, yet nevertheless, said Halleck, " Make Buell, Grant and Pope major-generals of volunteers, and give me the command of the West. I ask this in return for Forts Henry and Donelson."

It is unnecessary to comment upon that despatch. It is significant that the wise and inspired head of the nation fathomed it and followed his own conclusions. Just one name was at once sent to the Senate for recognition as the result of Donelson. In the clear mind of Abraham Lincoln no vestige of doubt beclouded the right of the commander on the spot—the man who planned and persevered, who personally led the fighting line, and finally forced that unconditional surrender. Ulysses S. Grant was named Major-General of Volunteers to date from February 16th, and was as promptly and unanimously confirmed by the Senate.

Later on, along in March, when all the reports were received, there were other and deserved rewards for Donelson. McClernand, Smith and Wallace, five weeks after Grant, were accorded their double stars—Buell and Pope going up with them, so that they, too, practically owed their promotion to Donelson and to Grant, as nothing else outside of Halleck's recommendation had occurred to call for it—Pope having only just begun at Island No. 10, and Buell not yet having ventured a battle. Quite a little crop of brigadiers, too, sprang from the battling ranks of Donelson; five Illinois colonels—Oglesby, Cooke, W. H. L. Wallace, McArthur and Logan rising to the stars, also Lauman, of Iowa. So, too, on this date there were others for which Donelson was not the cause, but the opportunity, as in the case of Grant's classmate and fellow captain of the Fourth Infantry at Fort Humboldt, Henry M. Judah, colonel Fourth California; so, too, " Bob " McCook, of Ohio, Speed S. Fry, of Kentucky, VanCleve, of Minnesota, and Manson of Indiana, who had fought with Thomas at Mill Springs, but in spite of that spirited little victory no reward as yet had come to Thomas. On that same date, March 21st, Samuel R. Curtis, of Iowa, had been made major-general for the Pea Ridge battle, but not until a month after the rewards of Mill Springs and Donelson and Pea Ridge had been confirmed by the Senate could an over suspicious and obdurate War Secretary see his way to signing the commission of George H. Thomas as major-general. The man who planned and fought and commanded and won at Mill Springs, nearly a month before McClernand, Smith and Wallace fought as subordinates at Donelson, got his major-generalship a month behind them. Only four colonels fought under Thomas at Mill Springs, and all four were rewarded a month ahead of him. However, this is opening another story. Few men except those who served under George H. Thomas knew him at his full worth; even Grant came to misjudge and almost to wrong him, and if one as just and appreciative as Grant could fail to appreciate Thomas, what could be expected of Stanton, who misjudged so many and suspected all?

And so Abraham Lincoln and the applauding North made it obvious that whatsoever Halleck might think or say or ascribe to himself, the name that deserved to be heralded foremost in connection with Donelson was that of Grant. It was the only name for many days that was heard, and Grant's headquarters were bombarded with telegrams, letters and messages of congratulation, sometimes coupled with suggestion, and frequently with request for favors. Grant's headquarters were besieged by callers, visitors, gifts and correspondents. Callers were made welcome and entertained as far as it was possible with the means at hand. Grant at first chatted frankly and cheerily in his open-hearted way with any and all comers, with the result that all manner of misquotations began to appear in the public press, and Rawlins took alarm and occasion to warn his chief. Gifts, almost the first he had ever known, came, heartily tendered and frankly and gratefully received, but correspondents thereafter were not, and censors innumerable have declared that Grant would have been wiser had he reversed the issue, declined the gifts, but received the correspondents. The gifts included creature comforts of many kinds, especially cigars, for that unlighted weed with which he galloped to the front at Donelson had started the story that Grant was an inveterate smoker—something he never had been, though when first employed about Springfield he cherished a grimy little meerschaum pipe. But after Donelson cigars poured in by the thousand and Grant and his staff could not even by assiduous effort begin to consume them.

The Commander-in-Chief of the Army and Navy had gone further in his reward and recognition of Grant. He had ordained, dating from February 15th, that the Military District of the Tennessee should be given to that officer, and as no limits were assigned, and as Halleck had not yet at least been announced as in supreme command in the West, the victor of Donelson found himself charged with new and important duties and responsible for all that might occur in a wide range of territory. Many men would have become inflated with importance, and many more would have looked upon it as an independent command. Grant was level-headed; he did neither. Men about him and his staff—not Rawlins—pointed out that of all the generals now on duty not one stood as high in public estimation as he, and that Halleck, Fremont and even McClellan might well look to their laurels and be jealous. Fremont had failed and been superseded in Missouri. Halleck had simply thwarted and obstructed. McClellan had built up and assembled a magnificent army, but kept it cooped about the encircling forts of Washington. People east and west were chafing at the inaction along the Potomac, and all the North was hailing Grant as the one man who really " did things."

Then there were other considerations. He had stepped from behind the counter of a country store to the command of a regiment, had been named nineteenth on the list of brigadier-generals, first appointed, and of all that list of forty brigadiers he was the first to rise to the grade of major-general. Where were the men who had forced him from the service years before? Neither one of them had yet been mentioned for even a brigade command and one of them never would be. If Ulysses Grant had picked up the troops along the Tennessee and gone careering off after Polk and Sidney Johnston, then marching to the defense of Nashville, all the North would probably have applauded, whether Halleck approved it or not.

But Grant was a graduate of West Point, schooled in discipline and subordination. Halleck was still his superior, and therefore to Halleck in all deference Grant submitted his next plans. It was his profound conviction that a strong column sent southward at once would split the Confederacy in twain, would find hundreds of adherents to the old flag, would crush the rebellion in the West and cripple the Richmond government beyond repair. It was his belief that the South staggered under the blow of Donelson, and that sound generalship demanded instant pursuit and incessant pounding.

With this purpose in view Grant had pushed C. F. Smith, his surest division commander, forward to Clarksville on the Tennessee. Then he deemed it necessary to personally meet and confer with Buell, who by this time should be close at the heels of the retiring Confederates and camped over against Nashville. All this was absolutely within his rights. With Smith commanding his advance and Tecumseh Sherman looking after communications at the rear, his rough-hewn army of Westerners seemed in the best of hands. Now for a blow at Nashville—the Richmond of the West, a position of the same relative importance on the one side of the Alleghenies as was the Confederate capital on the other.

But here came a strange and most unlooked-for misadventure. Loyally and subordinately had Grant reported his movements and intentions to his senior in St. Louis. All proper telegrams and written reports and returns had been prepared in his field office and placed in the hands of the government telegrapher, or in custody of its mail agents. It seemed odd that from Halleck there came no word of acknowledgment or commendation. It seemed odd that there should be no response to Grant's urgent request for steamers to enable him to move his men at once to Nashville. Smith had found Clarksville abandoned. Buell had found Sidney Johnston retiring southward from Nashville. It was most important that Grant in person should hasten to the front, yet no reply whatever had come to his despatch suggesting that " unless otherwise ordered " he would take Nashville about March 1st. Then when tidings came of its occupation by Nelson's division of Buell's army, Grant further wired that he would himself go thither on February 28th " if no orders came to the contrary," and thither accordingly he went, and with most surprising and disheartening results.

All these days a traitorous official in the telegraph office had been suppressing certain of Grant's messages to Halleck and Halleck's to Grant—the latter becoming more and more acrid as they seemed to produce no effect, and just at the time when, in the full flood of his triumph, the new commander of the District of the Tennessee was vigorously at work at the extreme front, planning swift concentration of Buell's finely-drilled brigades with his own rough-and-ready campaigners, far to the rear the wires between St. Louis and Washington, between Halleck and McClellan, were humming with schemes for his undoing. The general in chief command in the valley of the Mississippi—he whom McClellan later described as "the most hopelessly stupid official" he ever met, and a man destitute of military ideas—he whom the soldiers, ignorant of all these happenings, and impressed mainly by the gravity and deliberation of his movements, later christened "Old Brains," he who was indebted mainly to Grant for the successes achieved in his military bailiwick, was wiring McClellan, still in chief command of all our forces in the field, words to the effect that ever since Donelson Grant had ignored him, that Grant without his authority had quit his command and gone to Nashville, that Grant, "satisfied with his victory, sits down and enjoys it without any regard for the future. I am worn out and tired out with this neglect and inefficiency." This of the man who had almost worn himself out trying to get Halleck to let him do anything, and who was now fairly brimming over with eagerness and impatience to do more.

And McClellan, he who, secure in his high place, could find no time or inclination to listen to appeals for action coming from the over-patient President, or for justice, coming from his imprisoned comrade, Stone (another victim of calumny unqualified), he who possibly recalled old days in the quartermaster's cabin at Vancouver, and lent ready ear to rumor of renewed lapses, wired back to Halleck authority to arrest Grant and relieve him of his command.

If this, as said a Christian gentleman and gallant soldier, "wasn't enough to make a saint swear, nothing else could be," and yet it is a matter of fact and record that, when it all came to the ears of Grant, he never so much as uttered an expletive. But what C. F. Smith and Sherman said of that episode and of Halleck would make in both cases interesting, and in one inflammably lurid, reading. Like Grant, Smith was averse to blasphemy; Sherman was an impetuous expert.

And so for a time, thanks partially to the treason of

the telegrapher, who fled southward between two days, bearing the suppressed dispatches with him, but due quite as much to the prejudice, the distrust and possibly the jealousy of Halleck and the credulity of McClellan; thanks, too, it must be owned, to the fact that there had been times when McClellan had seen and Halleck had known Grant's over-indulgence in liquor, the man of the hour stood temporarily discredited at headquarters of the armies of the United States, but not in the hearts of the people.

CHAPTER XVIII

FROM DONELSON TO SHILOH

"I FEEL myself competent to command a regiment," Grant had written to the War Department in May, '61, but officers of his staff say that while at Cairo, before Donelson, he wished that he had a brigade of cavalry in Virginia; he believed he could "do things" with such a command, and, left to himself and his own devices, there is no reason to doubt he could. Placed under McClellan, who knew no use whatever for cavalry, he would have had no chance, and now, placed in command along the Tennessee where he had no cavalry worth mention, he was speedily in position to need it at the front quite as much as he had need of friends at the rear. It is characteristic of Grant that he rose superior to the need, both in front and rear, and got along without either.

Not for nearly a fortnight did the situation clear itself along the Tennessee, but meantime Sidney Johnston had retired, unpursued and unmolested, to Murfreesboro, and then still southward. History has failed to mention the rewards heaped upon a certain Southern sympathizer in Northern service—that elusive telegrapher—when he reached, as we are told, the Southern lines, "bearing his sheaves with him"—all those messages which should have passed between Grant and Halleck. If the breaking up of an aggressive campaign and the creation of illimitable discord in the camps of the enemy are legitimate acts of war, that faithless employe of the United States had abundantly served the South. Possibly such men as Sidney Johnston, Polk and Hardee cold shouldered such methods.

As Philip Kearny said early in '61, " It is a gentleman's war," and as such they sought to keep it.

Astonished and humiliated, Grant had received the curt order assigning to Smith the command of operations along the Tennessee, and the intimation that he, the conqueror of Donelson, would be expected to remain at Fort Henry. " Why do you not render the reports repeatedly called for?" was the telegraphic inquiry that finally opened his eyes to the fact that before deserting the telegrapher had been faithless to his trust. Then in all subordination Grant sent copies of the despatches previously penned. Then the senior major-general, much perturbed, began gradually to realize that all these things he had been saying to McClellan in condemnation of Grant were actually without foundation. Then it as gradually dawned upon him that grievous wrong had been done a loyal, gallant and most efficient subordinate, and then, it seems, " Old Brains" (not yet so nicknamed) was at his wit's end to "square himself," as soldiers say, with his superiors at the War Department and with his junior in rank, yet superior in soldiership, at the front. He had little difficulty in settling with the former. He could throw much of the blame upon the telegraph operator. He need have had no difficulty, though there might have been deserved embarrassment, in setting with his wronged and aggrieved junior. A frank, straightforward statement would have done it and swept away at once the cloud that long had hovered and that now and henceforth lowered between Halleck himself and his most distinguished junior, soon destined to become his superior officer. Moreover, Halleck had with him as friend, adviser, chief-of-staff and fellow graduate, his elder by six years in the army and decidedly his better in counsel —George W. Cullum, of the Class of '33. If Cullum had heard the stories to Grant's detriment he had little heeded them, and while Halleck had found no words in which to commend and congratulate the victor of Donelson, Cullum had penned most cordial and graceful expression of appreciation. Cullum gloried and rejoiced in Grant's exploit. It was a feather in the cap of the Alma Mater he loved. Cullum, who had won Grant's trust and gratitude, could speedily have mended the now serious breach between the two major-generals of the West. An honest, soldierly statement of the rumors that had reached St. Louis and of the reports and despatches that had not—of Halleck's consequent embarrassment and distress, resulting in his having reported to McClellan the rumors as they were reported to him—these, with as frank and soldierly an expression of regret, would have ended the trouble then and there. Grant was far too sensible of the weakness that had been his, and far too broad, generous and magnanimous to blame any man for believing as Halleck believed in the silence that fell after Donelson.

But Halleck was not man enough for this. He could stoop to subterfuge, but not to a subordinate. Explanation he had to make, and he who had asked the supreme command in the West, " in return for Henry and Donelson," excused himself to Grant for having relieved him of the charge of operations up the Tennessee, because the War Department had been worrying over his failure to communicate, to the end that McClellan had ordered his arrest and full investigation as to his alleged " condition." All this, said Halleck, had been stopped by his personal intervention—all this, he had the deep sagacity *not* to say, had been initiated by his personal reports.

And so after twenty days of confusion, days precious to the cause yet lost to the country, Grant resumed control at the front, believing McClellan the enemy who had downed him in mid career, and Halleck the friend who had interposed to save, and somehow Grant did not wish to be indebted to Halleck. As for Halleck, there is the old saying that he who has deeply wronged a man grows insensibly to hate him. Halleck regarded Grant with no such vehement dislike as that, but, having wronged Grant, he was ever ready to accept and welcome evidence or indication that after all he was right. And so, on one side at least, there was leaning toward the later and renewed humiliation that was to follow Shiloh. Of that hereafter.

On the other hand, consider the attitude of the aggrieved officer in the case and compare it with that of his accuser. A salient characteristic of Ulysses Grant was absolute truthfulness. His classmates at the Point, his associates of the old Fourth Infantry, his chums at Fort Columbia, in the days of his pining for wife and home, his despondency, his discontent with army life and his occasional resort to drink, his staff throughout the Civil War and even his political enemies in the years that followed, all bear testimony as to that. Rufus Ingalls and General Henry L. Hodges, who were his house mates at Columbia Barracks in '53, are most emphatic on this point. Horace Porter in his inimitable Memoirs tells of how the general-in-chief of all the armies impressed every one about him with the minute accuracy of his every statement.

It must be insisted that, as every one who intimately knew him dwells upon this rather unusual trait, implicit confidence should attach to the statement made in his own Memoirs as to his relations with Halleck, and it emphasizes all that has been claimed for Grant's modesty, patriotism and singleness of purpose.

"It is probable that the general opinion was that Smith's long services in the army, and his distinguished deeds rendered him the more proper person for the command. Indeed I was rather inclined to this opinion myself at that time, and would have served as faithfully under Smith as he had done under me."

FROM DONELSON TO SHILOH

O that unkind fate had not so soon thereafter robbed Grant of that chivalrous second, his ideal commandant, his ideal supporter! A pall spread over the Army of the Tennessee that bowed all heads and saddened all hearts when, only six weeks later, gallant "Charley" Smith breathed his last, almost within long gunshot of the field on which Albert Sidney Johnston, the lion of the Confederacy, died leading the last charge of the Southern line at Shiloh. Physically much alike, tall, slender, sinewy, and one at least "handsome as Apollo," these two soldiers of the old army were the heroes of their men, the objects of their unstinted admiration, and in their loss in the midst of the campaign of the spring of '62, Death, the conqueror, had taken equal toll from both North and South on the banks of the beautiful Tennessee.

In the same paragraph in which Grant refers to the temporary assignment of Smith to the command, he speaks of Halleck's unfounded accusation at his own expense. Never until after the war did he learn the true story, unearthed by Adam Badeau in some of his researches among the records of the War Department. Had Grant known the facts when, shortly after Shiloh, Halleck a second time relegated the now grim and silent soldier to the *rôle* of second in command, the chances are that Grant would have abandoned the Army of the Tennessee and sought another field for his activities, as indeed he came within an ace of doing when at Corinth; but here, luckily, Sherman swayed and stayed him. Grant remained at his unconspicuous post until a few months had demonstrated Halleck's utter inaptitude for fighting in the field, and once again the command of his old army, now strongly reinforced, fell fortunately to Grant. From this time on, until promoted to still higher sphere, he never left it.

But meantime what of Shiloh? Driven back by Grant from the line, Bowling Green-Donelson-Henry and Columbus, to a line stretching from Memphis toward Chattanooga, the Confederates had been further weakened by Pope's success in March at New Madrid. The Memphis & Charleston Railway, running eastward through northern Mississippi and Alabama, was crossed at Corinth, Mississippi, by the Mobile & Ohio, running east of south from Columbus. This made Corinth the strategic centre of the Southwest. Thither Sidney Johnston and Breckinridge had marched their legions, and thither, as March wore on, Grant desired to head his column. Corinth lay some seventeen miles west from the great elbow of the Tennessee, the point where the stream, after long, placid flowing from the Gateway of the Gods through the fertile fields of northern Alabama, turns sharply and suddenly northward and goes winding away to its far junction with the Ohio. Navigable for light draft, stern-wheel, river boats, its banks were dotted here and there by wood-piles, with attendant log cabins ("landings" in the vernacular of the river men), points from which country roads led away into the interior. Tyler's Landing, twenty-two miles east of north from Corinth, lay just at the northeast corner of Mississippi. Around the long bend northward into Tennessee and some ten miles by river, lay the little cluster of cabins known as Hamburg. Four miles further and still around another bend lay still another little bunch of woodpiles, cabins, etc., perched on the west bank, known as Pittsburg. Five miles northward stood Crumps, and about nine miles northeastward, and around another bend, yet only six miles as the crow flies from the Pittsburg Landing, lay on the opposite side the hamlet of Savannah.

Exploring the Tennessee shortly after the surrender of Fort Henry, a daring officer of our navy, Lieutenant Commander Phelps, had run his gunboat clear to Florence, Alabama, and found no foe worth mention. Scout-

back in the bush. Rabbits and squirrels came bounding in from that direction as though driven from their haunts by invading enemies, and still it did not dawn upon our generals at the front, or appear to Grant at the distant rear, that Sidney Johnston and all his men were simply anticipating the move which Grant had planned at their expense. In the light of later day wisdom, it seems strange that neither to Grant nor Sherman had it occurred that the Confederate leader by April 1st must know of their presence in his front, with an unfordable river behind the Army of the Tennessee, and separating it from that of the Ohio, still several marches distant. It seems strange that Grant did not believe Johnston capable of doing that which he himself would have been sure to do—namely, advance promptly to the overthrow of the men of the Tennessee before they could be joined by the men of the Ohio; but that is just what Johnston essayed to do, and might possibly have made an overwhelming success, but for slow and dawdling marches, but for the fighting spirit of that " devil-may-care outfit," the Army of the Tennessee. Starting on April 2nd, with Shiloh church less than twenty miles away, not until Sunday morning, April 6th, were his exuberant, untrained, unterrified Southerners straightened out in three long lines and ready to attack. Then at last the advance was sounded, and at half after six the memorable Battle of Shiloh— the bloodiest in the West, started in good earnest. " Before night," said one of their gifted leaders, " we'll water our horses in the Tennessee or hell."

CHAPTER XIX

SHILOH—THE ONE SURPRISE

THE nation knows the story of that tumultuous Sunday meeting at Shiloh church. Many of Sherman's men were still abed when the startling summons came— a reveille such as they had never heard before. The veterans, as they called themselves, of McClernand and Smith were less taken aback. They had heard the far-famed, far-reaching rebel yell at Donelson. Moreover, they were camped far to the rear of the foremost brigades and had abundant time in which to breakfast and form ranks and march to aid their fellows at the front. The men of Prentiss, many of whom never yet had rammed home a ball cartridge or felt the kick of a Springfield, had been called to arms at dawn, and were listening in amaze to the crash of musketry and the ear-piercing chorus to their right, where the tide of assault first broke on the lines of Sherman's centre, and the first sight of the blood-red battle flags, the first shell bursting in their midst from the haze of sulphur smoke along the fringe of timber in front of them, shook their nerve and stampeded horses, mules and many a man, and yet in all that desperate day's work, no more desperate, determined fighting was done than later by Prentiss himself and the devoted men whom he was able to rally about him.

It is as difficult to describe that morning's battle as to account for it. It seems incredible now that the Southern host had been able to march up, form for action within a mile of our lines, and do it with so much undisciplined straggling, shooting and shouting that Beauregard begged of his chief to call off the whole affair and hark back to Corinth. It was impossible, said he, that the federal troops could be in ignorance, even though Jordan, his chief of staff, assured him that he had ascertained that Sherman's men were not entrenched—were utterly unsuspicious. " It is incredible," said Beauregard, " it means that Buell has reinforced Grant—that they have full seventy thousand lying in wait for us—that they are simply leading us into a trap."

But Sidney Johnston had come to fight and fight hard, as heaven knows they fought, and could he have struck two days, or even one day earlier, before Nelson, Crittenden and McCook, of Buell's army, were fairly within supporting distance, the Army of the Tennessee might have been driven into the river from which it took its name. The rains, the roads and the flooded ravines were all against Johnston, and when he struck, although he struck an unprepared and unexpectant line, and sent its cowards and weaklings whirling toward the river, he presently found himself battering at tough and elastic barriers that hit back as hard as he, that yielded slowly, yet dealt heavy blows even in retiring—the " solid men " of the Tennessee that finally held fast and firm, for the Northerners had still their chosen leader; the Southerners had lost theirs.

Buell it will be remembered, had been marching since mid March to join Grant on the Tennessee; the latter had been halted there waiting Halleck's pleasure. Little by little the force on the west bank had been increased until by April 2nd Grant's daily visits showed him five divisions in camp between the bounding creeks, and still another, Lew Wallace's, to the northward. The old divisions, Hurlbut's, McClernand's and Smith's (W. H. Wallace commanding), camped on the interior lines; the new divisions, Sherman's and Prentiss'—the latter still incomplete—had been thrust further out toward the south and west. This seems strange. Halleck was expected any day. He had written Buell he would start " the first of the coming week," but Grant had looked for his earlier coming. Intrenching as a precaution had been suggested to Grant, and his gifted young engineer, McPherson, had been directed to make preliminary tracings. But, "what's the use?" was the other side of the question. "We are going to advance to-morrow or the next day." It seems never to have occurred to any one that they might be going to retreat, or that any one contemplated such a thing as attacking them. Grant and Sherman, the two schooled generals at the front, are explicit on this head. On Saturday, the 5th, said Sherman to Grant, "I do not apprehend anything like an attack on our position." On Saturday evening the 5th, said Grant to Halleck (both of course in despatches): "I have scarcely the faintest idea of an attack (general) being made upon us." And so when twelve hours later the general attack was made, although Sherman has stoutly maintained they were not surprised, it may be hazarded that they were astonished. The wonder of it is and was that, being unintrenched, unexpectant and almost unprepared, the Army of the Tennessee as a whole put up the magnificent fight that it unquestionably did. That was, after all, the greatest surprise of Shiloh.

Yes, even though two colonels of new regiments ran like the rabbits that came darting in, and their men saw and followed. Yes, even though stragglers and slightly wounded to the number of three to four thousand huddled under the bank back at the Landing, in panic and in terror. Yes, even though one light battery, officers and men, abandoned guns, caissons and everything, and fled in dismay when the first Southern shell exploded in their midst. Yes, even though there was consternation and confusion in the rear of many a brigade and battalion, yet, acting often independently, brigades, regiments and detached batteries fought fearlessly, savagely, long hours at a time, often against superior numbers, filling the ravines with Confederate dead and wounded, inflicting damage fully equal to that which they sustained; yet, in the thick of the morning battle, as Sherman's lines slowly fell back, McClernand, with his Donelson veterans in line, advanced sturdily, while everything to their right and left was in sullen retreat, and actually checked, then forcefully drove, a flushed and rejoiceful enemy full half a mile back upon its reserves. And yet, again, after Grant's arrival on the field, and his placid, cigar-puffing conferences with general after general as he rode the rear of his remaining lines, there were instances of tenacious "stands" in spite of heavy loss, inflicting heavier loss upon the foe, to the end that by dozens there were Southern commands so fearfully crippled that what was left of them had to be withdrawn from the fight. And yet, when the Confederates were enabled at points to burst a way through and completely outflank sturdily battling brigades along the Union line, there were many commands that took heart from the quiet, imperturbable leader who came along the lines bidding them "hang on, we'll beat them yet." There was even one command that because of his stern order, "Hold this at all hazards," clung to the crest of that wooded ravine (named "The Hornets' Nest," because of the stings innumerable received there), fought until everything was gone but honor, and then and not until then did gallant Prentiss, hemmed on every side, surrender his surviving two thousand to an overwelming force.

It was almost at the same instant that another gallant officer, W. H. Wallace, heading Smith's old division, met his mortal wound. It was here in front of our weakest division in point of battle craft, that Albert Sidney Johnston felt it his duty to personally lead a half broken brigade in final assault, and there receive through the boot leg a bullet that tore the artery, a scratch he disdained to notice at the moment, but from which the heroic soldier bled to death before any one about him realized that he was even hit.

It was just at half past two of this tremendous day that the word began to whisper along the Southern line that the lion-hearted leader was no more. It stayed for an hour the battle. It gave Grant and his chief of artillery time to align half a score of batteries along the ridge south of Pittsburg Landing. It gave a breathing spell to the hard-pressed men of Smith and Hurlbut, but away to the centre and right, to the north and northwest, the crashing fray went steadily on, McClernand and Sherman fighting hard and falling slowly, doggedly, back from ridge to ridge—Sherman looking ever to his imperilled right and for the coming of Lew Wallace, unaccountably detained.

We know the story of that momentous mischance. Grant had left his breakfast table, and the as yet unseen Buell at Savannah, had ordered Nelson to march at once to a point opposite Pittsburg Landing, and left word for Buell to hurry forward his foremost divisions due that very day, had then boarded his little steamboat and forced a way up stream through the multitude of river craft, had stopped a few moments at Crumps to bid Lew Wallace put his whole division in readiness to act, and then had steamed on again to be greeted by the sight of hundreds of skulkers lining the river bank for half a mile—a sight to stir most soldiers into flights of fury and blasphemy, but that could not provoke him to even mild indulgence: the nearest he came to it was to refer to one hopelessly terrified group as "those poor devils." Once ashore, the first thing was to see that the ammunition train was in readiness to supply the soldiery at the fighting front. Then, mounting, he rode forward through the dreary woods, through forlorn and dejected throngs of stragglers, skulkers and slightly wounded—even in the moment of thrilling victory the rear of a fighting line is a depressing sight—

and emerged after this nerve-racking plunge, placid, serene, confident. The rebound must come, he argued, when the enemy can drive no further, and the enemy at the rate he had been losing would be in no shape to resist once he got them going the other way, and of going never a doubt had he. All day long until near sundown the battle raged here, there and everywhere, with alternations of rest and, in places, of reformation, with the gradual result that the battle line was squeezed into a semi-circle, a mile or so back from the camps where Prentiss and Sherman had uneasily passed the previous night. But now the South had fought to a breathless finish. Its men could do no more. They were swept, too, on their right flank by the guns aligned at Webster's ridge. They had done their best, but were halted short of the goal posts. The Army of the Tennessee now held, and with the morning would be ready to hit.

And then with night Nelson, of the Ohio, was crossing by boat, and Crittenden was close behind, and McCook, with his finely disciplined division, with all the precision of the drill ground, was just marching up from Savannah. Lew Wallace, too, soon after dark, was in line at last on the right flank, and Grant, underneath the calm exterior, was simply burning with eagerness for morning to come. Then though he might not recover guns and prisoners already spirited away to the Southern rear, he meant to recover every inch of the ground and to drive in utter flight the victors of the Sunday battle, leaving a bloody trail behind them.

That night he sought a few hours' sleep at the Landing, but the moans and suffering of the wounded were too much for him. He groped his way out of hearing and lay in a poncho and blanket under a spreading tree. That night the guns of the *Tyler* and *Lexington* sent huge shells screeching every few minutes up the peopled ravine which encircled the Union left, scat-

tering death among the would-be sleepers of the wearied
Southern host. Their dead and wounded fully equalled,
if not exceeded, those of the Union force, and in point
of generals the cost to them had been as ten to the
Union one. That night it rained in torrents, but at last
the morning came and with it the initiative. The first
gun bellowed from the Union side and with it Grant
and his drenched, shivering but determined men, swept
forward along the battle lines of the night before—Lew
Wallace and Sherman to the west and northwest,
McClernand toward the centre, and Nelson and Crittenden of the Ohio, facing southward, and backed by
the regular batteries which Mendenhall and Terrell had
managed in spite of mud to bring up with their divisions.
Fan-like these forces spread outward from the common centre where they lay cramped throughout the
night, and long before noonday, in spite of hard fighting everywhere, especially where Sherman's men a
second time battled over the fields of Shiloh Church,
the Southern lines were splitting apart and being hurled
backward through the very ravines and thickets they
had carried with yells of triumph but the day before.

Buell, too, had reached the field, and to him, at
Sherman's station, appeared Grant, covered with mud
and mire, sore from injuries received when his horse
stumbled over a fallen timber the previous day, and
stiffened from a long night in the pouring rain. Little
like a victor looked Grant, at the moment. Little
like victory looked the field, yet there was the serene
confidence in Grant's manner which told of both, and,
just twenty-four hours after Sidney Johnston breathed
his last—just before three o'clock on this second day of
bloody Shiloh—the Southern second in command, now
become chief on the field, gave the order which ever
since early dawn he knew to be inevitable, and, still
valiantly fronting the fierce attack of the Union lines,
Beauregard slowly withdrew his bleeding divisions

from the field of their fruitless effort. Except for half a dozen guns and a thousand prisoners, the net result of the tremendous essay, the Army of the South had gained nothing at Shiloh, and what were these when weighed in the balance with the gallant spirit lost to the Southern cause forever?

Sundown of April 7th proclaimed Grant a second time victor in pitched battle, and there were really two days or more in which he was permitted to so regard himself, and to accept the congratulations of Sherman and McPherson. It is even recorded of him that he was human enough to indulge in a brief moment of triumph on meeting in the person of Major Pitzman, of St. Louis, the nephew of the successful competitor for the county surveyorship several years before. Salomon, the local favorite and politician, easily won that contest, and was now serving somewhere in the southwest with the rank of colonel. "Hello, Pitzman," cried the senior major-general with a shrug of the shoulders that displayed the double stars, "you see I've beaten Salomon after all!"

But then came Halleck, the newspapers, new defamation, detraction and presently new humiliation. For the second time the hardest and most determined fighter of all our generals, east or west, was made to suffer at the hands of his superiors, the press, and even the people whom he had so loyally and gallantly served.

CHAPTER XX

THE SORROW AFTER SHILOH

There was no pursuit of Beauregard. The rains and hails of the clouded heavens deluged his wearied men and drenched and chilled his helpless wounded, dragging back to Corinth over those wretched roads. A few cavalry went out and reported the foe as falling back. Then Sherman was sent to keep in touch, was fiercely rebuked by Forrest's horsemen, and wisely, perhaps, refrained from further venture. Both armies had vast repairs to make before either would be fit for further fight, though the Army of the Ohio, it might be hazarded, could have been entrusted at once with the duty of bayonetting Beauregard out of Corinth. Buell and his five fine divisions (for Wood and Thomas joined him by the 8th) would probably have been too many for what Beauregard had left.

But Halleck was coming at once to take command in person. He had expected to find two armies, Grant's and Buell's, fine, fit and ready for action. He found Grant's sorely battered and depleted, but no more so than was Beauregard's, in spite of Buell's slur. Buell reported that when he reached Pittsburg Landing Grant was whipped, and that there were barely five thousand combatants left to him. In fact Buell always believed that he, not Grant, restored the battle.

Now Halleck came to refit and reorganize. Grant's idea would have been to bury the dead and to leave the sick and wounded to the care of the Sanitary Commission. Grant would have shaken himself loose from the leash, gathered up all the sound men on the southwest bank and started forthwith on the heels of Beauregard. Grant probably would and could have had Corinth before April was ten days older, but Halleck would have nothing further done until his coming, and that coming came not until April 11th, four days after the last shot at Shiloh. By this time Beauregard was once again within the works about Corinth, and wiring for reinforcements. By this time, too, Halleck was again listening to calumny illimitable at the expense of Grant, and the columns of the Northern press overflowed with it.

All the skulkers, all the human rabbits who had fled at the first shot, all the envious, all the self-seeking had their tales to tell of luxurious dawdling and drinking at the rear while his men shivered at the far front, of neglect of every precaution (wherein there *was* a vestige of truth), of tender handling of " rebel sympathizers," of returning to their cruel masters of weeping runaway slaves who had taken refuge in his camps, of favoritism toward Sherman, Smith and fellow West Pointers, and ostracism of gallant and deserving volunteers, notably from Illinois. One could readily find the source of most of these, and all of these Grant heard, and some of this he read, always in submissive silence, thinking sadly of the effect produced at home—of the sorrow, distress and indignation in the loved faces about that distant fireside.

These were hard times for hard-headed old Jesse, who, from expressing himself openly and sometimes contemptuously as to the usefulness of his first-born for two or three years before the war, had taken to the opposite extreme, and until sternly checked by the son, had himself been fighting doughty battles in print. These were mournful days for Julia Dent, gathering her brood about her knees and bidding them pay no heed to the taunts and jeers of playmates, taught by envious elders to stab and wound the childish breasts. These were days of temporary triumph to certain subordinates, secretly hostile—men who dared now to submit their reports of Shiloh direct to Halleck, instead of, as military usage and regulation required, direct to Grant; and Halleck, so far from rebuking, received, tacitly encouraged, and presently, with comments of his own, forwarded to the War Department—all to the end that it was Halleck's, not Grant's, report of the great battle that was filed at Washington. The commander on the spot, flouted by some of his juniors, and slighted by his one senior, being thus deprived of much of the needed material, declined ever to submit a report. Halleck had taken this duty, as indeed he took the command, off his subordinate's hands. Over these days of new sorrows, slights and wrongs, we may better draw the veil. Of earthly witnesses to his sorrow—told only in his letters to his wife and to Elihu Washburne, and barely alluded to in a talk with Sherman—even among his staff there seemed to have been but one or two. These were matters on which he felt too deeply to trust himself to speak. He knew by this time that even in far-away Washington there were men who, self-seeking and resentful of his growing influence, had done their worst to poison the minds of both Lincoln and Stanton against him. He did not know—what infinite cheer it would have brought him—that when Stanton sent to the President the paper setting forth the story of Grant's intoxication, and urging his removal, the paper came promptly back endorsed: " I cannot spare this man—he fights."

However, let us turn and see how Halleck took up the reins snatched from the hands of the farmer-soldier, and what he did in the brief time in which his headquarters were actually in the field. The critic and analyst of many another man's campaign had now come to conduct one of his own.

Less than twenty miles away from the thronging camps where by the 1st of May Halleck had gathered one hundred thousand men, crouching behind well-planned fortifications lay the beaten army of Beauregard. With Halleck were Grant, Buell, Pope, Rosecrans, Sherman, Thomas and a score of division and brigade commanders now famous in the West—Pope fresh from his triumph at Island No. 10, which Halleck had officially proclaimed a splendid achievement, " exceeding in boldness and brilliancy all other operations of the war," a something " memorable in military history and sure to be admired by future generations." Yet historians and future generations, so far, seem to mention it but seldom in comparison with Donelson. But Pope was ever a pet of Halleck, a man much of his own kidney, except that Pope was an impetuous, though later a luckless, fighter, while Halleck never fought at all. Just as after Donelson Halleck sought to divert attention from Grant to Smith—the far more chivalric figure—so now he sought to exalt Pope and to " shelve " Grant. Wisely, probably, he broke up the existing barrier and merged the armies of the Ohio and the Tennessee, shifting divisions from one to the other, then reorganizing the mass into three grand divisions, right, left and centre. The right he placed under George H. Thomas, senior major-general of the Army of the Ohio. The centre he gave to Buell himself; the left, and as luck would have it, the one nearest to Corinth when finally they closed in, he gave to Pope. To Grant was assigned no command whatever. Designated in orders as " second in command," he was destined for the time to occupy a position, as pointed out by Colonel Church, about as influential and distinguished as that of Vice-President, or, as his old comrades of the Tennessee would have it, of a fifth wheel to a farm wagon.

And with his great army thus reorganized, refitted and again ready for the field, the man of whom so very much was expected, and whom the soldiers proceeded to dub " Old Brains," because of supposed yet unproved superiority to their immediate leaders, now proceeded to the reduction of Corinth and the crushing of Beauregard, whose force on paper approximated his own, but in fact was not much more than half. Away across the Alleghenies and down on the peninsula between the York and James, and just about this time, a single division of Southern troops led by that genial *bonvivant* and famous dinner giver of the old Army, " Prince John " Magruder, had been sufficient to stop George B. McClellan, backed by the entire Army of the Potomac. If only their beloved and admired " Little Mac " could have been induced to let them go, they could have swept past Yorktown and well nigh swallowed Magruder. But McClellan was an Engineer, steeped in siege craft, and, to the hilarious glee of all Richmond, there he sat him down before Magruder, sent for batteries, guns and ponderous mortars, and lost a precious month.

Almost in like manner, here at the far west, " Old Brains," with the slow, stealthy movement of some huge boa charming a fluttering pigeon, began that solemn and cautious advance upon the doomed strategic centre of northeast Mississippi. Each day the mighty army made a mile or so ; each night it was made sure of it by heavy intrenchments, until from Shiloh Church the face of the earth southwestward was one vast zigzag of corrugations ; until April had blossomed into May, and May had seen two changes of its moon, and then at last, twenty miles in twenty days, the great army coiled down in front of the entrenchments of Beauregard along the heights overlooking Philips Creek, and blinked its eyes at the distant chimneys of Corinth, and wondered what would come next. " If it took us a month with no opposition to make a day's march," asked a Tennessee man of Tecumseh Sherman, furiously chewing and spitting over a dry cigar, " how long's it going to take us to get in yonder, if they show fight ? " All the same the constrictor had at last its grip on Corinth.

And all this time, chafing inwardly, but silent and subordinate, Grant had followed the movements of his massive chief, neglected and ignored except by a certain few of his former comrades of the Tennessee, and ever attended, faithfully and loyally by Rawlins and Rowley. Other staff officers he had, but while every day was adding to the usefulness of Rawlins and the loyal energy of Rowley, it seems that two or three of the original staff might better have been left at home. There was something almost intolerable in existing conditions, and concerning them Grant unbosomed himself to his now devoted friend and comrade, the nervous, irascible, but most loyal Sherman. Here he was, by presidential order, the actual commander of the District of the Tennessee, yet, at the beck of the general commanding the Military Division of the Mississippi, required to follow meekly in his train without command, without escort, without functions of any kind. Thrice after Donelson he had asked to be relieved from service under Halleck, and Halleck had temporized and placated. Now again he had time to read the volume of marked copies or clippings from the Northern press, and realized how numerous and active were his enemies, how few and passive seemed his friends, for, as he himself would not deign to enter into newspaper controversy, they had followed suit. He therefore turned again to Sherman, who was very busy beating the bush at the far right flank, and reaching out for the Mobile and Ohio Railway. Beginning those thirty days as a division commander under the orders of his classmate Thomas, Sherman had developed more pent-up, high pressure energy than half a dozen other division commanders combined, and yet Sherman found time to plead with his now deposed superior and to urge him to bear and forbear a little longer until the country could hear the truth and Halleck listen to reason. Sherman, having known Halleck in San Francisco days, had higher hopes of him than had Grant, who now claimed that self-respect demanded that he quit the service, so far as the jurisdiction of Halleck was concerned. But Sherman prevailed, and Grant, luckily for the cause and the country, agreed to bide his time.

Corinth fell on the 30th, but Beauregard and his sixty thousand had slipped serenely out of the coils. Pope, being southernmost, followed swift and smote hard at the rearmost. Halleck stayed at captured Corinth and wired as to his captures, which consisted of abandoned earthworks, an empty town, but, of course, a great strategic position. So far as men and munitions of war were concerned, he had not taken a tenth part of what Grant garnered at Donelson. Still, something might yet be done further south, whither Pope was pursuing and where the woods for miles were reported by division commanders as full of stragglers from the enemy, half starved and wholly ready to surrender. "Not less than ten thousand are thus scattered about who will come in within a day or two," wired Pope to his chief, whereupon that strategist and statistician telegraphed to an exultant and rejoiceful war secretary at Washington: "General Pope is thirty miles south of Corinth, pushing the enemy hard. He already reports ten thousand prisoners and deserters from the enemy, and fifteen thousand stand of arms captured," and great was the sensation throughout the North, and greater still the depth of disappointment and disgust when it turned out to be, to put it mildly, premature.

And thus did Halleck capture Corinth and report the results. It is safe to say that Grant would have done both otherwise.

CHAPTER XXI

GRAND AND RAWLINS

THE summer of '62 was ushered in and from east
to west Union loving people were reading explanations
and reaping disappointment. McClellan made slow
progress on the Peninsula. Halleck had divided his
forces and sent them hither and yon. Six weeks after
Corinth the War Department summoned to Washington the leader of the left wing at Corinth, and sent John
Pope to command the left-over and scattered corps
McClellan had not succeeded in taking to the Peninsula.
One month later still it sent for Halleck and placed him
chief in command of all the armies in the field, with his
headquarters at Washington. Pope, hastening forth,
had established his, as he announced, in saddle. Thus
two men from the West had come to take high command in the East, and the Army of the Potomac, devoted
to its own commanders, could hardly be expected to
effusively welcome the newcomers.

Pope's first essay was a spirited address to his new
army, made up in part at least of men that had served
in and with the Army of the Potomac, and were proud
of it. Pope shared a not uncommon delusion that about
the only fighting yet done was in the West, and in his
address telling the Eastern armies that he came from
where they were accustomed to seeing only the backs
of the enemy, something the Easterners had yet to experience, and bidding them drop words and methods
hitherto in vogue and to learn the language and ways of
the men of the Mississippi Valley, he succeeded only in
rousing the antagonism of most of the Union Army then
in Virginia. Then he set forth to hammer Jackson and
Longstreet, and by the end of August his entire Army

was flung back to the Potomac, while a victorious enemy was marching for the heart of Maryland. It took less than ten weeks to end Pope's career as a field general. He had been appointed brigadier in the regular army in mid July, thereby making him a permanency in the service, but a command was found for him in the far northwest where he had no more fighting to do, and with McDowell, also deposed and relieved, he found leisure to study and criticise the campaigns of their brethren at the front, something in which each excelled. Few better exponents of the theory and art of war were ever found in these United States than Halleck, McClellan, Pope and McDowell, but for some strange reason their methods proved inoperative with American troops against troops even more aggressively American, and over American topography in the sovereign State of Virginia. There the whirlwind tactics of Stonewall Jackson swept our legions from the field, and there commander after commander of the Army of the Potomac found the road to Richmond blocked and impassable, until at last "the stone the builders rejected" came rough quarried from the distant West, and these and others who had signally failed, yet could concede nothing but luck to him who had "in spite of foes" succeeded, stood at last as silent spectators of the closing campaign, the final furling of the colors of the hard fighting, hard dying Confederacy, as the sword of Lee, the worshipped leader, lay at the mercy of the homespun and indomitable Grant.

But meanwhile other campaigns had to be planned and fought, other foemen had to be overthrown, but when Henry W. Halleck was summoned from the West to Washington—and well did President Lincoln understand this—Ulysses Grant stepped at once from second to supreme command in the Valley of the Mississippi, and it would seem as though the great President who was so patient in council, so painstaking in argument, and so set in mind when once his mind was made, had determined that in spite of every story they could bring to him, the best leader and fighter of them all was the stoop-shouldered, silent soldier from northwestern Illinois. And so again in the summer of '62, called from his headquarters at Memphis, Grant rode the lines at the far front, puffing almost continually at a long black cigar, seeing everything there was to be seen and saying next to nothing until about the evening camp fire, when he sat in conference with Rawlins and felt that he could open his lips awhile without fear of misquotation.

By mid-summer of '62 the great army with which Halleck had crawled on Corinth had been broken up and scattered, and Buell, with most of his old division chiefs in the Army of the Ohio, was already in eastern Tennessee, looking after the menacing force under Bragg. In the West Grant found himself with much of the old Army of the Tennessee. Among his division commanders, fortunately for him, was his stanch ally and subordinate, Sherman. Among them, too, were others, like Rosecrans and C. S. Hamilton, who had risen rapidly from civil pursuits which had occupied their time and thoughts since the brief years of service after graduation, and both Rosecrans and Hamilton, though both men of brains and ability, had characteristics that made them " difficult " as subordinates. Hamilton was a classmate, a fellow infantryman in the Mexican war, yet not one of Grant's intimates. Two of the division commanders, prominent at Shiloh and closely attached to Grant's fortunes or misfortunes from the start, were Hurlbut and McClernand.

It will be remembered that in the quartette of Illinois' original brigadiers, Grant was named foremost. Prentiss, the third in rank, quit his command, as we have seen, almost at the outset, rather than serve under the orders of Grant—an error he probably long regretted and surely atoned for at Shiloh. Hurlbut and McClernand were from the start envious of Grant, and the fact that he was a West Pointer, of long service in the army, and of distinguished record as a fighter in the Mexican war, seemed to weigh with them not at all. That each had been of more consequence in civil life than the humble clerk at Galena was all that either Hurlbut or McClernand seemed able to consider, and it resulted that from the former only half-hearted and perfunctory service could be expected, while, as it soon transpired, from the latter there emanated many of the reports to Grant's discredit. Before long, therefore, as will be shown, the embers of envy and dislike were fanned to the flame of downright defiance.

With such elements to contend with among his generals it was more than essential that the commander should be surrounded by a trustworthy and efficient staff, but here as hereafter, it seemed that Grant lacked the gift of estimating men at their true worth. Absolutely loyal, straightforward and simple himself, he doubtless expected the same traits in others, and appears to have been quite at a loss what to do when the men of his choice proved unreliable. Grant hated to give up in anything—even his faith in a friend.

By the time Iuka and Corinth had been fought and the winter wore on, over and over again the general had found it necessary to suppress some of his subordinates, and to rid himself of at least one who quarrelled so much with others that for a time they seemed to lose sight of the supreme importance of concentrating every energy on the enemy. By this time, too, Grant's most loyal adherents had determined that it was also necessary to rid him of certain of his staff, whose influence both with him and with the army was the reverse of good.

But here lay the difficulty. That very loyalty which Grant ever displayed toward superiors in rank or station, he extended to those whom he had called to his side. Once having given his faith to man or woman, there it clung. Once having chosen a man for his military family, he could see no evil in and would hear no ill of him. Later still in his career this blindness and deafness or dullness as to the moral traits of those about him—this disbelief of any suggestion detrimental to a man of his choice—led to consequences infinitely more serious than those which threatened him in the fall of '62.

But these were sufficiently serious to be the cause of grave apprehension to the men who best loved and served him. McPherson, his brainy, brilliant engineer, at Grant's own recommendation had been made a brigadier in the summer, and this promotion had been followed in October by another which made him major-general commanding a division of volunteers—still, of course, under Grant. But this took him out of the staff, where in many ways Rawlins had learned to lean upon him. Chief of that staff was Rawlins, the big Galena lawyer, whom Grant had had the consummate good fortune to select in '61, and Rawlins deserved and has had biographers of his own.

A charcoal burner for some years of his life, earning money enough to sit for two terms in the Rock River Seminary and then to study law, Rawlins had pushed into politics, had been a Douglas Democrat in 1860, but became the most fervent of Unionists when the war broke out in '61. He had prospered modestly, had married, and might have been earlier in the field and lost to Grant, but for the illness and death of his wife. When he joined his quiet-mannered general at Cairo he knew nothing of military matters, but much of men. His recent bereavement, added to austere views of his own, kept him aloof from camp festivities of any kind. He learned all he could of army methods, of papers, reports, returns, etc., from Grant, and soon mastered all mere matters of routine. Then he began taking more active part in the details and doings about him. He was " bold, virile and patriotic," as General James H. Wilson described him, and so imbued with a sense of the immensity of the duties before them all, and the importance of bending every energy to the maintenance of the Union, that he could tolerate no laggard and brook no laxity.

Knowing Grant thoroughly and well, delighting in his strength and dreading his main weakness, Rawlins stood by and clung to and watched over his commander with a fidelity and a vigilance which warded off many an insidious enemy, and which resulted, as Grant said in '63, in making Rawlins " more nearly indispensable to me than anybody else." When it is remembered that by '63 Grant had assembled about him a staff really great in their personal and professional traits, and all this time, too, Sherman and McPherson were in close touch and communion with him, it shows that Rawlins was the born manager Grant believed him. There, at least he made no mistake as to his man. A year later in the winter of '63 and 4, Grant wrote to Sherman the famous letter saying: " To you and to McPherson" his gratitude was mainly due, but he never wrote or told—possibly he never fully realized—how very much he owed to Rawlins.

By the fall of '62, however, Rawlins was so thoroughly assured in his own position that he felt the time had come when he could properly, and with some promise of success, proceed against the " detrimentals " who still clung like military parasites to the fortunes of their commander, and who might yet drag him down. It was just at this time that there came to him from the army in the East that other son of Illinois, a soldier, and the son of a soldier who seemed to beget nothing but soldiers (for three brothers were from the beginning of the war gallant and brilliant officers), one of them rising to almost dazzling prominence and distinction.

MAJOR-GENERAL JAMES H. WILSON
At the close of the Civil War
From his own memoirs, "Under the Old Flag"

The father had served with Lincoln in the Black Hawk war, and was known of old to most men in the history of the Prairie State. It was partly because of this that Rawlins so cordially welcomed the young lieutenant, Wilson, of the Engineers, when he reported for duty at Grant's headquarters, highly recommended by the generals he had served in the East.

The war was nearly a year and a half old when James H. Wilson joined Grant's staff. He had been graduated at the Point in 1860 under the eyes of the tactician Hardee, had served with McPherson on the Pacific coast, had been hurried East with him in '61, and after vigorous service on the Atlantic seaboard, had made the Antietam campaign with McClellan. He had also made close and curious study of the several generals with whom he had been brought in contact, and it is fair to assume that he had heard something of the talk about Grant indulged in about McClellan's headquarters. It so happened that Grant had gone to Memphis when this new arrival reported to Rawlins, the chief of staff. It is characteristic of Rawlins that he should have cordially greeted the newcomer, and then gone straight to the heart of the matter which at that moment was giving him most concern. " I know all about you," he said: " I knew your father and I'm damned glad you've come." Rawlins, it may be observed, was often " rude in speech and little versed in the set phrase " of polite society. Rawlins was as frankly profane as Grant was characteristically pure.

And then Rawlins opened his heart to the young West Pointer, told him that there were men on Grant's staff who were sure to harm him sooner or later. " I hear you don't drink," said he, and went on to ask Wilson to enter into an alliance with him, offensive and defensive, against the evil elements about them. A total abstainer in the army in those days was a rarity. Wilson in his youth had become convinced that alcohol in any shape is a bar to efficiency. Wilson was, like Rawlins, desperately in earnest in the matter of the war, and he welcomed eagerly the opportunity of usefulness held forth in an alliance with Rawlins, even though when he stood in the presence of his new general, just returned from Memphis to the front, he could see nothing whatever in Grant's appearance to warrant the faintest anxiety.

Accustomed to the pomp and dignity which surrounded the commanding generals with whom he had served, Lieutenant Wilson was presented to a simple-mannered, soft-spoken, rather stooping and unsoldierly-looking man, utterly unostentatious and utterly free from any appearance of the dissipation attributed to him. Grant, the graduate of '43 and one of the famous fighters of the old Fourth Infantry, welcomed the young graduate of 1860 as though he were one of the family, chatted with him as to affairs at the front, as though he had quite as much regard for the opinions of the lieutenant not yet twenty-five, as he had for the seniors about him, and made the newcomer, in consequence, quite at home. To see the " Chief " mingling, as it were, on terms of comradeship with those about him was something that made on Wilson a deep impression. To see that there were a certain few of the staff, notably those earliest appointed, who took advantage of this and assumed airs of greater intimacy and closer relationship was something obvious to others at the time and probably to Wilson, though in his vivid Memoirs he does not say so. But, however unfavorably he may have been impressed with these objectionable few, however strongly he was impressed by and drawn to his new commander and future chosen chief, it was evident that the young West Pointer at least had from the outset begun to appreciate the man who more than any other was Grant's right arm throughout the war—John A. Rawlins, of Galena. " He was then," said Wilson,

" about thirty-two years old, five feet seven inches tall, broad-shouldered, stout limbed and of strong, vigorous health. With jet-black hair and brown, steady eyes, swarthy complexion, fine teeth, a firm mouth and a clear resonant voice, he impressed me as a very earnest, able man." Earnest, able and efficient he proved himself from first to last, and the stanchest, steadiest of the remarkable military family which gradually became a council of ten of the surest and strongest men in their respective lines it was possible for a general-in-chief to draw about him. Graduates of the great National Academy occupied the headship of each department, except the medical, but chief of them all by common consent, and second only to the commanding general in their faith, favor and respect, stood Rawlins, the man who did not hesitate when occasion required, but for very different reasons, to whisper to his chief as did the chosen slave to the hero of old—" Remember thou art mortal."

CHAPTER XXII

GRANT AND McCLERNAND

" THE winter of our discontent " was that which followed the summer of Second Bull Run and Antietam in the East, and of Perryville, Corinth and Iuka in the West. Along in November McClellan had managed to march his loyal friends and followers of the Army of the Potomac to the neighborhood of Warrenton, Virginia, where at last the over-patient President had been compelled to relieve him of the command. Along in November Grant had his columns in northern Mississippi, striving to force a way southward. But here the country was sparsely settled; the enemy retired before him, and then, when every wheel of his train and batteries was hub deep, and the men's brogans were clogged with sticky mud, the Southern cavalry circled his flanks and fell upon the supply stations at the rear. The most important post of Holly Springs had been left to the care of a colonel who had already shown the white feather, and should earlier have been shot or sent home. A second time, and without even a show of fight, he miserably surrendered.

While the roads, or rather the lack of roads, in central Mississippi had more to do with the turning back of Grant's columns than the loss of supply depots at the rear, it seems strange that Grant should have trusted such responsible duty to such an irresponsible man. Soft-hearted we know he was, and sympathetic to a remarkable degree, yet he was firm and strong enough to " break " a brilliant division commander—a classmate and comrade of old—and send him home, because he was perpetually in a wrangle with the generals about him. Again Grant, who could not bear the sound of suffering among the wounded after Shiloh, could hold out firmly against the pleadings of a mother for a worthless son, could rebuke his own kith and kin when, in one of the rather numerous essays to " work " him (we seem to have no authorized English which exactly expresses the meaning conveyed by the vernacular), they sought to induce him to take upon his staff a young officer most justly sentenced by court-martial to suspension from rank and pay. But there had been something about that unfortunate colonel's case which induced Grant to give him another chance and the command at Holly Springs. That, however, was the end of him.

Now, all this time when there was anything worth reporting Grant reported it to the general-in-chief at Washington, but up to January little had occurred to call for correspondence except as to mere matters of routine, and nothing that could call for congratulation. Public attention for the time had been attracted elsewhere—to McClellan's halting tactics along the Potomac—to Buell's foot race with Bragg from the Tennessee back to the Ohio—to the indecisive fight of Perryville. The public noted with mixed emotions that the President had had to remove both McClellan and Buell. The public noted that when Buell stepped down and out the next in rank in the Army of the Ohio, and the only one who had won a battle, did not step up to his place. Instead of George H. Thomas then and there becoming head of what had so long been referred to as " Buell's Army," the command went to William S. Rosecrans, of Ohio, and the public at first did not know that Thomas, loyal to his chief and to his flag in spite of Stanton's suspicions, had actually registered a protest against the treatment accorded Buell, and thereby had increased the disfavor of Stanton, and brought about the promotion of Rosecrans instead of himself.

These matters settled as winter came on, attention

once more began to centre on Grant and his campaign, when condensed on a sudden by the momentous mid-winter battle of Murfreesboro, between Rosecrans and Bragg, beginning in the overthrow of McCook and Crittenden at the right and centre, and bringing up eventually against that strong and steadfast bulwark of the national defense in this and every fight in which he figured, George H. Thomas, the loyal Virginian. People in and about Washington, the White House and the War Department, were so busy over the details of that narrow escape from another disaster that Grant and his affairs for the time being—the month of January—were left to look after themselves.

And at this very juncture it seems that Grant had taken the bit in his teeth and, dropping the fruitless inland campaign in central Mississippi, had set forth upon another, down stream, just in time to checkmate an insidious move to deprive him of the opportunity which proved the turning point—just in time to harness the tide which, taken at its flood, was destined to lead on to fame and fortune.

All these months of the fall and early winter rumor had been busy with McClernand and his plans and projects. Bold, aggressive, ambitious, a man of no mean ability in any line of life, and a capable and proved division leader in battle, McClernand was possessed with intense desire to rise to the supreme command in the West and to down Grant; and while Grant, having little to tell, was telling the War Department practically nothing about himself or his plans, McClernand, supplying information of his own devising, was apparently having the ear of Secretary Stanton and even of the President. McClernand had innumerable means of conducting his campaign against his chief. He had been a fellow townsman of Lincoln, and claimed fellowship on that account, but in reality there was far less to this than was believed by him and his friends, or by the loyal friends of Grant. Lincoln and McClernand had dwelt together in Springfield, but hardly in touch. In politics they had differed widely. In social affairs they had mingled little if at all. McClernand was a vehement Douglas Democrat in the National House of Representatives; Lincoln was an ardent exponent of the new Republican faith at home. From having been a backer of Southern rights and slavery, McClernand, with Logan, Hurlbut and other prominent Illinois Democrats, had followed the noble lead of Stephen A. Douglas, whose thrilling speech to the Illinois legislature in April, 1861, had turned wavering spirits to warlike and determined stand for the Union.

Few men realized, as did Lincoln, the desperate need of the nation in this hour of threatened dissolution. It was, as he saw it, his duty and the proper policy to encourage and develop this Union sentiment among those whose political sympathies had led them hitherto with the South. It was this in great measure which prompted him to reward the magnanimous support of Douglas with the tender of a major-generalship. It was this that led to the appointment at the outset of McClernand, Hurlbut and Prentiss as brigadiers from the State of Illinois, when older and larger States were accorded but one or two or none. Far better soldiers in the regular service meanwhile went utterly unnoticed.

Now, true to his habit of seeking advice and information, true to his policy of encouraging and conciliating, it seems that in this autumn of '62 when so little was being done to his comfort or satisfaction, the President was giving ear to McClernand, who was urging the formation of a strong column with which to sweep down the Mississippi, capture Vicksburg and Natchez, and open the Father of Waters to the flag and the fleets of the Union. The next heard of McClernand at Grant's headquarters in the field, he, who had left the front in the early autumn, was conferring with Gover-

nor Yates at Springfield, and busying himself in the recruiting of new regiments, the organization of a separate force to be known as the Army of the Mississippi
and to be the independent command of Major-General
John A. McClernand.

Now, Vicksburg was the strategic centre of the
Southwest, the true objective point of the campaign,
and the very core of the great military department of
which Grant was the legal head. Yet here was one
of his juniors—it is misleading to refer to McClernand
as his "subordinate"—planning to conduct an independent expedition under the very nose of the commanding general. Grant, unsuspicious as ever, had not
seen the danger: Wilson and Rawlins, far younger but
far shrewder men, had scented it from the start. Wilson, indeed, had heard of the project before ever he left
Washington to join the army in the Southwest. Wilson,
after the mud march of the early winter, ventured to
open his heart to his approachable and friendly chief,
and tell him frankly what he feared—that Grant was
being undermined at the War Department, and that his
proper course was to drop the land route forthwith, and
head an expedition of his own at once by river. This,
it seems, was exactly what Grant had already determined to do—not because of McClernand, but because it
was now the obvious move. It was his entire right and
the orders were therefore issued without consultation
with higher authority. Having nearly completed his
preparations Grant, it is true, notified Halleck, as
general-in-chief, of his intention to accompany certain
of his troops on an expedition toward Vicksburg, and
Halleck, for once, never interposed an objection. He
probably saw at a glance that this would render it impossible for McClernand to succeed in his scheme of
heading a separate expedition, and Halleck had come
to know McClernand well, to respect his abilities as a

statesman and his courage as a soldier, but to distrust him utterly as a general.

Then, too, just when it may have seemed to McClernand and his intimates that the hour of their triumph had come, the President took a hand in the game and issued, all unsolicited by Grant, the order which, without the faintest reflection on McClernand or reference to his aims and ambitions, was none the less a cogent reminder to that chafing and restless junior that he was still under the orders and control of Grant. It was a bitter blow to McClernand, and it intensified the antagonism he so long had felt toward the man whom he presumed to regard, not as his legitimate superior, but as his rival.

Dividing the military forces of the Southwestern Department into four army corps, the President made McClernand head of the Thirteenth, Sherman of the Fifteenth, Hurlbut of the Sixteenth, and McPherson of the Seventeenth—all to constitute the Army of the Tennessee, under command of Major-General U. S. Grant. Here, therefore, were four fine *Corps d'armée* of seasoned soldiers, commanded by four experienced leaders, two of them Ohio " regulars," unselfishly loyal and devoted to Grant, and two of them Illinois volunteers, as selfishly disaffected toward their chief, though otherwise loyal to their country.

But how can a soldier be loyal to his colors, his oath of office and his country, without being loyal to his immediate superior? At the very moment when Grant was setting forth upon his first exploring expedition down the river, a general court-martial was sitting at Washington for the trial of a major-general whose devotion to one chief had led him into disparagement and suspected disloyalty toward another.

And now it is best to follow to its conclusion this matter of McClernand's disaffection and then refer to it no more.

15 225

Believing that he had been promised the independent command of what was to be known as "the Army of the Mississippi," and the conduct of operations at the heart of the Confederacy, declaring that he had been defrauded of these by Grant, McClernand set forth on the Vicksburg campaign an embittered and disappointed man, full of wrath toward his immediate commander in the field, and still believing that he had influence enough with the President and the War Secretary to rid himself of that obnoxious obstacle to his hopes and ambitions. The stories of Grant's inebriety became common talk in Washington in the spring and summer of '63, and were whispered far and wide throughout the army. The President and Stanton and Halleck seem to have heard them time and again, and yet when Mr. Charles A. Dana, Assistant Secretary of War, was sent as confidential adviser of the administration to accompany Grant's headquarters in the field—(a most unusual adjunct to the *entourage* of a commanding general, and one to which many a general would have strenuously objected)—only once could Mr. Dana detect a symptom of the lapses declared to be habitual, and it was not long before Mr. Dana became decidedly drawn to Grant, and, as the result of his own observation, averse to McClernand. His letters to Stanton clearly show it.

Now, while Grant was ever courteous and considerate in all his dealings with McClernand—calling him into conference quite as much as he did his other corps commanders, and inviting his presence whenever he invited theirs—it was noted that McClernand preserved at all times a stiff, formal, and distant manner toward his chief. It became noticeable that McClernand early in the campaign displayed irritation and annoyance whenever he received an order from Grant, that he was slow and indifferent as to obeying. Little by little the breach seemed to widen, notwithstanding the efforts of Rawlins and Wilson, both of whom held McClernand in esteem and admiration for his many strong, virile and valuable traits, and in spite of Rawlins's every effort so to word every letter, order or endorsement as to give McClernand no excuse whatever for misunderstanding, misunderstandings would occur—McClernand seemed determined to take offense.

It is a marvel that the final " break " did not sooner come, but it is certain that Grant strove to humor his surly second in command, unwilling to humiliate so true a patriot and so brave a soldier. McClernand, on the other hand, seemed as firmly bent on forcing a rupture. The beginning of the end was hastened when Grant was urging the utmost speed in ferrying the army across to Bruinsburg for the forward rush on Jackson, and, according to Mr. Dana, McClernand made preparations to bring his bride, her maid and all her paraphernalia over into Mississippi with the army. Then when not a moment should have been lost McClernand wished to hold up the entire movement that he might tender a review of his corps to Governor Yates, who had come down to visit the army. Contrary to instructions, also, McClernand ordered a salute fired in honor of the Governor, and one brigade, at least, lined up for review. It was absurd, as McClernand probably had sense enough to know, but Grant's refusal and prompt orders to move at once seem to have incensed him the more. In his anger McClernand dared to disobey positive instructions to leave his wagons at the landing when the column took the route for Port Gibson. Grant and his staff, including Mr. Dana, left behind them everything but the clothes they had on, and made the march to the front on borrowed horses sooner than miss the first fight—a battle brilliantly won mainly by McClernand's men, they having the advance. And here again McClernand wilfully and defiantly flouted the orders of his commander present on the field. Grant, knowing the importance of harboring ammunition, late in the action directed the batteries to slacken fire: McClernand, hearing this, loudly and instantly ordered them to continue, declaring that he had fought this battle himself, meant to fight it through and would not be interfered with by anybody.

Yet a little longer he tarried with them, utterly spoiling Grant's combinations at Champion's Hill by slow, dilatory, half-hearted methods, when bold and impetuous advance was ordered and expected. For this in part Grant could not blame him, for the orders sent McClernand on the previous day were to " proceed with extreme caution and not provoke a battle," so that when the heavy fighting began about Champion's Hill early in the morning, McClernand, still several miles to the southeast, took until midday to begin the advance. Indeed it was not until then that he received Grant's urgent orders for haste. Hasten, however, he did not. McClernand could fight boldly and well for himself, but not at the beck of Grant. Presently came the siege which might have been averted had Pemberton been " rounded up," as probably he could have been at Champion's Hill, and here McClernand's unruly spirit burst all bounds. A perfectly legitimate and reasonable order was borne to him by the man of all others who, with Rawlins, had shown himself to be a friend and well-wisher. Very possibly Lieut.-Colonel Wilson had been selected because of the close friendship between the McClernand and Wilson families, the comradeship of the elder Wilson and McClernand in the Black Hawk war, and because, with Rawlins, Wilson had striven hard after Port Gibson to bring about a better understanding between the two senior generals. By that time, however, Grant had been affronted too much and too often.

At all events, it was Colonel Wilson, the Illinois West Pointer, who was sent to McClernand with a very simple order, nothing more than to strengthen the outposts of the Thirteenth Corps at Hall's Ferry, on the Big Black—an order which should have been received with soldierly appreciation and obeyed with cheerful and soldierly alacrity. To the utter amaze of the younger officer, the elder instantly and furiously replied: " I'll be G—d d—d if I'll do it! I am tired of being dictated to! I won't stand it any longer, and you can go back and tell General Grant," winding up, says Wilson in his Memoirs, " with a volley of oaths which seemed as though they might have been aimed at me as at our common chief."

This was too much for a soldier and a gentleman to hear. First being careful to repeat the order as given, and so to acquit himself of his official duty, the West Pointer proceeded to tell his fellow citizen and soldier from Illinois that even a major-general couldn't curse him with impunity, and that another word of the kind would lead to his pulling the general off his horse and "beating the boots off him " in front of his men.

It sobered McClernand instantly. He promptly begged Wilson's pardon, assured him of his friendship, begged him to come to his tent and have a drink with him —he who couldn't say enough about Grant's ever doing likewise—and strove to explain the incident by the singular euphemism, " I was simply expressing my intense vehemence on the subject matter, sir."

But Wilson, thoroughly incensed at such exhibition of disloyalty and insubordination, refused the proffered amende—he always refused to drink—and rode back to headquarters and very properly reported the entire affair to Grant, and Grant, far from being filled with wrath, was apparently filled only with merriment. Those words of McClernand had furnished him with just the phraseology he needed in frequent and mild reproofs to those about him, notably that *fidus Achates,* Rawlins, who swore like a trooper when even mildly warmed up. Time and again thereafter when Grant had occasion to note or reprove some outburst of rank blasphemy within his hearing, he would turn to his nearest associate, as Wilson tells us, and say, with a smile, " He's not cursing. He's simply expressing his intense vehemence on the subject matter." And so even this flagrant bit of defiance on part of McClernand was passed over. But the next settled it.

McClernand had submitted a long detailed report to headquarters of the Army of the Tennessee, setting forth the deeds, the services, the sufferings of the Thirteenth Corps from the start of the campaign to the repulse of the grand attack on the 22nd. One has only to read it as it stands to-day (Official Records, Civil War, Series 1, Ch. xxiv, Part 1) to see that it exalted the Thirteenth and slighted every other corps. It was meant, of course, for the eyes of the administration at Washington, and it was duly forwarded by Grant, but with the comment that it was " pretentious and egotistical." Then there suddenly appeared in the columns of the Northern press, widely circulated over the entire country, a copy of what purported to be a general order issued by the authority of Major-General John A. McClernand, eulogizing the heroism, skill and services of the officers and men under his leadership throughout the campaign culminating at Vicksburg, and correspondingly belittling the deeds of the men of Sherman and McPherson. Copies of the papers speedily reached the camps in Mississippi, and great was the wrath in the tents of the 15th and 17th—the rival corps. Sherman and McPherson promptly, Sherman in a most indignant letter, laid the matter before Grant. If any such order had been issued by one of the corps commanders, regulations demanded that a copy be sent to Grant's headquarters, and none whatever had reached him. There could be little doubt, however, of its being genuine. Every word smacked of McClernand, but the matter was " respectfully referred to Major-General McClernand for explanation," and that misguided officer as promptly replied to the effect that the order was not only correctly printed, but he was prepared to stand by it and its allegations.

Then came the dramatic sequel. McClernand had of course automatically severed his connection with the Army of the Tennessee, and could have no hope of future use or usefulness therein. It is probable that he had determined that the time was ripe for final rupture with Grant. He believed himself Grant's superior in everything but the date of commission. He probably believed that he could convince the President and the War Secretary that he and not Grant should be the commander at Vicksburg—that he, rather than Grant, was entitled to the credit of the campaign, and that he, not Grant, would be the man to complete the capture of Vicksburg and reap the great rewards of the crowning exploit. But he reckoned without his host. Grant's hold on the situation, on the President, the Secretary, and on the people of the North was such that nothing could unseat him. McClernand's official accusation that Grant was indebted to "the forbearance of his officers" for his retention in the service fell on deaf ears. The appeal of the ultra-pious and prohibition committees for Grant's relief from command because of alleged indulgence in liquor drew from the long-suffering and ever tolerant Lincoln only a whimsical expression of the wish that he knew where Grant got his whiskey—he would "be so glad to prescribe some of it for some of his other generals." Little by little the star of Grant emerged from the clouds lowering for a time about it, and now seemed burning brilliant and serene. And so it resulted that gallant but wrong-headed McClernand, utterly baffled and disappointed, dropped into the background and finally, after repeated effort to have his case reopened, tendered his resignation at the close of 1864.

It was a dramatic scene that night in the camp of

McClernand, when, between one and two in the morning, he was aroused by his orderly with the information that the Inspector-General of the Army of the Tennessee had come with important orders. McClernand well knew what that meant; arose, and with dignity and deliberation clothed himself in complete uniform, placed his sword upon the table in the centre of his official tent, saw to it that the candles were lighted, took his seat in solemn state, then gave directions that the Inspector-General be admitted.

To him entered Lieutenant-Colonel Wilson, accurately uniformed as himself, belted, sashed and spurred, and standing at attention before him, and with soldierly salute, delivered himself of his message:

" General, I have an important order for you which I am directed to deliver into your hands and to see that you read it in my presence, that you understand it, and that you signify your immediate obedience of it," and with that the staff officer handed the seated general the sealed envelope containing the order which was to unseat him, watched him adjust his glasses, open and read. Then McClernand looked up and exclaimed, " Well, sir, I am relieved ! " A brief pause: " By God, sir, we are *both* relieved ! "

But if the deposed soldier meant that Grant, too, would be relieved as the result of the clash between them, he misjudged both the administration and the people. With the following day, with only his personal staff about him, the sore-hearted general was speeding northward, honored for his courage, his vim and energy on many a field, mourned by many a member of the Thirteenth Corps, even though certain of its generals disavowed his statements, and bearing to his self-imposed retirement not a little of deep regard even among those who deplored his intractable spirit, and his deliberate defiance of a commander who would gladly have been his friend.

CHAPTER XXIII

GRANT AND A GREAT CAMPAIGN

THE campaign of Vicksburg began in a series of tentatives at the bluffs east of the Yazoo " bottom," but in that network of bayous and tangled morass, the natural obstacles were more numerous than those devised by human agency. Only on the west bank could the army find suitable foothold, and there below them, perched on its commanding heights, the heavy batteries of the South guarded the approaches to Vicksburg and swept the wide waters of the Mississippi. The one plan of all others, after canals, cut offs, direct assault, and the Yazoo route had all been discussed, was to float the gunboats and supply steamers under cover of night down past the thronging city, march the troops through the forest and along the twisting estuaries of the opposite shore, reunite troops and flotilla miles below the batteries, ferry across to the Mississippi shore and strike inward at once. Bold, hazardous, " impossible," insisted Sherman, when it was broached in his presence. Impracticable, said others. " The boats will be blown out of water," declared the timid. But Grant, Rawlins and Wilson (Wilson who, starting as lieutenant of Engineers on the staff, had risen in less than six months to be Grant's Inspector-General and trusted adviser) stood together against all opposition, pointed out that Farragut's fleet had successfully steamed up stream against heavier guns and more of them, and that the navy's wooden walls at Port Royal had triumphed over the earthworks, thanks to better gunnery. It was argued that Farragut and Dupont had fine guns and gunners, and could shoot back, but that here the flotilla—a score of flimsy craft of all shapes and sizes, with only

233

six battle boats by way of convoy—could only float by and be shot at. The question was put to Porter, Farragut's plucky second-in-command at the taking of New Orleans, and now at the head of the gunboats acting in aid of Grant and his eager army. Porter's answer settled it. Suppose he did lose a boat or two? Most of them could probably run the batteries without great damage, and that meant success.

And so by devious routes, bridging the bayous and patching the levees as they went, the long columns marched away through the Louisiana lowlands opposite Vicksburg, emerged from the dense woods a dozen miles below, parked their wagons, pitched their tents, and then waited, wondering what was to come next, for only a senior or two was entrusted with the secret.

A wonderful night was that of April 16th, soft and moonlit. Too bright for the purpose, hazarded some, who feared and doubted to the last, but Porter marshalled his ironclads, six in number, and with a few experimental steamers close following, waved adieu to the commanding general above the great bend, and silently bore away on that tremendous mission. Grant, his staff, his wife and children, seated on the upper deck of the headquarters steamer, slowly followed in their wake until, almost within range of the northernmost batteries, the boat was held, and with anxiety intense, they watched and waited.

Then all on a sudden pandemonium broke loose along the heights above Vicksburg as it became evident that the Yankee gunboats were actually steering straight into their teeth. All at once the huge guns began to bellow, and the shells to burst with fearful crashings above and about those devoted and deserted decks. Every man except the helmsman and certain necessary watchers had been ordered below on the ironclads, each of which as it could bring its guns to bear, took up the thunderous chorus. Wooden buildings along the water

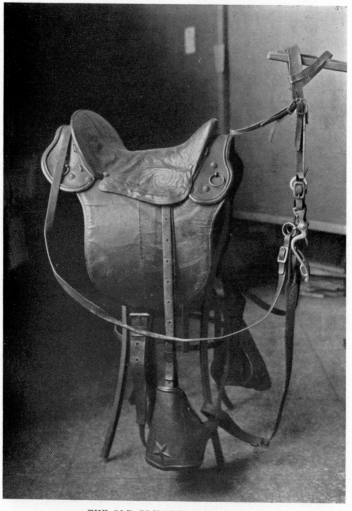

THE OLD GRIMSLEY AND BRIDLE
Grant's favorites while with the Army of the Tennessee

From the originals now in the library of the Chicago Historical Society,
Courtesy of Miss Caroline M. McIlvaine, Librarian

front, suddenly bursting into flame, lighted up the surface of the swollen river, and all too plainly revealed every vessel of the daring fleet. Full three miles or more they had to run the gauntlet of those fire-belching batteries, and, marvellous as it may seem, all but one steamer managed to float securely by. Long ere morning came, army and navy were exchanging greeting and congratulation at New Carthage, away below Vicksburg—the citadel of the Mississippi was turned.

And when the last boat vanished in the dim and mystic light beyond the bend and below the lurid glare about the batteries, Grant, the most impassive of the watchers, could bear the suspense no longer, and in spite of the not unnatural and quite outspoken opposition of his wife, long accustomed to domestic dominion over him, ordered horses, called to Wilson, the best rider of his staff, to accompany him, and set forth at the peep of day on a seventy-five mile trot over those devious roads and bridges, to reach the appointed rendezvous far down stream and get the details fresh from the lips of Porter himself. "My husband is a very obstinate man," sighed Julia Dent, but it was a trait that hitherto, in her experience at least, had not been unconquerable. A new and different and almost unrecognizable Ulysses was this who had so eagerly welcomed her and the beloved children, when they came to join him at Memphis, and if the usually tractable husband and father of the Hardscrabble and Galena days could be so different while still far from the actual concern of imminent battle, how much the more should he be " different " here at the far front, and in the face of tremendous responsibilities? It was probably not until the outset of the Vicksburg campaign that the former belle of the old barracks, the future mistress of the White House, began to realize that there were occasions on which her long devoted liege could and would act independently of her views and wishes. But this is mere " digression from our purpose," which was to tell of Grant in one of his greatest campaigns, leaving to later pages the discussion of his attitude as husband and as father, wherein the true Grant shone as tenderly and truly as, ever tenaciously and truly, he held to the line in head-long fight.

Seventy-five miles rode Grant between dawn and dusk of that April day, to congratulate Porter and con-fer with McClernand long into the night. Seventy-five miles he rode back again the following day, he and Wilson well nigh using up their mounts and orderlies, but seemingly returning fit and ready for even harder riding. Speedily Grant sent southward all the other boats of his flotilla, laden with the needed food, forage, ammunition, medical supplies, and the inevitable im-pedimenta without which an army cannot move. Speed-ily he decided on the landing place on the Mississippi shore just below the mouth of Bayou Pierre. Straight from the hamlet of Bruinsburg Grant launched his columns to the interior, first battling and beating the enemy at Port Gibson; then, to the amaze and consterna-tion of the Southern leaders, and to the outspoken re-monstrance of Sherman, cutting loose from his base and all communication with superior authority, led straightway northeastward for Jackson, the capital, there to overwhelm and put to flight the Southern forces under Joseph E. Johnston, hastening to the aid of those of Pemberton. Then, having smashed the army in his front, back more leisurely he turned to challenge the army in his rear, driving Pemberton before him; well nigh trapping him at Champion's Hill, bridging the Big Black and storming his lines on the westward bluffs, and finally, in just twenty days from the hour of his setting foot on Mississippi shore, penning Pemberton and his thirty thousand within the walls of Vicksburg.

Twenty days of a campaign in which, as military experts have said, the generalship was absolutely perfect—a thing that so rarely can be declared of any general that it becomes remarkable in case of one so often denounced and derided as Grant. Twenty days of swift marching and sharp fighting in which, night and day, Grant was alive with energy and electric force, in saddle from dawn till dark, sending orders and despatches hither and yon, receiving reports from front, flank and rear until after midnight, snatching short hours of sleep, rolled in his blanket in a fence corner, and seldom undressing, even when bed and roof were provided by certain wide-awake members of the staff. Twenty days in which he gave his generals and his officers but little rest, his enemy still less, himself least of all, keeping everybody on the move until he had split the Southern force in twain, flung one-half back across the Pearl, and chased the other within the lines of Vicksburg. Twenty days of a campaign which it is safe to say Halleck would never have sanctioned had he been given a chance to interpose, and which Sherman stood out against to the very last, and then owned up like a man and said, with Shermanic emphasis and embellishment, that Grant was right and he was wrong. Twenty days in which Grant's strategy and tactics stand unchallenged, and which might and should have wound up the entire campaign but for the few precious hours lost on the Union left the day of Champion's Hill. That misunderstanding with McClernand cost us the support of his strong Western division just at a time when McPherson, reaching far around the northern flank, had flung an arm about the retreating foe, and Hovey's men had even barred and blocked the road to Vicksburg and to temporary safety.

Forty-five days longer, once he reached the cover of that long chain of skilfully-planned intrenchments, Pemberton was able to withstand, first the fierce assaults and later the slow, methodical siege approaches, with every day bringing him nearer and nearer the verge of starvation, and no nearer relief or hope. Everywhere just then the forces of the Confederacy were vehemently occupied, and no column could be spared and sent to hew at Grant's flanks or rear, and make him loose his inflexible hold. Away to the east Lee was marching into Maryland and on to the great and dramatic three days' pitched battle with Meade on Pennsylvania soil. In the middle west Bragg and Rosecrans were crouching like Japanese wrestlers manœuvring for an advantage and poising for a spring. In eastern Mississippi Johnston was striving to rally in sufficient strength to once again try conclusions with Grant, but already the South had found itself without reserves. And so it happened that while Pemberton could not get a man to help him, Grant, whose thin lines had wrapped the long concave of outer heights, from the Yazoo above to the Mississippi below, who with less than forty thousand had penned his foeman, now by mid June had twice that number at his command, and absolute confidence in the final result.

It came just as the nation, with a gasp of relief and thanksgiving, learned that Lee, after tremendous battling, had recoiled before the arms of Meade, and was falling back from Gettysburg. While the issue in Pennsylvania was yet in doubt, while Lee's sullen lines still confronted Meade across the drenched and sodden fields at Gettysburg, in no uncertain tones came the announcement from the West: Pemberton had surrendered at discretion; Grant again had triumphed over his foes; Vicksburg had fallen, and the Father of Waters rolled "unvexed to the sea."

CHAPTER XXIV

GRANT IN THE HOUR OF TRIUMPH

DURING that " winter of our discontent " in which the Army of the Potomac was fearfully misled and as fearfully hammered at Fredericksburg, and the Army of the Ohio was fearfully hammered and well nigh overthrown at Murfreesboro, and the Army of the Tennessee was mired in the mud of northern Mississippi and compelled to put back for supplies, the people of the North became insistent. The administration could not explain how or why it was that with bigger armies, better equipment, and the best of intentions our generals were apparently getting the worst of every encounter. Something had to be done to bring about better results, and after long pondering Mr. Secretary Stanton hit on the happy expedient of sending a letter to certain commanders of separate armies in the field in which he promised the victor of the first decisive battle a major-generalship in the regular army. Mr. Stanton had little faith in human nature. He doubted the existence of the governing principles of a soldier. He could not believe that pure, unadulterated patriotism existed among our generals. Without the promise of unusual fee or reward, reasoned the lawyer, no man could be expected to exert himself; hence his offer to the professional soldiers at the head of his forces at the front.

As an illustration of temperament the effect was interesting. Rosecrans raged in spirit, and wrote a vehement and indignant reply to the effect that he desired no bribe in the performance of a soldier's duty. Grant read his, stowed it in his pocket, smoked and said nothing. Hooker, at the head of " the finest army on the planet," was speedily eliminated at Chancellorsville by a much smaller force under Lee, and by the adroit use of Stonewall Jackson's pet device, one which every general in the Potomac Army should have confidently expected, and which both the division and corps commander on the exposed flank refused to believe, even when reliably and repeatedly warned of its coming. Hooker was driven back to his camps, and Chancellorsville added to the array of our humiliations.

Even Grant's spirited campaign in central Mississippi, and the bottling up of Pemberton, hardly served to restore Union hopes. Then came Lee's northward spring, the clinch at Gettysburg, the final repulse after a tremendous conflict, the unmolested return to Virginia. The North thanked God for the relief that followed that three days' battle, so close was the issue, so narrow the escape from fell disaster. In spite of the urging of the President, the War Secretary, the General-in-Chief, Meade, the victor on the spot, had felt the pulse of his almost breathless army and doubted its power to stand another round. Lee should never have been permitted to recross the Potomac, thought Mr. Lincoln, and surely it seems so to students who read the conditions and figures. But the flower of the South was in those stubborn ranks of Lee, Longstreet, and Ewell. Fighting on the defensive Meade had lost one-fourth of his array in the three days' battle. How very much more might he lose if he hurled his wearied men on those sullenly inviting, retiring lines? Better leave well enough alone, was the counsel of some of Meade's ablest advisers. It was all well enough to clamor from a safe distance for instant pursuit and attack. It was what the administration prayed for, and probably most of the Northern people, but, as Longstreet distinctly told the writer in New Orleans in 1872, no more fervently than did the men of Lee, especially when intrenched at Williamsport.

And so, in spite of partial triumph and relief, Gettysburg was not the half that Lincoln, Stanton and Halleck hoped for, whereas, up from the far southwest, came the details of another great surrender to that incomprehensible Grant; and now, at last, even Halleck threw up the sponge with which he had smudged the earlier successes of Henry and Donelson, the stubborn stand at Shiloh, the skill and strategy which turned Vicksburg and led on to Jackson. With Pemberton fairly penned and Johnston held at bay, with Vicksburg captured and the Mississippi freed, Halleck owned that Grant after all stood pre-eminent in his line, and the prize of the major-generalship in the regular army went forthwith to the man who nine years before stood sadly in the streets of San Francisco, discredited, destitute, well nigh friendless and alone.

Halleck himself, as we know, was in San Francisco at that time. Hooker, recently trounced on the Rappahannock and later tricked by Lee, was also then prominent in California circles, and presumably conversant with the circumstances connected with Grant's resignation. And as for the men who had compassed and compelled that resignation from the regiment Grant had grown to love—though not as he loved wife and children at home—where were they? No man who ever knew Buchanan could accuse him of malignity. He had looked upon his junior with a soldier's eye that liked not the stern task he had in hand. He had done simply that which he conceived to be a duty in ridding the service of a man who would neither come up to his standard as to soldiership, nor control at all times a desire to drink. Bonneville, the aging colonel, now in '63 was serving as commander of the barracks at St. Louis, and never rose to higher grade. Buchanan, "Old Buck," as his admiring juniors dared to call him, still the picture of the soldier and the gentleman, had commanded the regular brigade through the battles in

Virginia, had been appointed brigadier-general of volunteers in November, '62, but the Senate said " No," and the appointment lapsed with the 4th of March. Like Bonneville, Buchanan then accepted duty at the rear, until in '64 he became colonel of infantry and joined his regiment in New Orleans.

It may be confidently declared that with Buchanan's humiliation at the hands of the Senate Grant had nothing whatever to do. That friends of his, still rankling over the past, may have sought revenge by defeating the richly-deserved promotion of Buchanan, is something of which Grant probably knew nothing. It was not in him to injure a deserving man. It *was* in him to work and work hard later for the restoration to command of men like McClellan, who had injured him—of Buell, who had slighted and belittled him.

More than one officer had said or written of Grant before Vicksburg that which later he totally forgot until most unpleasantly reminded. The Damon and Pythias attitude in which Grant and Sherman ever appeared, had stirred envious souls to recollection of something written by Sherman in '62—something to the effect that " had Charley Smith been spared to us Grant would never have been heard of," something which in the light of later events Sherman thought he never could have written, and said so. Whereupon, as the word of an officer who had been drawn into the controversy stood disputed, it seemed necessary to publish a photograph of Sherman's own letter. After all it only said that which Grant himself had said and felt as to Charles F. Smith. Both Grant and Sherman honored and looked up to their old commandant as the finest soldier of their day. Grant ever felt embarrassment in sending Smith orders of any kind, and, as he says, would have served Smith as loyally as Smith ever served him. If any man thought to break or even strain the bonds that united Grant and Sherman by the publication of that character-

istic statement, great must have been his disappointment. Grant was too magnanimous and Sherman too
genuine. If anything it only served to weld the friendship.

The conquest of Vicksburg and the surrender of
Pemberton's army had made Grant the greatest of our
generals in the eyes of the nation, and put an end for
many moons to the clamor at his expense. McClernand,
to be sure, fought hard in public and in private for his
own restoration, and for an " investigation " as to Grant,
but the President had to deny them both. In spite of
the fact that McClernand had still a strong following
at home—a host of honest people who had known him
long years, believed in him and honored him—there
were too many million people by that time who could
see nothing but Grant. The McClernand cry against
him, therefore, was but a mote in the broad sunshine
of popular acclaim. For long weeks the modest victor
could bask, if he chose, in public adulation, but he did
not so choose. Telegrams, letters and tributes rained
upon him, all expressive of praise and congratulation.
Grant read, put them in his pigeon holes—there was no
longer room in his over-stuffed pockets, the usual receptacle—smoked and simply said " thank you " or nothing. He could not begin to answer the letters, neither
could his staff. He had, too, the delighted missives from
the wife and children whom, all save adventurous Fred,
he had earlier sent up stream again. Fred had managed,
to the father's humorous delight, to pick up a mount
at Bruinsburg—he and Mr. Dana sharing a venerable
pair of carriage horses the night of the landing—and
to accompany the staff throughout the campaign. " He
looked out for himself," wrote the General, later, for
the father had no time to give to him, and as other
chroniclers have said, he was very much in evidence for
a fourteen-year-old, and sometimes as much in the
way. All the same the soldiers, as they expressed it,

"took a shine" to the lad, whose face was ever as cheery and smiling as by that time the father's was grim and set.

For a few weeks after the great surrender Grant and his staff were occupying quarters in the city. The General, with Rawlins and Wilson, moved in as not unwelcome guests at the commodious home of a planter whose wife had been suspected of Union sentiments throughout the siege. For some reason the Confederate commander, General Pemberton, whom we saw at San Cosme coming with Worth's compliments to Grant, had seen fit to assume toward his conqueror a cold and repellent manner which excited in Grant rather more amusement than it did annoyance. Pemberton, on July 3rd, had requested the appointment of a commission to arrange terms of capitulation, adding the customary platitude about a desire to avoid unnecessary effusion of blood. Grant sent his simple yet uncompromising response to the effect that commissions were unnecessary, and unconditional surrender all that was required. So a second time these "unchivalric," yet entirely proper terms were dealt out to the vanquished. Grant and Pemberton met between the lines and under the tree which later speedily was whittled to death. Grant was entirely at his ease, in no wise exultant or superior. Very possibly the utterly matter-of-fact manner which seemed to say, "this is all just as I planned and expected," may have been a cause of irritation to Pemberton, for when Grant and his staff on a very hot day rode in and dismounted at Pemberton's headquarters, the Southern general and his officers maintained their haughty and distant attitudes, offered not even a chair or a glass of water to the tired and thirsty visitors, and so were allowed to depart with empty wallets. Two or three young West Pointers in Confederate gray, however, came forward to shake hands with Wilson and were presented to Grant, who welcomed them sincerely and kindly. When they left to rejoin their dejected comrades their worn haversacks were bulging with all the good things the headquarters' mess afforded.

And just as soon as the veterans of Vicksburg's defense, having surrendered arms, flags and equipments, had marched away (unfortunately permitted to go and fight as much more as it pleased them—the one serious error of Grant's management of the surrender) Julia Dent reappeared at the far front, and took up her abode with her conquering husband in a house full of attractive women, in the midst of a new-budding romance. The most beautiful and attractive of the occupants was the governess of the planters' daughters, a New England girl of excellent family, who became at once the object of unstinted admiration and of some undesired attentions. The former were genuine and lasting, the latter were presently routed and replaced by devotions as sincere as was the man. Rawlins, the hard-headed, pragmatical chief of staff, who had buried his wife at the outbreak of the war, had fallen promptly, deeply and devotedly in love, and to the sympathetic interest of General and Mrs. Grant, began his determined wooing. It is recorded of this uncompromising and incomparable aide that he who had been the most absorbed and austere of men, became in this presence the gentlest and least aggressive. Long years of his vehement life Rawlins, when aroused, had been accustomed to vent his views in hair-raising expletives. The lady was from the land of steady habits where long years of the pillory had done much to banish " profane swearing," and Rawlins, whose language hitherto had known no trammel, even in the presence of him who swore not at all, his soft-spoken chief, registered his vow to break himself of the habit of a lifetime, and a mighty struggle did he have with himself; and hereon is where that selfsame chief was stronger than his mentor. Habits as deeply rooted as Rawlins's blasphemy Grant could and did conquer and put aside without so much as a sign of a struggle.

But the love affair thus born in Vicksburg went on to blissful consummation. A joyous wedding was that to which the staff was bidden in December following, and a noble union was that which ensued and lasted until that " most untimely taking off " which later robbed Grant of his own war secretary and his loyal, devoted and indispensable friend.

CHAPTER XXV

WHAT FOLLOWED VICKSBURG

FIRST came weeks of reports, of letters and congratulations, of calls, callers, gifts and givers. Many letters had to be answered and there was not time in which to do it. Many calls had to be returned, and it would have been better had some of them—notably that of Banks from New Orleans—been left until the war was over. Many of the gifts might far better have been returned, but were not. He who never had an "ulterior motive" could not see it in another, and then, while he had little use for many things that were sent him except such as cigars and saddlery, they were a delight to Julia Dent, who, like Alice in Wonderland, had an almost childish pleasure in an "unbirthday gift." There were gifts that set Rawlins's nerves on edge in his effort not to swear. There were even some which he urged the General to decline outright; whereat Grant looked gravely, keenly, at the flushed and bearded face, puffed thoughtfully a moment, turned and went silently away. Wilson sometimes was called in by Rawlins to second the urgings of the chief-of-staff, but while in matters military, and even in some matters personal to himself, the General heeded what those men had to say, some influence more powerful than theirs actuated Grant to the last in that matter of accepting gifts. Bribes they never were, because bribed he could not be; but as bribes, no doubt, a number were sent, and the effect upon the public mind in later years a thousand times outweighed their value.

But the weeks that followed Pemberton's surrender were very happy ones to Grant, and full of bliss and triumph to his wife. The contrast between her state as consort of the conqueror of the West, the chief of the great army and department of the Mississippi, courted and flattered on every side, and the humility of their lot when he was grubbing at " Hardscrabble " or clerking at Galena, was enough to turn many a head, though it never seemed to disturb his. Military critics claim to see a perceptible falling off in the conduct of affairs for a month or two after Vicksburg. Certain it is that much that might have been done was not done, but for most of this Halleck, not Grant, was responsible. It was in no wise the fault of Grant, for instance, that Lee was able to take Longstreet and his famous corps from under the aquiline nose of Meade, and send him around by rail to northwestern Georgia, there to join Bragg and enable him to fall upon Rosecrans and hammer him at Chickamauga, that terrific battle which wellnigh neutralized the summer victories, and which restored the credit and confidence of the South. With Stanton's elaborate system of spies and secret service it is remarkable indeed that one-third of Lee's army could march away from the Rapidan unguessed by any one at Washington. Yet even this might not have harmed " Old Rosy " had he been reinforced from the West as Bragg was from the East. The Army of the Mississippi broke up after Vicksburg. The Thirteenth Corps were floated down to aid Banks in Louisiana. Sherman had been sent to whip Johnston out of Mississippi and came back without having done it—saying his men were tired and Johnston too nimble. McPherson, with the Seventeenth Corps, was holding the line of the Mississippi as far down as Natchez. A strong division had been detached to aid Steele in Arkansas, and another to Burnside in far east Tennessee, and Sherman's splendid corps might well have been sent up to Memphis and then shipped to Chattanooga by rail, and with this aid from their old rivals of the Tennessee the chances are that the men of the Cumberland could have beaten

Bragg, even had he been reinforced more heavily than he was, both by Longstreet and by quite a number of Pemberton's late defenders of Vicksburg.

This, however, was not urged upon Washington by Grant, nor was he much impressed by the arguments in favor of it, advanced principally by his youngest, yet one of his ablest counsellors, Wilson. Ever since Donelson there had been some intangible, indefinable uneasiness between those two armies, the Tennessee and the Ohio. Even after their welding at Shiloh, their merging before Corinth, that feeling existed. The men of Donelson resented it that their leader should be " sidetracked " by any man from the Army of the Ohio —even the grave, dignified and honored soldier whom the men of Mill Springs and their comrades already hailed as " Old Pap " Thomas. It had stung the Tennessee to note how much Halleck exalted Thomas at the expense of Grant, and it was probably the foundation of the deplorable coldness which little by little developed between Grant and Thomas—but of that hereafter.

At the time when this move to aid Rosecrans was proposed to Grant, Sherman had been for some days back from his dusty marchings to and fro; his men were rested, and most of them eager to be at the throat or heels of the enemy. But Rosecrans, ignorant of the preparations being made to receive him south of the Tennessee, was in the full flood of a skilful campaign of manœuvres. The papers were predicting all manner of success and triumph, and it may be that Grant believed that, as the Army of the Tennessee had absorbed most of the glory thus far, and the old Army of the Ohio, now known as the Army of the Cumberland, was really launched on an independent campaign with promise of a crowning victory, it would only spoil it all to interject the aid of their rivals. It is more than possible that at this stage of the game Rosecrans would have been embarrassed by the coming of Sherman, and might have been exasperated.

Be this as it may, Grant did not urge the move. On the contrary, much to the disgust of Rawlins, he decided that this was a favorable time to visit the lower sections of his military domain, and to return the call of Banks. With this in view he took steamer for New Orleans, accompanied by his personal staff, leaving Rawlins to finish the reports of the campaign, to " run " the routine of the great command during his absence, and for the time being Grant disappeared from the view of his faithful friends at headquarters. Just as Rawlins dreaded, no good whatever and not a little harm resulted.

Galloping to a review at Carrollton, above New Orleans, Grant's borrowed horse slipped, fell and crushed his rider's leg beneath him. Grant went on crutches for nearly ninety days and no end of calumny was again started. Given a reputation for having once indulged in drink and anything will revive it. It would seem that in many a mind there is nothing so impossible, if not unforgivable, to man as ability to drop the vice at will.

Fortunately at this juncture Rawlins himself had carried to Washington the priceless records of the Vicksburg campaign, had been received and heard with marked respect and consideration by the President, by Halleck, and even by tempestuous Stanton. (It would have been a case of Greek meet Greek had the latter taken occasion to " turn loose " on Rawlins, as he so often did on others.) But all that Rawlins had to tell of the campaign and of the personal energy and activity of his chief came in good time. A story was current in the fall of '63, and revived with circumstantial detail a year later, to the effect that seeing his General yielding on a certain occasion in June, '63, to the alleged weakness of his Galena days, Rawlins had written a strenuous letter, telling Grant in so many words that he could not bear to see the splendid powers of his chief clogged or clouded by liquor, that he had noticed that very night— it was written at one A.M.—that even in the presence of "the eyes of the Government," Mr. Dana, Grant's staff officers were drinking and inviting their chief to join. Moreover there were indications which prompted him, Rawlins, to believe that Grant had yielded. Possibly it was this story which McClernand sought to stir; at all events it was told that Rawlins had said in so many words that the next time these symptoms appeared he would tender his instant resignation and go home. It is recorded that in his wrath on the occasion referred to, Rawlins impounded every bottle he could find about headquarters, even a basket of champagne kept to celebrate the surrender of Vicksburg when it came, and smashed them before the eyes of their owners. It was a noble letter, but it was hardly a noble motive which prompted its publication in full in the memoirs of an unsuccessful general of the eastern army.

Unlike Sherman's missive as to what might ever have been heard of Grant and himself had Charles F. Smith been spared to us, this was not a photographic copy, nor was the original produced, but all the same it bore tremendous weight and was probably authentic; it certainly had all the " earmarks " of Rawlins's style. Nevertheless Wilson and others who were with Grant throughout the campaign aver that there was precious little on which to base the belief that Grant had been drinking either before or after the occurrence in question.

But the luckless fall of that horse at Carrollton gave rise to all manner of gossip, eagerly believed and circulated wherever Grant's would-be rivals held sway. There were other disturbing tales abroad, of which Rawlins heard not a little and Grant had apparently heard not at all, nor heeded if he heard. He long since had learned the futility of combating newspaper slander, and had come to accepting all such as the inevitable accompaniment of success.

One tale that hurt him to the extent of writing to Mr. Washburne, was that of capturing and returning to their masters the fugitive slaves who had sought his lines for protection after Donelson. Now came others which sought to implicate him in cotton speculation. Of course there had been abundant opportunity, for he controlled the situation, and to officers eager to accumulate wealth the temptation was greater even than the opportunity.

Here in all the country about Vicksburg lay thousands of bales of the now almost priceless staple, and presently by every boat came eager would-be investors, some with and some without authority of the War Department. To insure his command against the inevitable demoralization which would result from such a traffic, Grant had issued positive orders against it. He could have reaped a fortune of one hundred thousand dollars in thirty days had he seen fit to lend himself, or the power of his name, to such a scheme, but he would have none of it.

Now, it is not to be imagined for a moment that the eyes of so keen a money-maker as Jesse Grant had been blind to this opportunity, or that, had he retained the old dominion over his son which in '39 had prompted the latter to " think so too if he did," the elder would have been among the foremost seekers after cotton; but Jesse, the father, had lost that domination, and he knew it. He would not spend a cent to get his son the horse and uniform he needed as colonel of the Twenty-first Illinois, yet within six months was importuning " General " Grant, commanding at Cairo, to help him get a contract for making harness for the artillery and transport. He had helped the son not one cent's worth to his high position, but was speedily writing him to give staff appointments to one Foley, then to "Al Griffith" and later to a Mr. Nixon. Failing in these he wrote begging that a pass to go South, obviously for purposes of speculation, be given to a Mr. Leathers, and in all these and in kindred appeals the son for good and sufficient reasons had stood out against him. Finally, as has been pointed out, the General had found himself compelled to write bidding his father, in no uncertain terms, to cease meddling in military affairs. "You are so imprudent that I dare not trust you with them" (particulars of recent events). "I have not an enemy in the world who has done me so much injury as you have in your efforts in my defense. . . . For the future keep quiet on this subject."

It was useless to try to "work" Ulysses, but there were other ways of attaining the object, and hardly had the smoke of the last battle about Vicksburg cleared away when there came a kinsman of the commanding general, and with a permit from the Secretary of the Treasury. The canny Grants had reckoned that Mr. Salmon P. Chase, of Ohio, would be loath to deny the request of a near relative of Ohio's greatest soldier, now the central figure of the war. Grant, the general, when confronted with this officially authorized arrival, smoked and said nothing. If the administration saw fit to do thus and so, it was not for him to protest. But Rawlins reasoned otherwise, and, never waiting to consult his chief, wrote a peremptory order banishing the cotton buyer from the lines, and when Grant checked it as being harsh and unnecessary, where a word would be sufficient, the chief-of-staff burst into a fury of wrath and blasphemy. The scene and sequel are best described in the words of General Wilson himself— probably the only eye and ear witness.

"This was more than the rugged and determined chief-of-staff could stand, and, evidently fearing that it meant a relaxation of discipline, if not a defeat of justice, he burst forth perhaps unconsciously with a volley of oaths, followed by the declaration that if he were the commanding general of the department, and any kinsman of his dared to come within the limits and violate one of its important standing orders, he would arrest him, march him out and hang him to the highest tree within five miles of camp.

"Thereupon, without waiting to note the effect of his stentorian speech, he turned about and, re-entering his own office, violently slammed the door behind him.

"It was an embarrassing episode—the only one of the kind I had ever witnessed—and as the punctuation of his remarks was both profane and disrespectful, I followed him and said:

"'Rawlins, that won't do. You have used language in the General's presence that was both insubordinate and inexcusable, and you should not only withdraw it, but apologize for it.'

"Without a moment's hesitation he replied: 'You are right. I am already ashamed of myself for losing my temper. Come with me.' And walking back into the General's presence, he said, in his deep, sonorous voice: 'General, I have just used rough and violent language in your presence which I should not have used, and I not only want to withdraw it, but to humbly beg your pardon for it.'

"Then with a pause and a blush he added: 'The fact is, General, when I made the acquaintance of the ladies at our headquarters I resolved to give up the use of profane language, and blankety blank my soul if I didn't think I had done it.'

"At this naive expression Grant's face lightened with a smile and he replied: 'That's all right, Rawlins, I understand. You were not cursing, but, like Wilson's friend, "simply expressing your intense vehemence on the subject matter."'

"It is needless to add that the incident passed off to the satisfaction of all concerned. The order was suspended, but discipline was vindicated by a quiet intimation on the part of the General that the intruder's health would be improved by an early return to the North, and he went the next day."

And so for a brief spell the family efforts to "fatten at the public crib," as the papers put it, through their connection with their one famous member, received temporary check. But the time was to come when, in added numbers and potent influence, they returned to the charge. But that was after Grant quit the tented field for the White House.

Hardly had the General commanding returned to

WHAT FOLLOWED VICKSBURG

Vicksburg and begun to hobble about on his crutches when the nation was stunned by the news of Chickamauga. Dana was with Rosecrans at the time, and his vivid pen-picture of the crushing effect upon Rosecrans, of the possible result to Burnside, now in peril at Knoxville, of the overthrow of McCook and Crittenden, whose ill fortune had become proverbial, and finally of the indomitable stand of Thomas, led to most important measures on the part of the administration. As the only successful commanding general of the four armies in the West, Grant was given supreme control, and summoned to oust Bragg from his triumphant perch on the heights overlooking Chattanooga, where, grim, defiant, destitute of forage and short of rations, the Army of the Cumberland held to its fortified lines.

And so, in mid October, journeying, as required by his orders, *via* Cairo and Indianapolis, Grant, with his staff, arrived at the capital of the Hoosier State, and found explanation of the roundabout route in the person of Mr. Secretary Stanton, who had come all that way to meet and take personal measure of the man of the Mississippi. Stanton boarded the car, promptly grasped Dr. Kittoe, staff surgeon, by the hand, confident as ever in the infallibility of his judgment, and impulsively exclaimed: "How do you do, General Grant? I recognize you from your pictures."

And so met the two men who henceforth to the end of the war were to be the dominant factors—Stanton at the War Department, Grant at the front.

CHAPTER XXVI

GRANT AND THOMAS

To Louisville together journeyed Stanton and Grant, sitting apart from the staff, and conferring gravely upon the situation. At Louisville they parted, Stanton to return to his duties at the Department of War, Grant to hasten southward, each rather relieved to get away from the other. Acting together loyally until after Appomattox, Stanton backing Grant, and Grant subordinately conferring with Stanton, there was never between them any pretense of personal friendship. In the performance of what he conceived to be his public duty, Stanton had given his assent in the past to measures which had humiliated and reflected upon Grant—especially after Shiloh—and Grant had never forgotten it, but had deliberately shaken himself free of all possible hindrance from the Halleck-Stanton influence when he "cut loose" at Bruinsburg and launched out for Jackson. Each had now learned to respect the ability and the patriotic purpose of the other, and, for the sake of the common cause so dear to both, their official acts were thereafter to be in concert. But this did not prevent Stanton from keeping his eyes and ears open, his spies and sycophants alert, for anything amiss about Grant, his associates and his habits; nor did it make amends in Grant's eyes for words and deeds to his detriment in the past; in fact it made him watchful, if not expectant, of new and similar demonstrations in the future.

But in going Stanton left to Grant full authority to manage his now immense command practically in his own way. This included the relief of Rosecrans from duty at the head of the Army of the Cumberland, the assignment thereto of George H. Thomas and the promotion of Sherman to the command vacated by Grant. The wires that very day bore to Thomas the tidings of his new duties, with Grant's injunction to hold Chattanooga at all hazards, and in thrilling words came Thomas's spirited answer to Grant: "We will hold the town till we starve."

And then, all breathing more freely after the departure of Mr. Stanton, Grant, with two or three of his chosen, scandalized Rawlins by going to the theatre. Rawlins would have had out a special train and set forth that very night to join Thomas at the imperilled Gateway of the Gods.

Accompanied now only by his military family, Mrs. Grant and the children having been "detached" at Cairo and sent to safe refuge, while the husband and father returned to the front, Grant arrived two days later at Stevenson, beyond which the railway could not carry him. Eastward the Tennessee was lined along the south bank by sharpshooters in butternut or gray, and communication with Chattanooga was by steep and devious routes over the high ridges and plateaus. Nevertheless, the indefatigable Mr. Dana had ridden to meet them and to give Grant full information as to conditions at Chattanooga—officers and men hungry but plucky, horses and mules, more than half of them already starved to death. There could be no doubt of the sincerity of Dana's welcome. He had learned in the Vicksburg campaign the true value of Grant, had set him higher in esteem than any of his generals, had learned to know and believe in Rawlins as a "naturally born" chief-of-staff, and to regard Wilson and Bowers as the General's most trusted aides. He rejoiced in the War Department order, with the final issuance of which he had doubtless had much to do, assigning Grant to the command of the entire military division of the Mississippi, embracing the departments of the Ohio,

Cumberland and Tennessee and the armies therein engaged. He rejoiced in the arrival on the *Tennessee* of Hooker, with the Eleventh and Twelfth Corps from the Army of the Potomac, and the tidings that, far away to the West, Sherman was already in march to join them. It promised under God's providence the final exclusion of the battle flags of the South from this section—the stronghold of the Middle West. Taking Wilson with him, the "eyes of the War Department" remounted at Stevenson and set out for Chattanooga, leaving Grant and his staff to make the slow and painful progress necessitated by his still serious injuries.

But first came interesting meetings with two former rivals—generals recently commanding armies as great as his own, if not greater and far more conspicuous—and the manner of the two men, as well as of the meetings, is illustrative of the mental attitude of each. It was here at Stevenson that the famous and successful leader of the victorious Army of the Tennessee met the deposed heads of the defeated armies of the Potomac and Cumberland—Hooker still smarting from the stigma of Chancellorsville, Rosecrans still suffering from the stings of Chickamauga.

It was characteristic of Hooker that he should assume a superior and patronizing attitude at the outset in the possible hope of attaining the old ascendency of captain over subaltern, or the glory of the headship of the "finest army on the planet" over the "hayseed" leader of those "hoodlums" of the Tennessee, which descriptives were attributed to and certainly sound like, *el capitan hermoso,* as "Fighting Joe" was known in Mexico. Having in mind the Grant of Vancouver, Humboldt and San Francisco days, and ignoring the fact that he too for a time before the war had been well nigh as poor and otherwise quite as open to criticism as Grant—ignoring, too, the immensity of Grant's later services and successes, and daring to ignore the fact that Grant was now his superior officer to whom it was his duty to show every military deference, it pleased Hooker at Stevenson, as it had Buell at Savannah, to omit the prompt and soldierly call for the purpose of "paying respects" and reporting conditions. The custom in all armies is as old and as thoroughly recognized as that of the salute to superior rank. But Hooker sent a staff officer with the airy message that he "wasn't feeling very well and would like to have General Grant call on *him*."

That message fell into the best possible hands when it was delivered to the chief-of-staff. Rawlins looked up from his improvised desk and never waited to hear what his mild-mannered chief might wish to say, for if Grant really believed that Hooker were ill he would take his crutches and set forth at once to see what he could do for him—which was the way of the Army of the Tennessee. Rawlins was too quick for his chief; Rawlins saw through the artifice in an instant, and his resonant voice informed the Potomac-schooled aide-de-camp, and a score of staff officers sitting about, that "General Grant himself is not very well and will not leave the car to-night. He expects General Hooker and all other generals who have business with him to call at once"—a message which opened the eyes of Hooker and his staff to the soldier stuff there was at Grant's headquarters, and taught a much-needed lesson.

And then came Rosecrans and a contrast. Cordiality toward the general who had come to supplant, and had already relieved, him was not to be expected. Rosecrans had looked upon Grant's earlier success as accident, upon his promotion as luck, and upon his conduct of affairs at Shiloh and later at Corinth and Iuka as far from sound. Rosecrans, so believing, had so declared himself in talk about the camp fires, and it had all in time reached the ears of Grant. But after Vicksburg Rosecrans saw that in the silent man of the

Tennessee there was generalship none of them could match, and, like Halleck, he surrendered, though long years thereafter that relief rankled and stung. Here, however, in candid and soldierly subordination Rosecrans reported to the man he had not seen since Corinth and had been moved to lightly regard. Frankly, courteously he was received, and the two held a long and important conference. Rosecrans was full of information as to the country and the opposing forces, and loyally gave it to the new commander; then went his northward way with the respect and sympathy of those about Grant, and the undoubted affection of his old command. Each general for the time felt for the other an access of soldierly regard, though as it happened they never had been cordial friends, and later became still further estranged.

But there was yet to come a meeting with the new commander of the Army of the Cumberland—he who twice had saved it and who twice before, but for persistent loyalty to his immediate superior, might have been assigned the command. George H. Thomas stood waiting at Chattanooga to receive his new commanding general, and throughout the Army of the Cumberland there was no little talk and speculation as to what that reception might be.

Ever since Donelson, as has been said, there had been this feeling between the Army of the Tennessee and that of the Cumberland. Ever since Shiloh there had been constraint between Grant and Thomas. Their common superior, Halleck, had humiliated the former in favor of the latter. They had not met or served together since the Mexican war until Halleck's cautious forward crawl upon Corinth, and when Thomas here encountered Grant the latter was under a cloud mainly of Halleck's creation—a cloud which seemed to envelop and hide him from the eyes of all save the ever faithful Sherman. No general of Buell's army, so far as is known, sought out Grant to say how much he regretted or disapproved the position of practical *surveillance* to which he had been relegated. It would have been an improper and unsoldierly act, and the Army of the Ohio, later of the Cumberland, was too well taught and disciplined. Moreover, what did they know of Grant and Grant's habits save what they had read and heard and could so readily believe? It is simple truth to say that that army thought it had many a general of its own who was Grant's superior in everything.

Then early in the second winter of the war, just after their fierce experience of Murfreesboro, the generals of the Ohio heard of that recommendation of Grant to create one big command out of the western armies and departments, all under one head, and the inference was that Grant wished to be that head. Perhaps he did, but he had not so said or written, and this was something neither Rosecrans nor any of his division commanders desired.

Then had come Grant's splendid campaign, closing with the surrender of Vicksburg, and his double stars in the regular army. Then had followed " Old Rosey's " brilliant campaign of manœuvring, closing with the sudden and amazing disaster of Chickamauga and the downfall of three prominent chiefs well-loved in the Cumberland—Rosecrans, McCook and Crittenden. The Army of the Cumberland was every whit as brave, as loyal and devoted as that of the Tennessee. Moreover, it contained no discordant factors, as had the Tennessee, and yet with all its loyalty, its fine soldiership and discipline, its proved spirit and knightly chivalry, it stood humbled and defeated, while its rival stood exalted in the public eye. Luck, superior forces and better generalship had been dead against it, and the Army of the Cumberland was sore in spirit, sore at heart.

And just at this time, as more ill luck would have it, there spread a rumor through the ranks, and it was common talk about headquarters, that Grant had said, and Sherman had echoed, that the Army of the Cumberland had been whipped and cowed—that now it could not be induced to come out of its works and fight. (Sherman's Memoirs later confirmed the statement.) Is it strange that now, as Grant drew nigh to become its superior, there was little welcome for him in the army at last led by George H. Thomas? Is it strange that these two great and loyal soldiers should feel the chill of that same enshrouding cloud the wet and wintry evening of Grant's arrival at Chattanooga?

He came to Thomas's headquarters after dark of a long, toilsome, painful day of riding over mountain roads, reaching the Tennessee wet and bedraggled, only to meet with further mishap on the southern shore. The injured leg had caused him intense pain all day, and now, to make matters worse, "Old Jack," one of his most reliable mounts, slipped and fell heavily, and that luckless leg was again pinned and crushed.

It was in this plight that he was assisted to limp heavily into the presence of Thomas, and presently the two were left together. Just what passed between them neither is known to have revealed. Wilson, hurrying in a few moments later, described the scene as follows:

"I found Grant at one side of the fireplace, steaming from the heat over a small puddle which had run from his sodden clothing. Thomas was on the other side, neither saying a word, but both looking glum and ill at ease."

Then, learning from Rawlins that nothing had been offered for their comfort, and knowing that Grant "would not condescend to ask," Wilson tells of his own appeal to Thomas, who the moment he realized that Grant was weary, hungry and in pain, as well as dripping wet, gave instant orders for warm, dry clothing, and a hot supper. Willard, long confidential aide to

Thomas, and in earlier days in Milwaukee the writer's teacher and friend, and Kellogg, the junior aide, long years later the writer's regimental comrade and correspondent, were among his authorities concerning these and other episodes at the time.

Whatever of rancor had cropped out in this ill-omened meeting between these two great leaders was presently swept aside in the courtly Virginian's resumption of the duties as host. Formality, too, was speedily smothered. For the rest of that evening the generals and their staff officers mingled and chatted with all apparent ease and cordiality, but Grant lost no time next day in selecting a house of his own, and then it was noted that once more constraint and distance separated the two establishments. The staffs, taking their cue from their seniors, became formal and punctilious, and out along the lines and among the camp fires the talk was fast and furious among the soldiery as they scanned the jagged earthworks on the commanding ridges east and west, and discussed the newcomers under Hooker, from the Potomac, and the slow approach of Sherman with the Tennessee, and passed from fire to fire, with characteristic American candor, their impressions of the man on crutches back in town, and of these experts from east and west—from the army in Virginia and the army in Mississippi—who were come or were coming to show the Army of the Cumberland how to fight. Small wonder there was little compliment or cordiality. When Pope in the summer of '62 was imported from the Army of the West to high command over the generals of the Army of the Potomac, he affronted the entire force at the very outset by the bombastic lecture with which he announced " Headquarters in the Saddle " and that he came from an army in which they had been accustomed to see only the backs of the enemy, which was no more tactful than it was true. When Grant in the autumn of '63 was imported from the West to supreme command over the loved generals of the Army of the Cumberland, he stood credited with having said they could not fight and that he was fetching Sherman and the Tennessee to show them how. It was most inauspicious, and it had wonderful influence in what followed. Eight weeks had Bragg and his veterans in gray occupied the long barriers of Missionary Ridge to the east of beleaguered Chattanooga, when Sherman finally came, and, crossing the Tennessee above the town, was sent in at the northward end of the ridge to take the Confederate army in flank and roll it southward, while Thomas, with the Cumberland in extended lines of battle in the westward valley, should face the parallel furrows bristling with Southern cannon merely to threaten, but not to be sent in to the attack. The Cumberland, so it was understood, was to take an object lesson in fancy fighting from the Tennessee—to "learn how," as it were—and Grant, with his staff, rode forward to Orchard Knob, midway across the plain and almost under the guns, where Thomas, grave and silent, greeted his superior with precise salute, and where the twain sat in saddle the livelong day, listening to the crash of Sherman's flank attack and watching the faraway clouds of sulphur smoke which, according to program, should have come floating steadily southward, but which somehow did not, for Sherman had been stopped at Tunnel Hill as flatly as in front of the Southern left at Vicksburg. And then at last, tired with its long wait, and even of satirical comment on the extent and value of its lesson in battle tactics, the Cumberland got its orders to "demonstrate," by way of driving off some of the tremendous force opposed, presumably, to the Tennessee. Then rejoicefully, in magnificent array and order, the four divisions—Sheridan and Wood in the centre—had marched to their stations, and there they received the order to advance, drive the enemy from the lower entrenchments and threaten—merely threaten —the ridge: *that* was to be the prize of Sherman and the Tennessee. The whole nation heard the rest in less than a week thereafter—how, like a human tidal wave, the long blue ranks struck the foremost line, sending the occupants scurrying for the shelter of the second, how like some huge breaker they had burst over the parapets and then rushed onward. They should have stopped short at the foot of the heights, those long, jagged ranks in blue. But they had been "stormed at with shot and shell," and now grape and canister were hurtling from the guns above. They had lost heavily, were losing more, had "got the rebels on the run" and what was the sense in stopping? It seems as though Sheridan's men had said, "Come on, fellows," to Wood's, and that Baird's and Brannan's had taken the cue. Be that as it may, that long, light blue wave of the Cumberland swarmed and swept on up those jagged slopes to the very summit, and in ten minutes more the men were tumbling into and over the Confederate works —Bragg and his astonished generals barely escaping with their lives.

It was an astounding victory, executed by no means as planned, but every bit as effectively as hoped. "Who ordered those men up the heights?" one historian declares that, in marked disapprobation, Grant said to Thomas. "No one," was the prompt reply; "they're doing it of their own accord," and so it proved. It is also recorded by the same historian that Grant's instant response was, "It is all right if it succeeds; if it doesn't, some one will suffer," to which Thomas said nothing. His men were talking for him.

The overwhelming of Bragg's army at Missionary Ridge clinched for all time Grant's hold upon the people as their great and successful general. To them it was a matter of little concern whether the battle was won for him by the Cumberland or the Tennessee. It redoubled the popular acclaim for Grant, but it failed somehow to bridge the chasm of constraint still growing between him and the noblest of his subordinates. If anything, it seemed to lead on to even graver misunderstanding in the future, to impel Grant to the very brink of what would have been the greatest wrong he ever dealt in a life in which knowingly, intentionally, wilfully, he never wronged man or woman—the relief of Thomas on the eve of the greatest and most decisive victory of the war.

CHAPTER XXVII

GRANT AND SHERMAN

THAT soldiers' battle of Missionary Ridge proved the turning point in the fortunes of several generals prominent on both sides. It practically closed the career of Bragg, whose reputation went to pieces with his army. Henceforth Joseph E. Johnston was to be the hope of the South in Georgia as Lee had been in Virginia since Johnston's disabling wound.

On the Union side, two or three generals whose reputations went up like a rocket at Chickamauga came down like the traditional stick at Missionary Ridge, notably Gordon Granger, whom Dana had proclaimed the "Ney of the Army," the soldiers could not quite see why. Granger had certainly made a swift march of a few miles from his post on the extreme left, and pitched in handsomely with two small brigades to the aid of Thomas in that immortal stand. This was something in line with Desaix's march *au canon* at Marengo, and led to his being given command later of the gallant Fourth Corps. But at Missionary Ridge he proved as great a disappointment as at Chickamauga he had proved a surprise.

On the other hand, there was Sheridan, the stocky, black-eyed little commander of Thomas's centre division. Two months before, serving in McCook's Corps at Chickamauga, he had been caught in the human torrent that swept through the gap when Wood's division was withdrawn by mistake. Far up on the ridge he rallied his men, marched them through the nearest gap to the road behind it, and took them away from the field where some of their fellows were still fighting; then fortunately filed to the right through a northward gap, and late in the afternoon reappeared in rear of Thomas and ready to support him. McCook and Crittenden, who had also been whirled away, never again recovered their commands, but "Little Phil" kept his with him until that evening of November 25th, where, taking the bit in its teeth, the whole division ran away from its general officers, stormed the heights in its front, and Sheridan had only to put spurs to his horse and follow on. Two months earlier he led that division out of action, and it well-nigh wrecked him. This wonderful evening it led him into action and well-nigh made him. When, half an hour after the start, Grant himself appeared in saddle on the captured heights, Sheridan and his men were far down among the eastward foothills, hurling Bragg's fugitives back to the very stream over which two months earlier they had swept triumphant. It was a great day for Sheridan, and from that time on Grant had him ever in mind. Moreover, it gave to Sheridan a confidence in himself and his men which he lacked before—the confidence which Grant ever had and which made Grant indomitable.

Sherman's repute was neither aided nor harmed by Missionary Ridge. He had made a brilliant crossing and had followed it with a fairly bold attack, driving the Confederate lines a short distance until they brought up on Tunnel Hill *and* Pat Cleburne—as superb a fighter as the South could muster, and it mustered them by scores. Cleburne was still there "standing off" Sherman when those four divisions of the Cumberland swarmed up the slopes behind him and whirled away every vestige of support. Cleburne therefore had to let go in order to save what was left of his command. Then Sherman too could advance, but not until the following day. It was the Cumberland that went snapping at the heels of the retreating host, Thomas close following his victorious men, and never stopping to ask Grant if anybody in particular was now to suffer.

Thomas had much dignity and little sense of humor. He took the situation seriously, but there were men in that rejoiceful Army of the Cumberland who presently found no end of fun in it.

The shades of night came slowly down when Grant reined up far over to the east of the heights whereon Bragg's headquarters had been perched for weeks, and still he had not overtaken his victorious army commander—"The Rock of Chickamauga." This may explain why no congratulations passed between them. Grant sent aides-de-camp to his leading generals to let them know that he was now returned to headquarters at Chattanooga, there to receive them or their reports. The aide sent to Thomas came back saying he couldn't find him, and as that aide had been longer with Grant than any other and seemed to accomplish less, Grant contented himself at the moment with telling Wilson to take up the duty the other could not perform, and Wilson says he groped for nearly two hours up the banks of Chickamauga creek before he ran into Baird's division, bivouacked and blissful, carried out his mission and rode until near dawn, getting back to his chief, finding Grant awake and remorseful for having given him an all-night ride after a long day in saddle—something Wilson did not mind in the least. Thomas had sent staff officers with full report and still Grant could not sleep. A tireless man in saddle himself, and one who hailed in Wilson a fellow horseman, he nevertheless hated to impose unnecessary fatigue, labor or exposure upon his staff. One and all they bear testimony to this—Grant's courtesy and consideration for them, and for those who served with and under him. But, to the grim satisfaction of Rawlins, he had at last to rid himself of the aide who "couldn't find Thomas."

Right here at Chattanooga Grant was to fill the vacancy by the appointment of Horace Porter of the Ordnance Corps, Wilson's classmate, roommate and intimate—as fine a soldier as his chum and even more valuable as an aide. Gifted with infinite humor and wit, Porter could be as reticent and close-mouthed as Grant himself. The acquaintance, begun the night of Grant's bedraggled coming to Chattanooga, ripened speedily into faith and trust, and then to fond and fervent regard which strengthened with every day of their association. It was high time Grant had strengthened his personal following, for Rawlins, Wilson and Bowers, his most valuable and reliable officers, were sorely overworked. It was through Wilson that Grant selected the military secretary so long needed, for after Vicksburg his correspondence became voluminous. Then, as luck would have it, the man he pitched upon, "unsight, unseen," was shot through the foot at Port Hudson, had a long, slow, painful convalescence, and was unable to join until after Missionary Ridge. He was a most scholarly, highly-educated, little fellow, had gone with the expedition to Hilton Head in '61, and made himself so popular that the officers recommended him for a commission, and it was given him. But they could not make him a soldier. Adam Badeau proved a success as a secretary, and in many a way was of so much use to Grant that the relationship lasted even through the sorrowful days of that second overthrow at the hands of Fate. Meantime Badeau had for nearly twenty years been a faithful friend, follower and a somewhat fulsome biographer. Until misfortune came he could see no star in all the constellations of the heavens to compare with that to which he had "hitched his wagon." With the final dissolution, however, the hitching broke.

The wintry months following the victory of Chattanooga were full of import. The people now would have it that Grant, the man of the West, was the one man of the war and should be recognized and rewarded accordingly. The President was much their way of thinking, and in Mr. Elihu Washburne and in Governor Yates he had fervent backers. But in large numbers prominent political leaders still doubted, still feared. Notably was this the case in the Senate. A bill to create the office of lieutenant-general had been prepared, and yet hung fire. Grant, never quitting his post at the front, set himself busily to the task of relieving Knoxville to the northeast, and of warding off Johnston to the southeast. Then, with Christmas over and campaigning for the present at an end, he began planning future operations, and while he was about it, writing recommendations for promotion of certain of the staff officers and generals about him, and for the re-employment of certain generals who, it is safe to say, were not agitating themselves and the powers-that-were in Grant's behalf. It seemed to him that McClellan, Buell and a few others, now shelved, were men of marked ability in certain lines, and that they and the cause might be the better off for their employment. Personal considerations did not enter into the matter. It is possible that the re-employment of McClernand would have occurred to him, even though that fiery opponent had stirred every possible friend and strained every nerve to induce the President to reopen his case and to bring Grant before a board of investigation. But when, about the end of November, the North began to realize the magnitude of Grant's great victory at Chattanooga, McClernand finally realized the futility of his appeal, and thereafter little was heard of it. Another year and he decided to resign. It was one of the most sorrowful endings of what might have been one of the most successful careers had McClernand been content to serve and follow instead of being possessed with the craze to undermine, overthrow and lead. It was said that he denounced West Point and the West Point influence as the cause of his undoing, but it must have been only a limited few of the West Pointers to whom he objected, for he was later seeking an appointment at large for his son, who, entering in '66—oddly enough, side by side with the son of General Grant—was graduated in 1870, in which achievement he distanced the son of the President, who, according to West Point's inexorable law, had had to fall back and try again. The younger McClernand proved himself to the full to have all his gallant father's bravery, energy and ability, coupled with a disciplined mind and a soldierly sense of duty which bore him on to his generalship in the regular service, honored by every man who ever served with or knew him.

And in the plans and preparations for what was to come with the spring, the man ever closest to Grant's elbow was Rawlins, and the man ever brimming over with helpfulness and suggestion was Sherman. Wherever the duties of his command might take him, Sherman's heart was there with Grant, who had come to be in his mind the great aggressive general of the war—the man of all others destined to win the final victory. If ever there was a moment in which Sherman would have welcomed the downfall of Grant and the substitution of his own name for that of the deposed general-in-chief, his closest friend or Grant's most malignant enemy could never discover it. Sherman's loyalty was something whole-hearted, spontaneous, absolute. He had differed with Grant on matters of strategy at times; he had opposed the running of the Vicksburg batteries, and vehemently argued against the Jackson compaign, but, like the man he was, had frankly owned up, and said Grant was right. Now, by the winter of '63–64, Sherman had nothing but admiration for his chief, and his only dread for him was that of Washington and the influences which would there beset him. For politics and politicians, in spite of his family connections, and for everything controlled by political influences, Sherman ever had a wholesome horror. He could not welcome the prospect of Grant's getting the lieutenant-generalship if it meant that he must take station at the War Department. He dreaded any move which might take Grant from the midst of the men who knew and believed in him—those men of the West with whom they two, Grant and Sherman, together had hewed their way to fame. He had a westerner's idea that the Army of the Potomac—which had been so superbly loyal and subordinate and self-sacrificing, no matter who was set over it—would not back this plain westerner as had "the Tennessee" through thick and thin. His antipathy to the War Department and its methods grew as the war went on and rose to fever heat against Stanton in '65, to the end that publicly he refused his hand at the great review, and would have none of him thereafter. Even when he became general-in-chief, with his own Grant at the White House, Sherman found the War Department intolerable and moved headquarters of the army to St. Louis.

But ever, from Vicksburg onward, he remained to the very last the loyal and unswerving friend of Grant. He declared him the greatest "all round soldier and general" of the war. He spoke of him with generous enthusiasm time and again. Nothing is more characteristic of Sherman than the frank and at the same time "acute and just analysis" with which, in his own impulsive and inimitable way, he favored Wilson, who had come to command all the cavalry of the West. It was just before the memorable March to the Sea. They had been in confidential chat long into the night and at last, in speaking of Grant, whom each had come to regard as the best and strongest of the Union leaders, no matter what had been his errors or his weakness, Sherman suddenly burst forth:

"Wilson, I am a d——d sight smarter man than Grant; I know a great deal more about war, military history, strategy and grand tactics than he does; I know more about organization, supply and administration and about everything else than he does; but I'll tell you where he beats me and where he beats the world. He don't care a damn for what the enemy does out of his sight, but it scares me like hell," adding further: " He issues his orders and does his level best to carry them out without much reference to what is going on about him, and, so far, experience seems to have fully justified him."

" And those who knew both," says Wilson—and this was penned long years after the war—" will have settled down to the conclusion that Grant was a far safer and saner general than Sherman."

With his one weakness, his few faults, his many foes, Ulysses Grant was blessed by the devotion and loyalty of such stanch and fervent friends.

CHAPTER XXVIII

GRANT AND THE LIEUTENANT-GENERALSHIP

EARLY in the spring of '64 the Congress yielded to popular demand and, recreating the office of lieutenant-general, enabled the President to confer it upon Grant, who was personally summoned to assume entire control of the armies in the field, and with a sigh of relief Abraham Lincoln affixed his signature to the commission, and Halleck and Stanton with the best grace they could command awaited the triumphant coming of the Conqueror of the West.

"U. S. Grant and Son, Galena, Ills."

wrote a travel-worn, bearded, somewhat stoop-shouldered man of middle age, in the register at Willard's Hotel, one gusty morning in early March, and the clerk in charge, who was figuring on a fifth floor room at the back of the house at first sight of the new arrivals, glanced casually at the name, began with " Show Mr. Grant to——" when somebody precipitated himself upon the unobtrusive stranger, seizing and vehemently shaking both his hands and exclaiming: " Why, *General* Grant, we didn't expect you till——" whereupon the clerk gave a gasp and the by-standers a start. And then came an impromptu reception all too hearty and insistent for the modest and embarrassed recipient, who wanted a bath and breakfast. Some biographers say that Mrs. Grant and Colonel Rawlins accompanied him on his arrival at the capital. Others have it that they came later, by way of Philadelphia, where certain shopping had to be attended to. At all events it was but a short time before Mrs. Grant's arrival at Willard's.

Meanwhile, however, had occurred the memorable scene at the White House of the 9th of March, in which the President formally invested the first lieutenant-general since the days of Washington with the credentials of his new rank. In so doing the President made a brief and pithy speech, closing with the words, " With this high honor devolves upon you also a corresponding responsibility. As the country herein trusts you, so under God it will sustain you."

Knowing well by this time that Grant was no speech maker, the ever considerate President had sent him in advance a copy of the remarks which he proposed to make, and, still further to put the recipient at his ease, Mr. Lincoln decided to read in order that Grant might do likewise. And so it is recorded that the quiet-mannered officer from the West, still wearing the coat of a major-general, and for once at least buttoned to the chin, listened gravely to the words of praise, encouragement and confidence, then fished from a pocket a half sheet of paper and, in low but audible tones, read the following reply:

" Mr. President, I accept the commission with gratitude for the high honor conferred. With the aid of the noble armies that have fought on many a field for our common country, it will be my earnest endeavor not to disappoint your expectations. I feel the full weight of the responsibilities now devolving upon me, and I know that if they are met it will be due to those armies and above all to the favor of that Providence which leads both nations and men."

The President and Mrs. Lincoln, of course, invited the new lieutenant-general and his wife to dinner, but the former had already hurried down to Fortress Monroe and could not return in time. Many another social diversion was in waiting for him when he reappeared, for people of every class seemed eager to meet, see, and hear him, and a more elusive celebrity never crossed the threshold of Willard's, a more obstinate and intractable arrival never baffled a caller or balked a correspondent. Conferences with the President, with Halleck, Stanton, Wilson (then at the head of the Cavalry Bureau), and the chiefs of the departments of supply took up every moment of his time. He *could* not, he said, accept social invitations. He *would* not, said Rawlins, accord interviews, or what at that time passed for such, for the art was in its infancy. He was bent on getting out of Washington and away to the front at the earliest possible moment, and, leaving scores of invitations unaccepted, the new general-in-chief took over the duties hitherto devolving upon Halleck, leaving to that scientific soldier the improvised office of chief-of-staff U. S. Army, while Rawlins, the indispensable, took the field as chief-of-staff to the lieutenant-general commanding. Just as unobtrusively as he had come, Grant vanished from Washington, and presently pitched his tent with those of the silently waiting Army of the Potomac—the most momentous coming, probably, in all its history.

For it was a noble command. Granted to the Cumberland and the Tennessee everything ever claimed for either by their most ardent friends, neither at Donelson nor Murfreesboro, at Shiloh nor Corinth, at Vicksburg, Champion's Hill nor Chattanooga had they encountered such generals and such troops as from the outset were pitted against the Army of the Potomac. The flower of the Confederate forces were these men of Lee, Longstreet and Stonewall Jackson. Time and again, valiant, subordinate and superbly self-sacrificing, had the men of the Potomac answered every demand, no matter how ill-advised, and loyally had their regimental officers and the rank and file supported every general appointed over them—no matter how ill-fitted for command. Whatsoever may be said of their immediate leaders, no man can ever justly asperse the loyalty, the devotion, the discipline and valor of the

Army of the Potomac. And now, silent and subordinate as ever, it stood to arms to droop its colors to the silent man from the West, and take its orders henceforth from him who came to them a stranger. At Gettysburg, so said Lincoln, their myriad dead had given the " full measure of devotion," but there were days to come in which in fuller measure still, duty to this stern, implacable soldier should demand of them their utmost endeavor—their uttermost devotion, for, far beyond the breaking strain of the disciplined soldiery of the old world, it was their destiny to be tried by Grant, and it is their deathless glory that to the uttermost they answered him, and died by thousands that in the supreme grapple twixt North and South the Union at last should triumph and the nation live.

Over that fearful progress from the Rapidan to the James, with its days of fierce hand-to-hand fighting in the Wilderness, of wild charge and countercharge at Spottsylvania, of human sacrifice and fruitless, senseless assault at Cold Harbor, it is not the purpose of this chronicle to linger. Every general yet pitted against Lee in Virginia had recoiled before him, and this Grant would not do. If in headlong assault he could not drive him from his intrenched lines, he slipped around the eastward flank and so bore ever onward. If beaten back at any point along that deadly front, he kept the columns ever winding southward, sending back the inspiring words, " We will fight it out on this line if it takes all summer." Never before had Northern general taken such punishment and still pushed on. " Butcher " they cried at the North, as the fearful list of casualties grew and multiplied. Cold-blooded and brutal they pictured and denounced him, sitting placidly and smoking and whittling while, in the execution of his implacable will, his men were dying by hundreds— and yet did not Rawlins and Bowers tell us how, when the tidings came that Gordon's furious onset had

smashed in Sedgwick's right, with heavy loss in killed
and captured, though with outward calm the commanding general gave every needful order to restore the faltering centre, no sooner were the adjutants sent scurrying
away than, turning from the silent few at his camp fire,
Grant hastily entered his tent, threw himself face down-
ward on his cot, and for the first time in his known life
gave way to emotion uncontrollable. Even Rawlins stood
awe-stricken. Sympathetic and tender-hearted as he
knew his chief to be, never had he dreamed that Grant
could so feel and suffer. The death of "Aleck" Hays,
shot dead the night before, heading his division, had
deeply moved the General, and now came this crushing
blow that wrecked his right wing, yet must not swerve
him from his purpose. Whatever happened, though the
Army of the Potomac died in its tracks and he with it, it
must never again turn back, and it never did. Though
thousands of its chosen strewed the pathway from Germanna Ford to the James, there was still left to Grant
enough to pen the army of Lee within the lines of Petersburg and Richmond. Once there he could hold him for
the final overthrow.

Daringly, brilliantly, bravely as it had fought from
the start, the Southern army outdid itself in that marvellous defense. The leaders well knew that this was to be
the supreme test, that at last there had come to head
the Northern host a man who never yet had lost a
battle, and who now took the field with an army in the
pink of condition, far outnumbering theirs. Lee could
muster but sixty-five thousand all told; the South had
sent its last levies into action, "robbing the very cradle
and the grave" for men to fill its depleted ranks. The
North, though divided in sentiment and cursed with
"copperheads," had far from exhausted either its men
or its means. Grant had still abundant resources on
which to draw. Lee had little or nothing. And yet Lee
and his officers rode into that campaign like Paladins of

old, for a wave of religious fervor had swept over the Southern camps during the winter agone, and, as though consecrated to their task, shriving themselves as did the Normans the night before Hastings, fared forth into battle with faith in their hearts and prayer on their set lips. Weaker in numbers they were, but never were they stronger, and so the Union army found before ever they reached the bloody angle of Spottsylvania, and the men of the Potomac could only strive on, fight on, doggedly, loyally, but with hardly a sign of cheer, enthusiasm and never of exultation.

It had been planned and hoped that the Army of the James, under Benjamin F. Butler, should so vehemently threaten Richmond from the east as to compel Lee to look to his rear, and leave fewer men to oppose the Army of the Potomac; but Butler compelled not at all. It had been planned that our cavalry, now under Sheridan, should do great things in aid of the slow-moving infantry, but the cavalry corps had not come to know their new leader, or he them, or even himself. It is no disparagement to the Union cavalry that even after its sturdy work under Gregg and Buford at Gettysburg, it was still, in the spring of '64, innocent of its higher purposes and possibilities. Even Grant sent and Sheridan led it astray on an almost fruitless raid. They dealt death at Yellow Tavern to the plumed leader, Stuart, of the Southern Horse. They might even have ridden into Richmond, but they rode back. Not yet did Sheridan see his powers, even though his great leader had predicted that in the little Fourth infantryman of the 50's, the snappy division commander of the Cumberland, there should stand revealed the great cavalry leader of the close of the war.

Oddly enough it was Halleck who suggested his name.

Grant had been impressed with the fact that, even after Stuart's overthrow by Gregg at Gettysburg and his senseless self-separation from Lee before it, the glamour of his previous achievements had given the Southern cavalry *prestige* over the sturdy horsemen by this time developed in the North. What was needed was a man to command and lead our cavalry. " How would Sheridan do? " asked Halleck, when the matter was brought up in conference at the War Department. " The very man," said Grant. And so in addition to Grant, imported from the West to " push things " in Virginia, and to " Baldy " Smith (whom the Army of the Potomac for old times' sake might have welcomed, as the Army of the James, its chief at least, did not), and to Wilson, speedily announced as division commander, there also came to them, raised from an infantry division to command a cavalry corps, that black-eyed, swarthy, short-legged son of Ohio from the Army of the Cumberland whom everybody knew as " Phil " Sheridan. The great mass of the Army of the Potomac, the infantry, accepted in silence and subordination the new dispensation. They still retained the generals under whom they had fought, and to many of whom they were attached. Meade, as commander of the army, Hancock, Warren and Sedgwick, heading the three corps, " Old Burn " commanding an outside organization independent of Meade, but acting under Grant—these were all Army of the Potomac men.

But it was different in the cavalry. It is true that their former commanders, Stoneman and Pleasonton, had earlier left them, that glorious John Buford had sickened and died, that fiery Kilpatrick had been shifted to other fields. They still had with them, modest, silent, but a superb soldier, David McM. Gregg. They had their younger brigadiers, Merritt, Custer and Davies. They took it much amiss that over the heads of these should be placed the infantry division leader, Sheridan, and over the heads of Merritt, Custer and others, as division commanders, should be set their junior on the

list of brigadiers, who, though the right-hand man of
Grant in the West, was in their eyes the "Engineer"
Wilson. Finally another importation from the infantry,
if not from the West, was assigned to them, General
Torbert, he being given one of their three divisions, and
so the cup of the cavalry was filled with bitterness. And
yet, almost from the start, they began to like Sheridan,
and when, in less than a fortnight of the start, Meade
and Sheridan clashed in emphatic and spectacular debate, and even the sulphurous battle fumes about them
lost by contrast something of their satanic character, the
cavalry began to swear with, instead of at, Sheridan.
After Winchester and Cedar Creek they swore by him.

Grant's reorganization of the cavalry corps of the
Army of the Potomac was later justified in the results
obtained; but that, too, was something for which he had
to wait in patience. He had troubles enough on his
hands as the summer of '64 came on. The plans were
admirable. Sherman with his now enthusiastic and
united army was to advance on Atlanta from the Tennessee, and keep Johnston busy in the West. In Virginia Lee's sixty-five thousand in the field were to be
assailed by Meade and Burnside with no less than ninety
thousand men, all under the eye of Grant; while Butler,
far down the James, was to threaten Richmond with
twenty thousand from the east. Ord and Crook, each
with a formidable column, received orders to descend
upon the upper James from the northwest, and it was
confidently hoped that long ere the summer solstice,
Richmond and gold would fall. But when the autumn
came Richmond was as stanch as ever, gold had gone
soaring to 290, and Grant had met with setbacks innumerable, and yet there he was indomitably hanging on,
his lines investing Petersburg, his supplies coming easily
by water to City Point.

Then by way of diversion Lee sent Early into Maryland and scared Washington out of its seven senses.

Then Grant sent Sheridan to the Shenandoah to put an end to all that sort of thing in future, and Sheridan's successes so broadened and inspired him and all who served with him—the cavalry and the Sixth Corps especially—that when in the early spring these travel-stained, but now confident and co-operating troopers trotted jauntily back to the Army of the Potomac, dull and dispirited after its ineffectual assaults and its long months in the trenches, and the jingling sabres and fluttering guidons came winding along the entire rear of the huddling groups in winter quarters, like some half-asleep, hibernating bruin the army seemed suddenly to wake and give tongue, and volleys of chaff and soldier satire went echoing through the sombre woods. It was the reveille of final victory.

CHAPTER XXIX

THE LULL BEFORE THE STORM

But while the Army of the Potomac had received without enthusiasm the news of the elevation to supreme command of this man from the West, there were a certain few that rejoiced with exceeding joy—West Pointers, men like Sherman, McPherson, Sheridan, Ingalls, Augur, Macfeely, Wilson, Comstock and Horace Porter—men of brains and soldiership who either had known and loved him in the old days, or had learned to know and love him in the new. The men of the Potomac had not heard the sweetest things of him in letters from their comrades of Hooker's Corps sent to aid him on the Tennessee. Hooker himself, chagrined at the failure of his attempt to take the upper hand, had been further aggrieved at the half whimsical but altogether true endorsement placed by Grant upon Hooker's characteristic report of his share in the battles about Chattanooga, in the course of which he claimed to have captured more artillery than, as Grant pointed out, was taken by the entire army.

Nor had there been effusive welcome for the quiet-mannered, plain-spoken Westerner when Meade, Hancock, Warren and Sedgwick first called to pay their respects. They were courteous, subordinate, thoroughly soldierly. Moreover they had heard that " in spite and not because of " the rumors as to Grant's so-called habits, the gifted journalist and keen observer, sent by a far from friendly war secretary to closely watch everything that occurred at Grant's headquarters and report accordingly, had come, had seen and had been conquered. Mr. Charles A. Dana, ten years Grant's senior, had become the stanch supporter of Grant, and declared

From the collection of F. H. Meserve

GENERAL W. T. SHERMAN

him in his opinion the strongest and surest of our generals in the field, even though of Sherman he had enthusiastically penned to Stanton, " What a splendid soldier he is!" They came to greet the new chief loyally, as " the spirit of old West Point " demanded, yet they would have been less than men had they refrained from curious study of the newcomer and commander, and among their individual cronies, from a certain confidential comment. Quiet, unassuming, courteous but not effusive, Grant had in turn welcomed each caller, chatting preferably over Mexican war days with Meade and Sedgwick, of St Louis and its hospitable homesteads with Hancock, who, like Grant, had many a sweet association with Jefferson Barracks. He found at first no common ground with Warren—who had saved the second day at Gettysburg to Meade and the army, and had been rewarded by the command of the famous old Fifth Corps, who had dared to refrain from expected attack on an impossible position at Mine Run, and was as yet an untried corps leader in actual battle. The test was to come all too soon.

But it was observed by those who had been with him in the West that Grant was not the hail-fellow-well-met of the Army of the Tennessee. There it had been: " Hello, Sherman!" " How are you, McPherson?" or the playful old army nickname by which he hailed Macfeely, or the cadet " handle" to his classmate Quinby. So far as Sherman, at least, was concerned, too, the answering hail was ever " Hello, Grant "— utterly democratic and unmilitary, but characteristic of both.

But now he had come to new and strange and far more precise surroundings. Now, from Meade down, except in personal chat with some old chum, the new commander addressed each officer by his formal title, save those of his staff and his deserved favorites, Sheridan and James H. Wilson. It was noted, too, that

Rawlins, the dominant man of the staff in the West—the man who stormed at anything and anybody, his chief not excepted, when he believed matters were going amiss— the man who had not scrupled to smash even Grant's champagne at Vicksburg, and who had never shrunk from urging his chief or dictating at times to division or even corps commanders—was now become somewhat silent and self repressive. Observant as ever, Rawlins deferred more to the commanding general, dictated less to the staff, and domineered not at all. It is well known that with three or four exceptions the " military family " about the chief in Mississippi needed just such a head as Rawlins, but now the keen Illinois soldier-lawyer found himself surrounded by men of far finer mold and character—regulars and West Pointers, as a rule, and both among them and in his dealings with the generals of the Potomac, Rawlins seemed no longer what he assuredly was in the West—lord paramount at headquarters. He much missed Wilson, even though he found in Horace Porter a stanch, but less aggressive, supporter. He was not in good health. He had remarried, too, and in conscientiously striving to conquer his one evil propensity had correspondingly robbed himself and the nation of that forcefulness of expression which had exerted such marked influence for good in the battlings of various kinds in the armies of the West.

There was, all things considered, something of constraint about the new dispensation of the Army of the Potomac, even though there was none of the state and style maintained in the long days of McClellan, the brief incumbency of Burnside, or the vainglorious reign of " Fighting Joe." With Meade came dignity and courtesy commingled—except under fire. The soul of civility and consideration ordinarily, Meade was absolutely unapproachable in battle. He seemed inspired with rage with every one about him. In this he was the antithesis of Warren, who was placid, suave and sweet mannered in the heat of action—and nowhere else. Until Warren got fairly into a fight he was captious, carping, critical, faultfinding, almost sneering —a man who " got on the nerves " of many a staff officer who came to him with an order, and it was this unhappy trait that led to the otherwise unjust undoing of one of the best and bravest of the corps commanders of the Army of the Potomac.

Even in his personal appearance and equipment the new commanding general had brought about a change, or some one had done it for him. Neat always as a new pin, Grant nevertheless wore his uniform loosely, and in the West had appeared in as few of the " frills " of his rank as could be dispensed with. Now, as lieutenant-general commanding all the forces in the field, he donned the new frock coat, fairly bristling with buttons, ordered the absurd regulation cape overcoat then pre-scribed for officers of all grades, bought the highest and most portentous of the black felt hats with gold cord and acorn tips, then affected by many of our generals, ordered the costly horse furniture, including the blue and gold *schabracque,* and the brass mounted bridle pre-scribed by the regulations (a something at which his " horse sense " revolted), and the first time he appeared in saddle on the march that beautiful May morning, with the Army of the Potomac trudging cheerily along to Germanna Ford, Grant sat in saddle watching them go striding by, his new coat buttoned throughout, his waist girded with brand new silken sash of buff net, and over it the gold-striped belt of Russia leather—all as trim and precise as any of the Potomac's own. Out West, where he hailed from, Herron was about the only "dandy " general, though McPherson, even in the final campaign in front of Atlanta, was conspicuous for the accuracy of his dress and equipments. Grant's old friends of Donelson and Shiloh would have looked in mild wonderment now, and the soldiers of the Army of the Potomac, as they trudged by, glanced quickly up from underneath the drooping visor of their forage caps, trying to take his measure as he sat composedly smoking.

Before they crossed that Virginia Rubicon, the Rapidan, it had been settled that the new general at least knew how to ride. Ten days later it was said of him that he seemed to dread no obstacle as too much for his men. Later still, down near the North Anna as Horace Porter tells it, the soldiers had satisfied themselves that he was as imperturbable under fire as in his daily walks in life. Sitting placid, unmoved and cross-legged at the foot of a tree, writing despatches to Washington, with the fragments of bursting shells hurtling about him, Grant attracted the attention of the wounded of a Wisconsin regiment being aided to the rear. They were doing no cheering just then for anybody, but in his own inimitable way the American volunteer gave audible vent to his views in the pithy vernacular of the camp: "Ulysses doesn't scare worth a damn."

Neither did they cheer him as, after that frightful progress to the James, they swung out across the long pontoons toward the southern shore. Cold Harbor had been the final test both for them and for him. Never again would Grant order frontal assault pushed home upon Lee's men in force and fortified or intrenched position. No good ever came of it, and after the experience of Spottsylvania—where, led by a peerless soldier, Emory Upton, the assaulting column pierced the centre only to find itself in a network of intrenchments—Grant's orders to attack Cold Harbor should never have been given. Heaven knows they cost us heavily and filled his heart with sorrow unutterable. And still he pushed on—on, ever relentlessly on, until brought to bay in front of the lines at Petersburg, which Butler, "Baldy" Smith, and their men had somehow failed to bag for him as had been hoped and planned.

THE LULL BEFORE THE STORM

It is said by certain Southern historians that Grant had been drinking during the campaign of the James. This gives an exaggerated idea of the facts. There were a few occasions on which, as Porter tells us, late at night about the camp fire, his officers brewed a toddy and the General would take a sip. There was one occasion after long and heavy strain, when in presence of Butler and " Baldy " Smith he took two drinks of whiskey in the course of an hour, and as he declared, in his utter frankness, that he had had one before, the effect was to be expected. Two drinks were quite enough to flush his face and thicken his speech, even though his vision and judgment might remain unimpaired. This incident was bruited to his detriment within that hot summer month of June, but the War Department could no longer interfere with Grant— and the President would not.

That summer of '64, however, had strained almost to the breaking point the faith the nation had learned to place in Grant, and had brought most grievous anxiety to the administration. As the autumn wore on, with no new gains and not a few reverses for the Army of the Potomac (notably the affairs on the Weldon railway), and notwithstanding the success of Sherman in the West and the triumph of Sheridan in the Shenandoah, "the war is a failure" was the cry of the opponents of the Union party all over the North, and even Abraham Lincoln at a time doubted the probability of his re-election. The nation was stancher and stronger than appeared in the public prints. November saw the cause of the Union vindicated at the polls. Then came the meteoric launch of Sherman's columns from Atlanta to the Sea, the utter collapse of Hood's army when Thomas struck it south of Nashville; and, in the hope of better things with the coming of spring, the administration and the people strove to possess their souls in peace until the Virginia roads were once again passable, and the armies about Richmond could hope to move. Meantime, little though they knew it, the patience and the fortitude of Grant himself had been tried to the uttermost, and he had been brought to the brink of the one wrong of his career—thus far, at least. Slow to wrath, patient and just, it is recorded of him that only twice during the entire war did he lose his temper and inflict personal rebuke or punishment, once to a coward in the West, once to a brute of a teamster who was beating over the head a helpless horse. On this latter occasion Grant flung himself from saddle at the sudden sight, and before any of his staff knew what was coming, had seized the hulking fellow by the throat and shaken him furiously. All manner of things Grant could see, smile at and take no offense; as when a Western colonel, ignorant of the General's immediate presence, damned young Fred for butting into him at blundering gallop; as when the young newspaper man, finding Grant and certain of his staff at breakfast, seated himself uninvited at the table with the calm assurance of his years and the remark, " I believe I'll take a snack myself, if there's no objection." But, Grant could never tolerate a bully; he hated a liar and a coward, and the one thing that seemed to make him impatient was incapacity to act at once when orders required—and this trait led to the famous, but mercifully arrested, order for the relief of George H. Thomas on the eve of the battle of Nashville.

When Sherman started on his renowned march to the sea, his army was thoroughly " weeded," as it were, and everything not in the very best of condition was left behind. Wilson, sent by Grant to reorganize and command the cavalry of the West, had been ordered by Sherman to fit out one division, Kilpatrick's, to accompany the march. In thoroughly equipping this command, therefore, Wilson practically stripped his own. The depleted and dismounted regiments were sent back to Nashville to refit, to be recruited, if possible, and rehorsed as soon as possible. The Fourth and Twenty-Third Corps were left to defend Tennessee in case Hood should decide on a blow at the North, rather than a pursuit of Sherman. George H. Thomas had been chosen to head the Union forces, consisting of two small corps, a number of broken-up commands, and a lot of broken-down men. A better defensive fighter had not been developed in the entire war, but he had to improvise much of his defensive army.

Later in November, long before Wilson had succeeded, even by strenuous efforts, in getting remounts for his cavalry, the Southern force came sweeping northward, driving before it the two corps led by Stanley and Schofield, inferior in numbers and lacking cavalry support. Hood's generals included such distinguished division chiefs as " Pat " Cleburne, Cheatham, Stewart and Stephen D. Lee, and his horsemen were led by N. B. Forrest, than whom there was no more aggressive trooper, north or south. Back from the line of the Duck River the Southern general drove the Union corps, many of Schofield's narrowly escaping capture as they slipped past Hood's encircling arms at Spring Hill. At the Harpeth Schofield and Stanley halted and faced about. Strong entrenchments covered the approaches to the little town of Franklin. Here that dull November afternoon was fought a battle furious in its character and fearful in its casualties. Time and again Hood's veterans charged the Union lines, only to be mowed down by hundreds, to suffer almost irreparable loss in generals, field officers, and in men. No less than six of Hood's division or brigade leaders fell dead along that blazing front—gallant Cleburne among them—and so tremendous was the punishment administered that when finally Schofield and Stanley resumed their northward march to join Thomas at Nashville, they were practically unpursued, save by Forrest's vigilant troopers, and even these were held at respectful distance. Franklin took the heart out of Hood's army for the time being: Nashville, which speedily followed, utterly destroyed it.

Yet when Hood's colors appeared along the line of the Brentwood Hills, some five miles to the south of Nashville, and the now cautious general proceeded to the investment of the state capital, the garrison was still in no condition for aggressive fight. Men enough to defend the fortifications had Thomas, and that was all. Moreover, for the moment, it was quite enough. The bloody and disastrous assaults at Franklin had taught Hood never again to attack the Union lines. He sat him down in sight of the capital and waited, while Thomas was bending every effort to gather about him the widely dispersed forces of his military domain, and while Wilson, with all the vim and energy of his nature, was calling in the cavalrymen of the neighboring states and getting them, somehow, anyhow, into saddle. Horses had to be had at any cost. Far and near his foragers impressed the private stock of friend or foe. The vice-president elect, still a citizen of Tennessee, and one of the " political " brigadiers of the volunteer army, found himself bereft of his own carriage team. But Wilson knew the supreme importance of the occasion: Cavalry in sufficient numbers must be improvised against these experts of Forrest. It was the first of December when the victors of Franklin fell back into the lines of Nashville. It was December 2nd when Forrest's guidons fluttered into view along the southward heights. By December 3rd Hood's whole army was lined up against the works of Nashville, the great supply depot and strategic centre of the southwest, and by December 5th the Northern press, never too wise, was clamoring for a " knock out." Gold was still soaring. Sherman was swallowed up somewhere in Georgia. Grant's army was stopped in front of

Petersburg. The people were impatient, unreasoning, unreasonable; the administration was worried and harassed; the President looked haggard; the Secretary of War, never saintly in temperament, had worked himself into a frenzy of nervous irritability. Even Grant, who was just returning from a triumphant visit to New York—whither family matters had called him, and where all Gotham thronged to do him honor and vainly besought him for a speech—began to worry under the rain of question, suggestion and criticism. " Thomas must attack and destroy Hood at once," was the burden of the cry, " or Hood will be crossing the Cumberland and sweeping on the Ohio."

By December 6th Thomas had over fifty thousand infantry and artillery, but his cavalry was still far inferior in number to Forrest's, and Thomas and Wilson knew the importance of cavalry in the attack of Southern troops in position, against whom a frontal assault, unsupported by attack in flank, was a wellnigh hopeless proposition. Wilson had assured Thomas that by December 7th or 8th he would have remounted almost every horseman, and could probably put ten thousand riders into the field. His men were in the "remount" camps on the north bank, over against Nashville. His five thousand effectives were getting rested and reshod after the strenuous work against Forrest. Hood was showing no disposition to attack, or even to reach round the flanks and reconnoitre the Cumberland. There could be no reinforcements of consequence coming to him. Everything else in the extreme south had been hurried off to oppose Sherman, yet by December 6th the War Department and the press of the North were in a mad rage of impatience with Thomas. Gone and forgotten were the plaudits that followed Mill Springs, Chickamauga, Missionary Ridge; gone and forgotten were the tributes, public and private, to his sound judgment and superb soldiership.

Even Grant, usually stolid, having begun to urge and prod, was now demanding. At a distance of something like a thousand miles from the field, Grant, Halleck and Stanton were sure they better saw and understood the entire situation than did Thomas on the spot—Thomas who had got Hood precisely where he wanted him, far from possible support, far from his impoverished base, and who fully meant, if given a few days' time and ten thousand cavalry, to fall upon that venturesome leader and wreck him utterly.

But meantime the fates had conspired with adverse influences in Washington and at Grant's headquarters toward the undoing of Thomas himself—the man of men in the Army of the West—"the noblest Roman of them all."

Early as December 2nd Stanton had wired Grant:

> "The President feels solicitous about the disposition of General Thomas to lay (*sic*) in fortifications for an indefinite period until Wilson gets equipments. This looks like the McClellan and Rosecrans strategy of do-nothing and let the rebels raid the country."

And Grant had wired Thomas before Hood had been there more than half a day:

> "If Hood is permitted to remain quietly about Nashville you will lose all the road back to Chattanooga. . . . Should he attack you it is all well, but if he does not, you should attack him before he fortifies."

And later the same day, December 2nd:

> "With your citizen employés armed you can move out of Nashville and force the enemy to retire or fight upon ground of your own choosing. . . . You will now suffer incalculable injury upon your railroad if Hood is not speedily disposed of. Put forth, therefore, every possible exertion to attain this end."

To this and to similar urgings from Halleck, Thomas replied, giving the situation in full, saying that he had

now sufficient infantry, but setting forth that in order
to dispose of Hood effectively he must have cavalry,
and that he would have enough in two or three days.

On December 3rd Thomas had again assured Halleck by wire that Hood was quiescent, that there would
be ten thousand cavalry in saddle in less than a week,
and then he could and would take care of Hood. But
it seems that assurance was insufficient. Halleck insisted, December 5th, that no less than twenty-two
thousand horses had been issued to the cavalry since
September 20th, and at 8 P.M. on the 5th Grant again
urged Thomas to action, and again Thomas, patiently
but cogently, said: " I do not think it prudent to attack
Hood with less than six thousand cavalry to cover my
flanks." Then later on, December 6th, as though
Washington and City Point could no longer brook the
delay, Grant wired at 4 P.M.: " Attack Hood at once
and wait no longer for a remount of your cavalry."

To this there could be only one reply—prompt acceptance of the order. Back came Thomas's despatch:
" I will make the necessary disposition and attack Hood
at once." It came late at night on the 6th, and all day
of the 7th Thomas and his aides were busily occupied
with the details of the attack in force. Frontal attack
on Hood's intrenched lines, as has been said, was not
to be thought of, and Grant, who had tried such attack
with disastrous result at Spottsylvania and Cold Harbor,
might have known it. Thomas's plan from the first
had been to send Wilson with at least six thousand
troopers out to the southwest to circle Hood's left
flank and rear, to push the Twenty-third Corps far out
on the heels of Wilson, to attack from the west, and
then when the Southern flank had been crumbled, to
turn the partial attack of his centre and left into an
assault in force.

Wilson and his men had still to be moved over
from the north bank. It all took time, and Stanton

waxed well-nigh frantic. "Thomas seems unwilling to attack because it is hazardous, as if all war was anything but hazardous. If he wait for Wilson to get ready Gabriel will be blowing his last horn," was Stanton's wire to Grant, on the morning of December 7th, and such his reference to two of the very best officers that ever fought.

And then said Grant over the wires to Washington: "You probably saw my orders to Thomas to attack. If he does not do it promptly I would recommend superseding him by Schofield, leaving Thomas subordinate."

On the evening of the 8th there came a despatch to Washington, not from Thomas or one in authority, but from a captain in the quartermaster's department, to the effect that the enemy had a large force of artillery along the south bank of the Cumberland below Nashville, also that the "rebel general Lyon holds the same bank, but does not fight gunboats." And though Thomas had gunboats and cavalry patrolling the Cumberland, closely watching for any indication of an intent to cross, and finding none, the administration and Grant, too, became possessed with the conviction that Hood was planning to send Forrest across the Cumberland, and to follow in his tracks, whereas Hood was doing the very opposite. On December 6th he had sent Forrest with most of his cavalry, backed by a strong division of infantry, to Murfreesboro, four days' march away. Yet on the 8th Grant would have it that Hood was bent on crossing the Cumberland, and wiring Thomas again: "By all means avoid the contingency of a foot race to see which, you or Hood, can beat to the Ohio." Then as Thomas on the spot could not be made to see that Hood was trying to cross, there was sent to Washington, at noon on the 9th of December, Grant's despatch: "*No attack yet made by Thomas.*

*Please telegraph orders relieving him at once and plac-
ing Schofield in command."*

Had that order been carried out, and Thomas deposed at the moment when his plans were complete and
his forces prepared for action, a wrong irreparable
would have been done, yet such was the attitude of the
administration, of the press, and of the general public
at the moment, that it probably would have been applauded. Even Halleck, who believed in Thomas and
who had exalted him above Grant at Corinth, had that
day wired him of Grant's extreme dissatisfaction. " If
you wait till General Wilson mounts all his cavalry,
you will wait till doomsday," he said, and Thomas, loyal
and subordinate to the last, sent his soldierly and
tempered reply: " I regret that General Grant should
feel dissatisfaction at my delay in attacking the enemy. I
feel conscious that I have done everything in my power
to prepare, and that the troops could not have been gotten ready before this, and if he should order me relieved I will submit without a murmur. A terrible
storm of freezing rain has come on since daylight which
will render an attack impossible until it breaks."

On the same day, December 9th, Thomas had also
telegraphed Grant direct: " I had nearly completed my
preparations to attack to-morrow morning, but a terrible storm of freezing rain has come on to-day which
will make it impossible for us to fight to any advantage.
. . . Major-General Halleck informs me you are
very much dissatisfied with my delay in attacking. I
can only say I have done all in my power to prepare,
and if you should deem it necessary to relieve me I shall
submit without a murmur."

That freezing storm lasted three days and nights,
sheeting the fields and hillsides in a glare of ice on which
horses slipped and fell, and men could not keep their
footing. It swept the valley of the Cumberland, an icy
blast, a pitiless, drenching, slanting deluge that stung as

it struck and froze as it fell and sent men and beasts cowering to cover. It would have been impossible to march a squadron of cavalry in face of it, and the men afoot could hardly crawl. When first informed of the new reason for delay, Grant wired suspending the order for Thomas's relief "until it is seen whether he will do anything," yet with what seems to have been a growing conviction that Thomas would not strike no matter what the weather, for, after waiting all day long on the 10th, hearing nothing but further details of the storm, and all the morning of the 11th, Grant could stand it no longer. At 4 p.m. he wired direct: "Let there be no further delay. I am in hopes of receiving word from you to-day announcing that you have moved. Delay no longer for weather or reinforcements." To which at 10.30 p.m. Thomas replied: "I will obey as promptly as possible. . . . The whole country is covered with a perfect sheet of ice and sleet. . . . I would have done so (attacked) yesterday had it not been for the storm."

It was the last of Thomas's despatches to his now utterly un-Grantlike chief. The storm was still raging in Tennessee, but all was quiet on the Potomac, save in the neighborhood of Stanton. The 12th of December passed without change at Nashville, and the 13th found Grant at City Point, unable longer to control his impatience or himself. It must be owned that he had been subjected to severe strain. Now, issuing orders for General John A. Logan to go at once to Nashville, and then, before Logan could have gone half way, Grant decided himself to follow; steamed around to the Potomac and up to Washington, where, on the evening of the 15th, he had a conference with the President, Stanton and Halleck, insisting now on the immediate relief of Thomas, then hastened to his room at Willard's to prepare for the journey by special train, and was stopped at or about 11 o'clock by the telegraphic tidings that Thomas at last had struck, that Hood's left wing was crushed. Turning to a trusted friend, Grant removed for a moment the inevitable cigar from his lips, quietly remarked, " I guess we'll not go after all," then sat him down, and, true to his truthful self, wired Thomas that he was on his way to Nashville, but now in view of Thomas's splendid success would go no further. To this he added his hearty congratulations.

And yet Thomas's splendid success was at that time only a moiety of the still more splendid success of the 16th. With Wilson and his cavalry whirling ever upon Hood's left and rear, capturing battery after battery, taking in reverse one position after another, doing everywhere the lion's share of the work and proving beyond peradventure Thomas's claim, that without cavalry decisive victory, if not successful attack, had been impossible, the great defensive fighter of the West had become the irresistibly aggressive leader who, by nightfall of the second day, had captured half the guns of the Southern host, and sent the beaten battalions of Hood's hard fighting army fleeing for their lives back to the sorrowing land from which they came, Wilson and his exultant troopers hacking furiously at their heels, that young whirlwind of a leader himself heading charge after charge, and holding up far to the south of the abandoned field only long enough to receive from Thomas in person most fervent thanks and congratulation, and to hear the nearest approach to an expletive that ever fell from those bearded lips—pure of speech as ever were Grant's—" Dang it to hell, Wilson, didn't I say we could lick 'em? "

CHAPTER XXX

OBSTACLES AND DELAYS

WHEN Grant set forth for Germanna Ford as the head of the armies of the United States, he appeared, as Porter tells us, in complete uniform. Somebody, too —probably his most potent counsellor, Julia Dent—had persuaded him to wear thread gloves as more elegant than buckskin, but by the third day little was left of the gloves, and riding gauntlets reappeared. By the same time, too, he had found sash and sword more or less in his way, as he was frequently dismounting, pencilling orders and despatches, or squatting cross-legged on the ground with his pad on his left forearm, or a knee, and his cigar gripped in his teeth. A week in the Wilderness had taken much of the " style " out of the Army of the Potomac. Men were ridding themselves of overcoats and even blankets, so as to " march light." Officers were shedding sashes and throwing loose their coats. Grant hated a buttoned-up uniform and wore his as loosely as possible, finally shifting with a sigh of satisfaction into the loose-fitting sack of blue flannel, suggested by some level-headed staff officer as more seasonable for hot weather. By the time they crossed the James the general-in-chief was about as unpretentious a soldier in personal appearance as rode in that entire array. Even in his general's coat he could hardly have been impressive, as it is recorded that he encountered one morning a small drove of beef cattle headed obstinately the wrong way, and a perspiring herder shouted to him, " Say, stranger, just shoo them back there, will you? " And Grant, schooled from babyhood in the ways of the farm, " shooed " as requested and shooed to some purpose.

But while the Army of the Potomac saw little to call for admiration in the general appearance of the man from the West, there was one thing every horseman noted, and that was his riding. A surer seat could not be found, even among the "dandy" riders of the cavalry corps. No matter how his mount might flounder, shy or stumble, Grant was "with him" and quick to gather and sustain. Yet in mounting and dismounting his was a method of neither the school nor the army. Grant swung out of saddle without the preliminary hold of the pommel, and in mounting seldom if ever found it necessary to grasp the lock of the mane or more than lay hand on pommel or cantle. Once he had his toe in the stirrup a mere straightening of the leg seemed to do the rest. In an instant he was seated lightly in saddle, and once there was entirely at home. "Posting" at the trot, except with an English saddle and the flat seat, was something unheard of in those days, and the old "Grimsley," now in its glass case at the Historical Society Library in Chicago, was still in '64 Grant's favorite saddle. The ponderous housings were far too hot for the summer campaign and were discarded until the staff settled down at City Point. Then "Cincinnati" sometimes appeared in the official robes, at which Grant more than once made a wry face. A horse, he said, had quite enough to carry on parade or march "without all that weighty jimcrackery." Another thing Grant had little use for was a military band. Every regiment originally had one, and greatly did some of them add to the cheer and spirit of the camp or march; but before the third year only brigade bands were allowed, and even these in Grant's ears were too much of a good thing. "What's the joke?" he asked, the day the army emerged from the thickets and struck out for the open fields of Spottsylvania, and a band had burst into joyous music and the retinue of staff officers into a laugh. "They're playing ' Ain't I

Glad to Get Out of the Wilderness?'" was the answer, and Grant, who frankly owned he knew only one tune and was not sure of that, grinned and shrugged his shoulders. Later, when an ambitious leader, eager to do him honor, came with his band and struck up triumphant music close to headquarters, the commanding general grimly stood it a moment or two, then whimsically begged that the "noise" might be stopped, as there were matters of importance on which he wished to hear and speak, and the bandmaster doubtless felt deeply aggrieved.

There was another adjunct to our military progress through Virginia toward which Grant felt antipathy, due in great measure to his evil treatment at the hands of the newspapers in the West. Sherman, as far as he possibly could, had banished correspondents from the lines of his army, but Grant found the Army of the Press strongly intrenched in and about the Army of the Potomac. Some of these recorders of public events were great and gifted, most of them tried to be just and fair; many of them were, however, ignorant of military methods, and all of them were imbued with such zeal in the service of their respective papers (and every paper of any standing at home had its special correspondent somewhere at the front) that "exclusive" and important information sometimes found its way into print in spite of injury to the army and aid afforded the foe.

Now, while Grant had about him as staff officers in Rawlins, Rowley, Bowers and Horace Porter a quartette of strong, silent, reliable men, he had had, as has been told, a number of detrimentals, most of whom had been discarded ere he left the West, yet one or two weak vessels were still with him when the forward move began. Correspondents, known to be such, were not harbored at headquarters of the army; nevertheless, there seemed to be "leaks." Correspondents were numerous among the camp fires of the army and hovering about the outskirts of that sacred little bailiwick wherein Rawlins sat, lynx-eyed, yet not as forceful as in the West. Grant had " grown," was conscious of his power, and constantly in correspondence with the President and the Secretary of War, and Rawlins could not presume now, as presume he had, with reason and good effect, in the West. Distinguished visitors came not infrequently from Washington, and brought friends with them and introduced them at Grant's headquarters. Among these came Elihu B. Washburne, still representative of the Galena district in Congress, and here at least was a man even Rawlins could welcome with open arms. And Washburne brought with him a friend whom he introduced as Mr. Swinton, and told Grant he was an accomplished literary gentleman desirous of riding with the army, " in order that he might write its history at the end of the war." Mr. Swinton was welcomed as Washburne's friend so long as Washburne stayed, which was only until after the first few days of fierce battling in the Wilderness. It is not unlikely that this now famous historian hoped and expected that Washburne's introduction would be an *open sesame* to the doors of Grant's headquarters' mess. But Swinton was already known to the Army of the Potomac as one of the most active and gifted of the correspondents in the field, and beyond the tin plate, cup and camp chair indulged in by the staff, no accommodations were furnished Mr. Swinton, and these probably only for a day or two until he could make permanent arrangements with some of his press associates. It may be that, being eminent in his profession, Mr. Swinton resented it that the commanding general did not make him a member of the military household, but certain it is he speedily made himself *persona ingrata* and an impossibility at headquarters.

The night of May 3rd Grant had called Colonel

Rowley, who was to be officer on duty until dawn, and given him some detailed instructions and information. To Grant's amaze, he read them reported *verbatim* in the columns of a Richmond paper three days thereafter. It was bad enough that they should appear in the columns of the Northern press, but that which was furnished one was almost instantly, in '64, made known to the other.

A night or two later General Meade came to confer with Grant. The officers of the staff hospitably greeted those with Meade and drew them off to the camp fire in order that the chiefs might talk in private. Not five minutes later, sharp-eyed little Bowers caught sight of what seemed to be a human form crouching near to the tent in which sat the generals in low-toned conference, and easily within earshot. "Who's that?" he demanded, sharply, of Rowley, big and muscular, and Rowley, striding thither at once, found a civilian squatted against a little tree, grabbed him by the coat collar, jerked him to his feet, with Western frankness expressing his opinion and with equal emphasis demanding the meaning, of such conduct. The intruder was Mr. Swinton, and the result Mr. Swinton's exclusion from the charmed circle at headquarters for all time. Grant says he never saw him again, but was shortly called upon to save his life. A few weeks later General Meade came spurring to headquarters in great haste and some agitation. Burnside, commanding a separate force and not under Meade's direct orders, had found fresh occasion to look upon Mr. Swinton as a pernicious and prolific source of information to the enemy, had arrested Swinton forthwith and, as empowered by the custom of war in like cases, had ordered him summarily shot. These were strenuous days in the history of the great republic, and even the press had sometimes to be chastened for sin against the common cause. But the nation was then in straits. Stern measures had to be adopted, and though Grant promptly issued orders staying the shooting, he no longer stayed the order sending Mr. Swinton North. It is a whimsical illustration of our American methods that the next time the nation became involved in a general war " the boot was on the other foot." The nation was not in straits in '99. Stern methods were regarded as unnecessary by the press, at least, and the general commanding the forces of the United States on foreign soil had his face summarily slapped in presence of his staff by a correspondent with whom he had presumed to differ.

And correspondents were not the only men to do Grant injury in many a way. Even soldiers whom he had most befriended turned spitefully upon him and found ready listeners at Washington. It was one of these that very summer of '64 who, owing very much to Grant, repaid him grievously. One of the McClellan clique of the old Army of the Potomac—an unsuccessful, even if able, division commander—he had found himself at Chattanooga without a command, when Grant set him on his feet, gave opportunity to his unquestioned talents, rewarded him by soldierly praise and endorsement, and finally won over a reluctant and long obstructive Senate to the confirmation of his promotion to the double stars.

When it later transpired that this officer could not subordinately serve under Butler, for which there may have been some excuse, and would persist in vehement criticism of Meade, for which there could be none, Grant realized that in estimating the real value of the man the Senate had been right and he had been wrong, and therefore released him from service with the army at the front without formally relieving him. The next thing known was that a prominent senator had a letter from this officer setting forth that Grant took whiskey and was perceptibly drunk the day he came with General Butler to visit him at his headquarters. General

Butler, he declared, noted Grant's condition and would surely make use of it. This, it may be said right here, General Butler did not and would not do, even after he himself had been relieved from his command by Grant. Savagely as he attacked Grant in his later speeches and writings, and heartily as he hated him, Butler declared that he had not seen him either drink or drunk.

And finally it was this officer who, long years later, published his Memoirs of service in the West and East, and as an appendix printed that remarkable and pathetic appeal, penned by Rawlins in the dead of night when he thought his chief lay sleeping off the effects of liquor, though it transpired that Grant was really ill, that the liquor he had seen him drink at Sherman's headquarters was prescribed by the senior medical officer there on duty, and that the wine bottles which stood upon the table near Grant's cabin door had been emptied by bibulous members of the staff. Barring a certain hesitancy in expressing himself in writing that evening, Rawlins had seen no other indication that Grant was drinking, but his anxiety was ever keen, his zeal was vigilant, his friendship and loyalty unbounded, and who could blame him?

On the other hand, who can commend the publication of such a letter by one who had once enjoyed the privileges of intimate association with Grant and his staff? Is it likely that Grant would preserve that letter for the information of future generations? Is it probable that Rawlins made a copy of that which he must have been an hour in writing, beginning at 1 A.M.? Is it possible that he would permit any one else to copy it?

Let us finish this topic here and now. Whatever may have been Rawlins's anxiety as to Grant's alleged weakness in the West, he seems to have recovered in great measure before the march to the James. Porter frankly refers in his Memoirs to the fact that the General would take a modest glass with the rest. It is refutation of the theory that Grant could drink nothing without showing ill effects, though it is certain that a little would affect him more than it did many another.

A comical incident grew out of this soldier custom prevalent in all armies since the crusades, and tabooed by only an occasional ascetic in the days of which we write. Generals there were, like Wilson and Upton—splendid soldiers, too, and manful men—who would not touch liquor themselves or tolerate it about them. But at nine out of ten headquarters—corps, division, brigade or regimental—no such abstinence prevailed, and there came a time when even the chief quartermaster of the armies of the United States found his supply running short. It happened to be one of the times in which Stanton had his wary eye on Grant's headquarters, firmly convinced that officers there were wiring confidential information to influence the gold market and were speculating on the strength of it. By his order all telegraphic despatches were rigidly scrutinized; and if any could be found which in the faintest degree departed from the strictly official and essential, they were to be at once brought to him. One day, in the long and dreary winter that followed the unsuccessful assaults about Petersburg, a despatch from an officer of Grant's staff to an old chum and comrade in Oregon days, then stationed in New York, was laid before Mr. Stanton, and the Secretary read, became suddenly charged with electric impulse, and, barely able to control himself, sent for an officer who intimately knew both the correspondents and who had scouted the idea of any covert or underhand measures on part of either. "Look at this, sir!" demanded Stanton. "Look at this! Here is proof conclusive of what I tell you—a damnable cipher code that no one here has ever seen before. Now, what have you to say? What can that be but a means of conveying forbidden information?"

The officer took it and read; then he, too, nearly exploded, but not with wrath. "If your cipher sharps had ever served in Oregon, Mr. Secretary, this would be no puzzle at all. It is nothing but a message in Chinook, which interpreted reads, 'Send me another keg of that same whiskey.'"

However, there was much less drinking at the various headquarters than the few chroniclers would give one to understand, and these few, it might be hazarded, have referred to the matter, not so much to call attention to others' indulgence as to their own abstinence. It is noted in telling how General this or Senator that asked for a drink of brandy or whiskey on reaching "my headquarters" that the narrator takes occasion to say, "While I never used it myself," the visitor's needs were presently supplied.

There was of necessity very much of "entertaining" at Grant's headquarters from the day they were established at City Point. All manner of men, from the President down, came thither from time to time—President, peace commissioners, politicians, relatives of ill or wounded soldiers, generals and their staff officers from other commands, and the incessant aides-de-camp of the Armies of the Potomac and the James. In very many cases the visitors were guests of the lieutenant-general himself, but many, as a rule, were invited to the staff table and very probably, after a hard ride in stormy weather, to a "nip" at the tent of some one of the military household. It once or twice happened during the protracted stay of Mrs. Grant and little Jesse that the General received the reports of night-riding staff officers at the camp fire, and adjourned with them to the tent of Colonel Dent or Colonel Ingalls, Colonel Parker or some other staff officer who happened still to be up, and when the chilled and wearied visitor had been refreshed by a stiff drink, he could then be interrogated until Grant had extracted all information possible. This probably was the foundation for the venomous story of his "surreptitiously obtaining whiskey" in spite of the efforts of Rawlins.

The General had moved his family East. The elder children had been placed at school (Fred, the first born, with the honors and a scar or two of Vicksburg, preparing for West Point), but Mrs. Grant came to join her husband about as soon as his cabin was ready for her reception, and here, to his obvious comfort, spent many weeks. Her brother, Colonel Fred Dent, was now the only family appointee on the staff—certain earlier selections, made in deference to her wishes, having proved unsuitable. Colonel Dent was an amusing talker, and although of no particular military strength to the staff, was popular among his brother officers as the source of most of the merriment about headquarters.

Among the visitors, too, was Jesse Root, the father, who came and spent some little time. As was to be expected in the man, he had his eyes about him, and the business instinct of the past was still dominant. Many a rebuff had come to Jesse in the course of the three years in which the star of the son had been at last in the ascendant. Filial though he was, the General had to set firm foot upon every scheme to profit through the methods or needs of Uncle Sam, and many a scheme had Jesse. "Business" was born in him; the lack of it in the son had made him the butt of paternal sarcasm and public slights. Father and father-in-law both had said many a cutting thing of the sad-faced, stoopshouldered son in those dismal years immediately following his retirement from the army, but never a sign of resentment or symptom of retaliation came from Grant. There was humorous twinkle in his eyes the day that Jesse broached his proposition as to gathering in the hides of the many beef cattle butchered for the use of the great force in front of Petersburg. The instincts of the tanner made Jesse quite importunate, but the soldier son had to deny the thrifty father. Yet what a chance to ship whole cargoes of hides to the nearest market—hides which had cost the shipper nothing! The time had been in the not very distant past when, at the beck of the younger brothers, the broken captain was not only a party to transactions in hides, but conspicuous in the meanest and hardest part of the job—the personal handling and hauling from seller to cellar.

It was during this winter, too, that Grant was completing the purchase of the lands about the scene of his courtship and marriage. His pay as lieutenant-general, owing to the price of gold (which had risen to 290) amounted in actual value to less than five thousand a year, and at war-time prices the purchasing power was pitiably small. Nevertheless, the moment the debts were paid, his first thought seems to have been to buy the old home for Julia Dent and the children. Every penny borrowed about Galena had been scrupulously paid before the war was a year old. Every little bill contracted along that dreary roadside between White Haven and the heart of St. Louis had been wiped off the slate. Some of the shop-keepers (there were still a few as late as the exposition of 1903) had lived to tell how Grant came back to them in '61 and '62, to say he still owed them such and such a sum, and to settle on the spot. They did not have to name the amount due. In every instance he knew it and reminded them.

It was during this winter of '64 and '65, too, that public-spirited citizens of Philadelphia clubbed together against that projected return to St. Louis at the close of the war, and presented Grant with a fine house and lot in their midst. That set others to moving in like manner. He had suffered much in spirit over the onslaughts in the papers—the " Grant the Butcher " editorials which followed the battling in the Wilderness

GRANT AT COLD HARBOR

1. John A. Rawlins. 2. Colonel Comstock. 4. Lieutenant Dunn. 5. U. S. Grant. 6. Colonel M. R. Morgan. 7. Colonel Babcock 9 Colonel Parker. 3 and 8 are portraits of junior officers not now remembered

and Cold Harbor, the latter the one assault which he owned was an error and ever regretted. He had borne in patient silence the innumerable slings that were dealt him during the presidential campaign of the fall of '64, resulting in the final defeat of McClellan—the logical candidate of the " War is a Failure " party—and in the triumphant return of Abraham Lincoln. There was even a symptom of grim satisfaction in Grant's receipt that winter of the superb sword which had been put up to popular vote at the mammoth fair of the Sanitary Commission in the city of New York. For long days, as the " most popular general " McClellan had led in the voting, and his name stood at the head of the list of all the candidates until toward the close, when better counsels and possibly the reserve forces and funds of the Union League prevailed, and Grant won by a big plurality.

All the same that winter of '64 and '65 was a trying one to Grant and all about him, even though Sherman had marched almost unopposed through the void and hollow spaces of a depleted South, and was striding northward through the Carolinas—though Thomas, firm, tenacious and absolutely sure in his judgment, had dealt the most telling blow of the war, and was threatening the approaches to Virginia from the west—though Sheridan, with his now well-handled cavalry, had thrashed Early out of the Shenandoah, and was preparing to swoop down upon Richmond from the northwest—though Wilson, with the strongest corps of horsemen ever assembled within our borders, was launching out upon the final blow at the central South, which was to leave nothing uncaptured from Eastport, in northern Mississippi, to Irwinsville, in southern Georgia. About Petersburg and Richmond, however, every blow had been skilfully parried and fiercely countered by Lee. The mine had been a miserable fiasco, the attempts on the Weldon railway emphatic failures, the wintry months in hut and trench had " softened " the Armies of the Potomac and the James, and still Grant sat there grim and determined, confident with the coming of spring and Sheridan he could turn the final trick, reach round the southern flank of Lee, compel him to let go his hold on those deadly parapets of Petersburg, then fall upon him in the open and, weakened by that time as his army must be, who could doubt the result? And yet how superbly those starving, tattered, jaded fellows fought to the very last! Superb as they had been at Malvern, at Antietam, at Gettysburg, in the Wilderness, never were they grander in their heroism than in those last stands at Sailors' Creek and Farmville, as they rallied with deathless valor and devotion about the battle flag of their beloved and chivalric Lee.

CHAPTER XXXI

THE LAST CAMPAIGN

Most loyally and faithfully had General Meade sought to carry out every wish or command sent him by Grant. It had been the latter's method merely to indicate the movement required of the Army of the Potomac, leaving to Meade the details. They were men utterly unlike in mode or manner, yet imbued with hearty respect, one for the other. Meade, who was the soul of courtesy and consideration when unruffled, became unbearable when aroused—stormed at every one about him, even at generals of rank and distinction, who, as a rule, could only submit in silence as became officers bred to the purple of the Army of the Potomac. When, as happened just once, the object of his temporary wrath was born of Irish stock and bred in the Army of the West, the instant result was a verbal battle the like of which was never fought in the East. Meade, it was said, could lose his temper twenty times a day, yet never lose a friend. Grant's temper was lost but twice during the entire war, yet his enemies seemed to multiply. Meade was irritable as Grant was serene, and as methodical as Grant was careless. Moreover, they differed widely in their ways. Meade was of the Engineer school, never until the war having set squadron in the field. Grant had learned the game from the fighting end at the start. Meade had the Engineer eye for a strong position, and was imbued with the defensive method of holding it. " What shall I do if the enemy pushes me here? " said he to Grant, pointing to a place on the map where his line seemed weak and where supports might not readily reach him. " Push him there," said Grant, pointing to a spot a mile away. Meade had thought only of the stop; Grant thought instantly of the "counter." Meade, most loyal and subordinate himself, looked for loyalty and subordination as instant and as complete as his own. Hancock and Sedgwick were examples of the admirable as subordinate commanders. Warren, with all his dash and bravery when once engaged, was cursed with the propensity to carp, cavil and criticise. It led almost to his relief from command before ever they crossed the James. It was the underlying cause of his dramatic and most undeserved undoing at the very climax of the last campaign.

But Sedgwick and Hancock both were lost to Meade as the spring of '65 came on. Sedgwick had been shot dead that fateful day in front of Spottsylvania. Hancock, disabled by wounds, had availed himself of leave of absence and had been set to organizing a new command. Wright, a fighting Engineer, had succeeded beloved "Uncle John" in command of the Sixth Corps. Humphreys, another fighting Engineer, with a record behind him, had succeeded to the command of the Second, while Burnside's old men were now led by that thorough soldier, another Engineer, John G. Parke, and what was left of the Army of the James by E. O. C. Ord.

The first expedition to Fort Fisher, conducted by Benjamin F. Butler, had failed in the moment when success seemed certain; and as the same troops, with a different leader, triumphed readily where Butler had failed, he, too, lost his command, and joined the array of Grant haters, of whom there were now so many. It had been Grant's lot to have to displace a dozen generals in the effort to find competent and efficient commanders, and every time such general left the field he and his friends flooded the press with sensational clamor at the expense of Grant, who heard it all, of course, and, true to his stoical custom, sat in silence, smoked and said nothing. McClernand, Rosecrans, C. S. Hamilton, Gordon Granger, Sigel, "Baldy" Smith and Benjamin

THE LAST CAMPAIGN

F. Butler—even loyal, but hopelessly slow, " Old Burn " and certain others, all owed their relief from duty, primarily, of course, to faults of their own, but directly to the order or request of Grant. Just in the nick of time he was saved from supplanting Thomas on the eve of splendid victory. It is sadly to be regretted that he himself could not have been at the far front that April Fools' Day at Five Forks, when Sheridan's brilliant tactical fight and spectacular overthrow of Pickett's famed division (what was left of it) was marred by the sacrifice of that brave and brainy leader Gouverneur Warren—the man whom Grant himself at one time would have placed in command of the Army of the Potomac had anything happened to Meade.

But Sheridan was the man of the hour and deservedly so. He had rejoined in the full flush of his triumphs in the Shenandoah and up the James. He had brought back his seasoned cavalry almost in the pink of condition—fit, so far as the men were concerned, for anything. He had launched out around Lee's southern wing, reaching for the Southside Railway and the rear of that impregnable line. He and his grim superior had fully decided that the time had now come to " end it all right here." The South, as Butler wrote, had " robbed the cradle and the grave " to put their last reserves into the fighting lines, for gray-haired men and laughing boys were shouldering the worn Enfields in the battered ranks. If Sheridan could reach the roads to the west of Petersburg, there could be no help for it, Lee *must* let go. Then what could be hoped for Richmond?

Yet, even at the last, it seems as though the gods had planned to balk the march of the Union. The rains fell in torrents and flooded the flat country to the south and west. The troopers had ridden away, defiant of wind or weather, had rounded the far flank and stirred up a hornets' nest of Southern Horse, fighting like fiends about Dinwiddie. The infantry and the gunners of the army had been summoned from their snug winter quarters, and now, soaked with rain and soft with their long hibernation, sulked along the dripping wood paths, even their generals moody, silent and depressed. Wright and the Sixth Corps, Sheridan's sturdy backers in the Shenandoah, were too far back now. It was Warren, with the Fifth, who marched nearest. They had all bivouacked for the night, seeking such shelter as ponchos and scant canvas could afford, and were huddled about the camp fires, dull and dispirited. Even Meade seemed ready to quit and put back to the winter lines; even Rawlins urged it, and the loyal little gathering at Grant's headquarters, by this time moved far out to Dabney's saw mills southwest of town, seemed to take the cue from him. It was Sheridan who saved the scene, Sheridan who came splashing in from the far front, chock-full of vim, confidence and energy, absolutely sure that with infantry to back him he could send Fitz Lee and Pickett whirling away northward, and then envelop the lines of Petersburg. It was Warren who was told off to his aid, Warren of whom the word had been passed—"He may fail you. If he does, relieve him," for Grant, with all his appreciation of Warren's fighting spirit, "when once engaged," had more than once found serious fault with his sluggish methods when instant action was needed.

And it all fell out as might have been foreseen. Warren, ordered to march at night, did not get fairly away until morning. Gravelly Run had risen again and could not be forded. All day long Sheridan fumed at Dinwiddie, waiting for Warren, and finally pushed ahead without him, and when at last he had marshalled his cavalry in front of the works at Five Forks, and needed only the infantry of the Fifth Corps to make the enveloping attack of the eastward flank, it seemed as though Warren could never be roused to the im-

portance of the occasion. The sun was fast setting,
Warren's men were still marching up from the rear,
and while Sheridan was striding about fretting, fuming,
swearing with wrath and impatience, Warren sat su-
pinely by, apparently indifferent and, as it seemed to
Sheridan, impassive, sluggish, even sullen. At last,
and only just in time, the rearmost regiments reached
their position; at last the word was given to go in, and
with a wild clamor of bugles and cheers the cavalry of
Merritt, Custer and " Tommy " Devin were flung in the
teeth of the enemy. Ayres's fine division of Warren's
Corps was checked at the eastward angle of the works,
and Sheridan felt himself compelled to rush in and
personally take a hand. With his battle flag clinched
in his gauntleted fist, spurring straightway among the
faltering ranks, he darted hither and yon, in and about,
cheering, cursing, driving, until the very force of 'his
meteoric example seemed to carry them in and over the
sodden parapets, even as the charging cavalry swept
over the long line from the south. Then when he
wanted Warren, as luck would have it, that brilliant
soldier was having a time of his own recalling a wandering division, and though he finally swung it in and led
it in magnificent wheel enveloping Pickett's staggering
line, and with it charged home upon their rear, he had
not happened to be where Sheridan's aides expected to
find him. He was personally conducting a splendid
fight in his own daring and decisive way; but through
the thick woods no sign of it had come to those about
the commanding general, and the ill-considered order
was issued in the very moment of triumph—the order
that sent Warren to the rear a heartbroken man.

Sore in spirit over the loss of their admired leader
and the death of gallant Fred Winthrop, shot down at
the head of his brigade, the Fifth Corps spent that
April night in sleep and silence, while the troopers of
the cavalry were exulting in their great victory. Now,

assuredly, the Army of Lee would have to abandon the impregnable works; the Southside Railway was within Sheridan's grasp. But, farther to the west the Richmond & Danville line was still open to the enemy. Squeezed out of Petersburg and southern Virginia, Lee might swiftly make his way into North Carolina, and there, uniting with Johnston, overwhelm Sherman, and then turn back on Grant. But the plans of the latter had already been made to block that very scheme. Lee was never to be allowed to reach Johnston or support of any kind. Early on the morning of the 2nd Sheridan had struck out and reached the Appomattox, west of the encircled city. Wright, Humphreys, Parke and Ord had swept over the outer intrenchments and completed the semicircle about the doomed city. Vengefully and fiercely Lee struck at his assailants but could not shake them off, and while Grant was sending encouraging tidings to President Lincoln, eagerly awaiting news at City Point, Lee's messenger to President Davis, coming in the midst of Sunday morning service, bore him the long-dreaded tale of disaster. For the last time the fated chieftain of the Confederacy bowed his head in that sanctuary and passed out into the April sunshine, leaving a stricken congregation to hear the sorrowful words of their loved old rector that there would be no further service that day. They could only hie them homeward and face the catastrophe Davis and his associates had brought upon a brave and devoted people.

That night the men of Lee slipped away across the Appomattox and struck out westward, safe for the moment from attack. That night the officials of the Confederate government were in full flight for the southwest, leaving Richmond to the mercies of its mob. Early on the morning of the 3rd the men of Meade had burst into the outskirts of Petersburg, Grant riding in their midst, while farther to the north the men of the old Army of the James poured into the smoking streets of the capital, and set to work to extinguish the flames. In one immense herd, at the southern end of the bridges at Petersburg, were massed the men of Lee's rear guard, squeezing across as fast as possible, yet presenting a broad target for the guns of the field artillery, such as never before had been afforded, and Grant, "the Butcher," gazing from afar on the helpless throng, their outward battalions still bravely, defiantly facing the swift advance of the blue skirmishers, stayed the order which would have brought the batteries lashing from the distant rear, to deluge with shell and shrapnel those thinned and devoted brigades. "I could not bear to kill," he said, "when it seemed so certain that in a day or two we could easily capture."

Then came the chase; Meade, with the infantry following close at the heels; Sheridan, with the cavalry, reaching even farther out to the left front, yet at every possible opportunity darting in and dealing savage blows at the sore and bleeding flank. Gallantly, stubbornly, in spite of hunger, desertion, battle losses, lack of sleep and rest, those heroic fellows in ragged gray faced and fought to the very last. With rations in abundance awaiting them at Appomattox station, they set forth eagerly on the dawn of the ninth day, confident that by noon they would be feasting and resting about their ladened trains, and lo! the onward way was barred by long extended lines of horsemen in faded blue, and when the bugles sang "Forward," and the cheery word was passed, "It's only cavalry; nothing else could yet have got here," and sturdily the gray ranks swept onward to brush aside the insolent, challenging troopers, then, right and left, the nimble riders drew aside, and lo, again there uprose solid, serried ranks of sturdy infantry, the hard-marching linesmen of the Army of the Potomac, and at last, at last, after four long years of almost incomparable battling, the Army of Northern Virginia—the "finest infantry in the world," as foreign commentators would have it—the flower of the Southern forces, as all admit, though by this time only the ghost of its once magnificent self—was beaten at its own brilliant game and blocked and brought to bay.

Another beautiful and outwardly peaceful Sunday morning was this on which the white flag suddenly shot up above the halted lines of Lee. Forty-eight hours earlier Grant had sought to stop further bloodshed and besought Lee to surrender, but there was still hope in the Southern ranks that they could reach the Danville railway and leave even Sheridan behind. That hope now was dead. Not only Sheridan but Ord was here in sufficient force to bar, while Meade's divisions were hammering at the rear and closing in on the southward flank. Moreover, nothing but parched corn had they now left to eat, and little enough of that. The remnant of the once proud and indomitable army had been worn down by battle, by suffering and starvation until barely the shadow was left. Everything was gone but honor. And so, toward noon that day they came again together, those two leaders of men whom we last saw meet at the wagon train on the eastern shore of Lake Chalco—Lee now, in spite of his army's straits, clad in immaculate uniform, brand new and brilliant to the last detail, with his costly sword gleaming at his side, erect, dignified, as he stood awaiting the coming of his conqueror at the little homestead of the Virginia McLeans. One staff officer only stood in attendance, the spectacled Colonel Marshall; and presently " up from the South," riding hard after riding long, and risen from a night of sick headache that left him pale and haggard, stoop-shouldered by habit, shabby in raiment by force of circumstances, and looking as little like a victorious general as Lee looked like the beaten man, came Grant, the conqueror.

Dressed like a private soldier, in loose blue sack, with baggy trousers and bespattered boots, his hair and beard

THE McLEAN HOMESTEAD, APPOMATTOX

unkempt, his hand ungloved, the general-in-chief of the armies of the United States swung out of saddle, climbed the wooden steps, entered the little parlor, and there the renowned leaders clasped hands a moment, called each other formally by title and by name, and with Rawlins and presently Porter, Babcock and Parker, of the staff, joined later by Dent and Badeau, and later still by Generals Ord, Sheridan and others, within, while swarms of officers of all ranks gathered on the lawn without, the two great commanders began their memorable conference. Grant was for indulging in reminiscence of the Mexican war, surprised to find that Lee could well recall him, and twice had Lee to bring him back to the more important business in hand—the terms of that historic surrender.

Then at the beck of the shabbiest looking, yet the greatest, soldier of the gathering, Colonel Parker swung a small table into the centre of the room, laid his writing pad upon it, and Grant swiftly penned the simple terms familiar to almost every school boy in the land, providing for the immediate disarming and disbandment of the Southern force—officers and men to pledge themselves not again to take arms unless properly exchanged, officers and men to take home with them such horses as they had, officers (a glance at the shining sword of Lee suggested this) to retain their prized side arms—the necessary rolls to be made out at once. Lee's fine, grave features softened a little as he read—so gentle, so magnanimous were the terms. " My men are nearly starving," he began, when Grant stopped him with prompt question as to the number in need, and the instant order for a full supply of rations.

And then they parted, Lee passing down the steps and out at the open gate to where gray "Traveler" stood awaiting him, every Union soldier facing his late antagonist at the salute, and then, when he had ridden beyond earshot, the jubilee began—Custer, seizing the

table on which the chiefs had signed and bearing it
forth on his curly head; bearded elders, with glistening
eyes, battering each other's backs; slender young staff
aides flying into wild gymnastics about the lawn, others
spurring off to bear the wondrous tidings, and start the
guns to thundering their rejoicing—a symptom stopped
on the instant by Grant's quick order. There should be
no " crowing " in his command over a foeman so dauntless, so daring, and even, after all was said, so dear;
for were they not brothers? He checked the shouts
with which the men would now have eagerly greeted
him, as presently he rode back to wire the news to
Washington. Never had there been a war of more
deadly, desperate fighting; never had there been a four
years' grapple to compare in valor and determination
with that fought out on the sacred soil of Virginia;
never in all the history of war was conqueror so
unconscious. Once again, on the morrow, he stopped
to chat for half an hour on his homeward way with the
gray-haired idol of the South, his conquered foe, and
then set forth to Washington to provide for the speedy
muster out of the vast army of volunteers, and to lay
before the President and Secretary of War the story
of his soldier stewardship—the most acclaimed and applauded man of all the nation, the soldier who, having
endured to the end, at last had worn out the sword of
Lee.

CHAPTER XXXII

PEACE AND PERPLEXITIES

GRANT'S own Memoirs close with Appomattox. Over the troublous days of reconstruction, of presidential impeachment, of political intrigue, of his own administrations, of all, in fact, that followed the great surrender, he draws the veil of silence. The last year of the war had been a severe strain upon the patience and patriotism of the North. It had been quite as severe a strain upon the general-in-chief. Just as the cynics of the Army of the Potomac had prophesied—the man who had whipped every adversary in the West had for the time been stopped by that great, gray captain, who, in succession, had defeated every chieftain, no matter with what preponderance in arms and men, the North had sent against him. From the Rapidan to the James Grant had slowly forced or flanked the army of Lee. From early May to July—" fighting it out on this line if it took all summer "—and full half his men—the inflexible Westerner had pressed at every point the flexible Virginian, and still, as autumn wore on, that skilled fencer stood dauntlessly on guard between him and the gates of the Southern capital. Even the stout and steadfast heart of Grant seemed for a time almost to fail him. Back at Washington the President and the War Secretary were silently filling his every requisition for means and men, but behind the President and his despotic minister the murmurings of the people and the menace of the press had begun to wear upon the iron nerve of the soldier in chief command.

It was characteristic of him that as soon as safety would permit, he should send for Mrs. Grant and some at least of the children, and it is remembered that during the autumn, when he was sought by a staff officer, the commander of the myriad forces of the Union was found rolling upon the floor of the little cabin in mirthful grapple with Jesse, the younger, and that on another occasion when "Cincinnati," caparisoned for ceremony, was becoming impatient in front of the General's field residence, the General himself was found at the back of it, himself bestridden by his lusty little son and heir, playing horse for that youngster's benefit. It is remembered by those who surrounded them that during the days of Mrs. Grant's sojourn at City Point the General spent long hours at her side. To his staff he would not talk of his troubles. If any one knew them it was his wife.

The long strain in a measure accounts for his impatience with Thomas, whose perfectly justifiable delay in attacking Hood at Nashville seemed inexplicable at City Point. The insistence of the press that Grant was "losing ground" in the eyes of the administration and the hearts of the people during that long "hold up" in front of Petersburg was another thing that told upon him. He had been North on a visit and found everywhere a sense of nervousness and apprehension over Sherman's dive into the bowels of the Confederacy. He believed, and by this time Sherman knew, the Confederacy was but an empty shell, with every available man on the surface and no one left at the core. He regarded Sherman as the most brilliant and gifted soldier of his day, and so proclaimed him whithersoever he went, saying much on that score at least and doing everything to restore confidence, all to the end that when Sherman wired from Savannah his Christmas present to the nation, it looked for a time as though popular acclaim and presidential perplexities might result in Sherman's being ordered to supplant his great superior. The move was actually in contemplation at Washington, and even that could not daunt the deathless friendship

From the collection of F. H. Meserve

Col. Ely S. Parker　　　Col. Adam Badeau　　　Gen. Grant　　　Col. Babcock.　　　Col. Horace Porter

GRANT AND HIS PERSONAL STAFF, 1866

between the two—even such temptation could not sap
the loyalty of such a man as Sherman or stagger the
faith of such a man as Grant. Just as in 1861, and on
to Shiloh, the latter held that "Charley" Smith was
best fitted to command, and he, Grant, to serve, so now
in '64 and '65, in spite of all that had occurred, or possibly because of it, there were days in which he more
than half believed that Sherman might have succeeded
where he had failed. Sherman was magnetic, meteoric,
aggressive, brilliant, a chieftain who aroused the enthusiasm of his officers and men. Grant was silent,
simple, even stolid—arousing no enthusiasm whatsoever.
About the best or most the men of the Army of the
Potomac ever said of him was that "the old man never
quit when once he took hold," or else that widely quoted
tribute in the vernacular of the Western rank and file,
"Ulysses doesn't scare worth a damn."

But Ulysses would have been less than human had
he enjoyed defeat, and Grant liked to win, whether in
battle, cards or horse race; and here, as the last year of
the war opened, he found himself in danger of losing
to a subordinate the laurels of a conqueror—the stars
of the chief command. To ninety-nine men out of a
hundred the prospect would have been a bitter blow and
to nearly that number the test would have been too
much for friendship. George H. Thomas, as we have
seen, was so great, so magnanimous, that when threatened with removal from command and orders to serve
under one of his own subordinates, he could announce
his instant readiness to accept the decision "without a
murmur." And now in his turn Grant, supreme in
command, was put to a like test, and met it instantly,
as had Thomas, with "the spirit of old West Point."
If there were no other lesson to be learned from that
war, the example of loyalty, self-sacrifice and devotion
set by Grant, Sherman and Thomas should live in history for all time. One can hardly read Grant's letter to

Sherman at this emergency without a gripping at the heart, a moistening of the eye. The bill to make Sherman, too, a lieutenant-general and therefore eligible to command the army, had been prepared. The moment Sherman heard of it he wrote to his brother, long the senator from Ohio, to stop it instantly, and to Grant in his silent sufferance came Sherman's golden words, " I should emphatically decline any command calculated to bring us into rivalry."

And then came Grant's reply. Fancy Marlborough writing thus to Prince Eugene, Cæsar to Antony, Bonaparte to Desaix, Johnston to John B. Hood, Sheridan to Thomas, aye, Lee to Longstreet! The famous friendship of Damon and Pythias knew no such strain as that which politics and politicians thrust into the lives of Grant and Sherman, and yet, strained to the breaking point of human endurance, superbly did those two soldiers bear the test and triumph over every adversary and adversity. *" If you should be put in command and I put subordinate,"* wrote Grant, *" it would not change our relations in the least. I would make the same exertions to support you that you have ever done to support me, and I would do all in my power to make our cause win."*

But Sherman, as we know, blocked through Brother John the bill for his promotion, even as later he blocked the project to set him over Grant. It has pleased many commentators and some historians to refer to Sherman as erratic, but where in all history can one read of finer constancy in friendship—of franker, stancher loyalty and self-abnegation? Sherman stemmed that " tide in the affairs of men " which unquestionably was flooding toward him after Savannah, then swept Grant skyward after Appomattox. North and South alike proclaimed the silent soldier from Galena as the conqueror, the undisputed chief. North and South alike welcomed and acclaimed him. A triumphal progress—in spite of his shy, retiring self—was that which awaited him whither-soever he journeyed in the Northland. People of all classes thronged about his carriage or his train, stopping his way, wringing his hand until he had to carry that hand in bandages and the arm in a sling. Audiences in theatres sprang to their feet and shouted when he arrived. Players forgot their " lines " and applauded wildly from the stage. Congregations stood when he entered church, and pastors called down the blessings of the Almighty on the bowed head and blushing face. Papers that had plastered him with charges and insinuations turned to fawn upon him now, with almost as offensive praise; but, high and low, rich and poor, great and humble, the people of the loyal North lavished upon him tokens of gratitude and admiration such as no American had ever before received; and the surviving men of the late disloyal South, disarmed alike by his measures and his magnanimity, hung above their mantels the swords he had spared to them in token of a soldier's admiration of soldierly valor and virtue, and swore that if any man could win them back to the flag of their fathers it would be this plain soldier of the West—the man who having asked only their parole of honor at surrender, now had to stand between them and the vengeance which Andrew Johnson, Stanton and a rabid few at first so fiercely demanded.

If ever man had reason for believing himself greatest of the great, as the people settled down " to bind up the nation's wounds," it was Ulysses Grant; but he gathered his military staff and his little family about him and devoted himself assiduously to closing up the affairs of the swiftly disbanding armies, and striving to adjust military conditions to the inevitable reduction in numbers and return to civil control. He had been received at Washington with almost adulation by every government official from our great President down to the pages of the House of Representatives. Members of the Cabinet, of the Supreme Court, of the Senate, vied with each other in effusive honors. Lincoln, sincere and swayed with an almost overwhelming gratitude under God to Grant, was at last beginning to realize the fruits of his patient, prayerful labor; the dream of the ship under full sail had not yet returned, the shadow of that fell coming event had not yet been cast before him. Heaven had granted to him four days of unutterable joy as recompense for four years of incomparable service. Then came the hideous crime that was to stun and horrify the nation.

Meantime Stanton, who never really liked Grant and probably never much loved any man, for those few days deferred to him as he never had to any one. Then came the awful shock of the assassination (a fate spared to Grant because he had promised to go that night to join the children at Burlington), the sudden disappearance from the scene of the one master mind Stanton measurably bowed to, the emergence from the obscurity of a hotel bedroom to the White House of the intemperate and ill-balanced politician destined for the time to sit as president, and then Stanton's prompt essay to gain the upper hand. Under Lincoln, and because of the tremendous issues involved, Stanton for a year had been unable to dictate to Grant. Now, with the war well-nigh ended and Lincoln gone, he sought to assume at once the supremacy he undoubtedly believed his due. Almost at the outset, however, his aggressive will and imperious temper led him into error and defeat.

The terms of the surrender of Johnston's army to Sherman, unlike those of Lee to Grant, were promptly disavowed by the administration, and indeed disapproved by Grant himself. But where the latter would have quietly stopped proceedings until suitable terms could have been substituted, it pleased Stanton privately to denounce Sherman as a traitor, and to publicly and offensively disown and renounce Sherman's actions.

PEACE AND PERPLEXITIES

For a moment, perhaps, public sentiment, ever excitable, was with the implacable Secretary, but another moment's reflection on Sherman's long and brilliant record of patriotic and soldierly service steadied the press and satisfied the people. Even Grant, usually so calm and undemonstrative, had been stirred to instant action and impulsive protest against Stanton's scathing rebuke of his favorite second. "It is infamous, it is infamous!" he cried. It was abominable that one so loyal, so gallant and efficient as Sherman had ever been should now by any man, even the War Secretary, be denounced as a traitor. The first symptoms of a breach between the new and accidental President and the general-in-chief of his armies occurred over this humiliation of Sherman. The next, and one more serious still, was that in which the President had sought to punish certain prominent Confederate officers who, under the terms of their surrender to Grant, were permitted to remain undisturbed at their homes so long as they observed the parole. Threatened with arrest, they promptly appealed to Grant, and now the new executive had a taste of the mettle there was in his foremost general.

"If those men are disturbed, Mr. President," were the words attributed to Grant—and there is no question that whatever the words the purport was a fact—"I tender at once my resignation and submit the issue to the people," and Andrew Johnson had sense enough to know that as between himself and Ulysses Grant the people would promptly and crushingly decide for the latter.

Early, therefore, as the summer of '65, differences had sprung up between the General-in-chief and the two men whom the law and the constitution made his superiors, yet the two had to stand in assumed gratification and complacency whenever they happened in public to appear with Grant, and to listen to the shouts of the multitude for the General, and to look in vain, in that presence, for any greeting for themselves. The day of the grand review, when the Army of the Potomac marched up the avenue with Meade at its gallant head, the throngs in front of the White House went wild when Grant stepped to his place on the platform, and hailed with only perfunctory applause the coming of the hat-waving, hand-shaking Chief Magistrate, followed by the grim, gray-bearded War Secretary. The next day the populace shouted itself hoarse when Tecumseh Sherman rode past at the head of his magnificently gaunt, sinewy, shabbily-dressed but superbly marching array—the men who had footed it over half a continent in his train. Sinewy and sullen they went striding by, those wiry Westerners, with eyes straight to the front and hearts resentfully beating—drooping colors and sabres as regulations demanded as they passed the constitutional commander-in-chief and the war minister beside him who between them had held their loved general up to popular execration. They were glad when it was all over—and so was Stanton, for publicly, and precisely as he had said, Tecumseh Sherman had refused the proffered hand of the spectacled secretary and scouted his tender of amity. Long years later, oddly enough, when general commanding the army, it fell to Sherman's lot to have to rebuke the Commandant of Cadets for a somewhat similar refusal to accept the hand of his immediate superior, the Superintendent, and when the Commandant had been officially lectured upon the gravity of his misconduct and the evil effect his example would have upon the undergraduate body at West Point, and assured that nothing could justify a junior in refusing the hand of a senior, the General was suddenly reminded of his own dramatic demonstration of the spring of 1865.

They all "harked back" to West Point that year that followed the great surrender—all save Sheridan,

who, the very week after he had rounded up the worn
army of Lee at Appomattox, had been despatched to
the Rio Grande. Sometimes in groups of two or three,
sometimes singly, the great generals of the war re-
visited the scene of their boyish struggles and studies—
Grant, Sherman, Thomas and a score of lesser lights.
Even the War Secretary himself came and peered curi-
ously about the barracks, the recitation rooms and
offices, and went away without making, or possibly receiving, a very favorable impression. When Sherman
came he breezed all over the premises, chatting cheerily
and shaking hands with everybody from the superintendent down to the shoeblacks—one of whom claimed
to have " shined him up " in 1840. When Thomas came
—grave, courteous and dignified—the officers and the
corps seemed to hang about him in something akin to
reverence such as the Southerners ever showed for Lee.
When Grant first came it was nearly dark and very
wintry, and a great soldier was being borne to his rest,
and the General-in-chief, muffled in huge cape-overcoat,
and with his high black felt hat pulled well down over
his brows, marched afoot at the tail of the procession of
mourners, grim, impassive and out of step with the
wailing music of the band and everybody about him.
That night when gallant little Bowers was crushed to
death under his eyes at Garrison's Station across the
Hudson, though filled with shock and distress of mind,
the iron leader of the war fell back behind the mask
of inflexible reserve which was now becoming habitual,
gave brief direction that the body be carried over to the
Point, and went his instant way to the duties awaiting
him at Washington. " The coldest blooded man I ever
saw," said a bystander, but he saw the surface only.

All through the Southland, too, Grant was sent by
presidential mandate during the year that followed the
war. Mr. Johnson desired to know at first hand the
actual condition of the people and the sentiments of

the soldiers and statesmen lately in rebellion. He knew that to no man in the Union service were they so drawn as they were to Grant. Everywhere they greeted him with respect, deference, often with gratitude, and at times with something akin to affection and appeal. Grant came back to Washington and made report to the effect that peace was possible and the people submissive, but it presently transpired that this report was not that which was now desired. The President had determined on reversal of his policy and the congress had taken alarm. A very different condition of things was reported by the next emissary despatched, and a very different man was the reporter—General Carl Schurz, destined from this time on to oppose in many a way the great soldier whom, five years earlier in the streets of St. Louis, he had passed unnoticed—an obscure and almost friendless man.

CHAPTER XXXIII

PROBLEMS AND POLITICS

EARLY as the summer of '66 the nation was beginning to forget the bitterness of the war days, beginning to tire of the sight of soldiers in uniform, beginning to say, even in the North, that the death of Lincoln in the hour of victory insured his deathless fame, beginning to realize in the South that the abominable deed of their self-constituted avenger had robbed them of their best and most powerful friend. Over the life and character, the fate and fame of Abraham Lincoln there shines a lustre so intense that mortal eye may not pierce the veil that shrouded the soul within him, but if ever God-like attributes descended upon man, if ever the teachings of the meek and lowly Son of Bethlehem were indelibly implanted in the human heart, that great heart beat in the rugged bosom of him who, like Him of old, was born in obscurity, bred in poverty, schooled in suffering, steeped in sympathy, love, patience and tenderness for all mankind. God alone could have been the strength and solace of Lincoln during those four years of almost intolerable strain, for about him, in his official household, there was not one man upon whom—as was otherwise with Grant—he could unreservedly lean; there was not one, on the contrary, whom he had not by patient pleading, or even cajoling, to persuade and lead. There was not one woman—and it was otherwise with Grant—ever at hand to comfort, to sympathize, to sustain. Over the pathetic sorrow of Lincoln's married life, foreseen, yet faced unflinchingly and borne with infinite patience and pity, it has seemed best to draw the veil.

Even in that first summer following the disbandment

333

of the armies, the people were realizing something of the greatness of him they had lost, and contrasting it with the littleness of him they had self-imposed—the majesty and magnanimity of the administration of Lincoln, with the machinations and " my policy " of Andrew Johnson. Yet the latter implicitly believed in himself and thought to rouse the people to a following such as they had denied his great predecessor. From having started with the threat of making " treason odious," he had veered squarely about to the restoration of every right " the States in rebellion " had less than six years earlier renounced and rejected. He sought to lead a new South to its old-time supremacy, and the North said No! He sought to swing by personal appeal the people of the thronging cities of the middle and western States, and while " swinging round the circle " to parade Grant in his train, as though Grant, a popular idol, approved and supported him. Grant could not disobey the lawful order of his chief, but before that pitiable progress fairly began, found legitimate means of escaping. He who had never known what it was to " manœuvre " was finding manœuvring indispensable at Washington. He listened now in grim silence to the inside history of that triumphal progress, so fatuously projected and so flat a failure, and read, with thankfulness for his escape, of how the head of the nation rode through curious crowds in the city streets, vainly bowing right and left to unresponsive throngs that withheld their cheers until Custer's yellow curls and starred shoulder-straps caught their eye from the fourth or fifth carriage. Never did President of these United States present a more melancholy spectacle than when Andrew Johnson uncovered to the salute of some of Grant's old regiment, once more quartered along the Canadian frontier and detailed for escort duty that day in Buffalo. Never was there sadder contrast between past and present eminence than when on the platform in Niagara Square, Millard Fillmore, white-haired erect and dignified, made the address of welcome to the man who, like himself, had stepped from the vice-presidency into the chair of the chief magistrate.

The acute stage of the difference between Johnson and Grant had not yet come. Congress, rejoicing in the triumphant closing of the war, had revived the grade of general, rewarded Grant with four stars and a substantial salary, and lavished brevets and honors upon all those who had served at the front and many who had not, all to the end that more than half the senior officers of the regular service were now wearing the uniform, though only a dozen were drawing the pay, of major or brigadier generals. Almost every field officer wore the yellow sash instead of the red. Full many a captain marshalled a little squad of men, no one of whom presumed to address him except as " the general." It was Fred Grant's first summer at West Point, and once or twice his illustrious father dropped in upon his old school and found assembled there almost as many generals as there were junior officers. The newly authorized regiments had not yet been organized. The army was full of men recently commanding corps, divisions and brigades, many of whom had to go back to company duty, some few of them even to " fall in " as file closers. The War Department was making it as easy as possible for them. Numerous courts, boards and commissions were in session, giving temporary employment on their volunteer rank to regulars who little relished the prospect of garrison duty. Andrew Johnson had signed the commission of Ulysses Grant as general, and that of Tecumseh Sherman as lieutenant-general. He could have done no less. Andrew Johnson had designated the eldest son of the foremost fighter of the nation a cadet " at large," and young Fred was pitched forthwith, neck and crop, into the military melting pot, where even paternal power could help him little with the officers, and not at all with the cadets. If anything, the troubles of the son of a Somebody were double those of the obscure and unknown—all the more had he to be taken down before he could enter on the plane of absolute equality demanded by that fiercely democratic autocracy—the Battalion of Cadets. Grant the general, who more deeply, tenderly and passionately than most men loved his wife and children, left Grant the son to the tender mercies of a lot of young fellows, many of whom, like gallant Griffith, Schenck, Hoxie, Sears, Davis and Morton, had fought valiantly under him in the Army of the West, were practically his appointees, and yet could no more depart from the stern traditions of the corps than could their instructors diverge from the standards of the Academy. That Fred's later career as a cadet was "eased up" in a measure was something the General never learned until long after. Possibly, as was the case when Mr. Lincoln would have welcomed the escape of Jefferson Davis if it could be accomplished "unbeknownst to him," the General, remembering his own failures in French, would have welcomed any legitimately-afforded lift his son might be so lucky as to receive, but Grant would never suggest or second it. The Academy passed that summer from the control of the Engineers, as has previously been recorded, to that of the line, and late in August, Halleck's right bower and chief-of-staff, the very Captain Cullum who had so heartily written his congratulations to Grant after Donelson, subordinately and silently turned over the control to the Captain Pitcher (both now uniformed as brigadiers), who, in May, '61, had mustered into service the Twenty-first Illinois, with Sam Grant at their head. There were sad and sore hearts among Grant's old friends and professors that day. There was, on the other hand, exuberant rejoicing among some of his gallant comrades of Worth's old division—the men of Molino and Monterey. It was the work of Congress, not of Grant, but he fell in with it, and there followed a brief term of years in which the tone and the discipline of the Academy suffered in consequence.

The death and burial of Winfield Scott, Grant's commander at the gates of Mexico and his illustrious predecessor in the generalship, occurred during the first week in June. Possibly it was this event which called him thither, but a confidential wire from Washington summoned him back within another day. The President had determined that, as Grant would not order the army to interfere in certain civil matters, he must have at its head some soldier more pliant and sympathetic. It was quite in his power to give orders direct to the army, but he was shrewd enough to see that a storm of disapprobation would be sure to follow, and he preferred that this should break upon Grant, not himself, for Mr. Johnson was planning for a second term, and General Grant, while shutting his eyes and ears to all suggestion, was inevitably looming up as the choice of the people. Johnson sought to make Grant the catspaw —to persuade him to order that which he himself had the sagacity to withhold, and then to place the odium upon the shoulders of Grant. The scheme failed. Grant would obey orders, but no suggestions. Finding it impossible to use him in this way, Johnson bethought himself of another. Grant had ever felt that the government owed reparation to Mexico for the wrongful war of '46. Mexico was now striving to repel another aggression, that of the Emperor of the French in his effort to seat Maximilian upon a Mexican throne. Mr. Johnson planned to send Grant as a diplomatic agent into Mexico, and to seat Sherman in his stead at Washington.

But again he failed. Grant flatly refused the " mission." He would obey any legitimate order as a soldier, he said, but this was diplomacy and beyond his province.

22   337

It further failed because wary Sherman as flatly refused to be party to any move toward ousting Grant. He came to Washington, as directed, but went at once to Grant; lived under his roof; stood shoulder to shoulder with him against the project. Refusing to supplant his general in command, he most adroitly suggested entire willingness to go in his stead to Mexico, and the President was caught in his own trap. Sherman went, and Grant remained to hold the fort.

The deplorable and memorable breach between the President and his War Secretary—bequeathed to him from Mr. Lincoln's administration—was the next serious episode involving Grant. Firmly and flatly Mr. Stanton, with Congress and the North behind him, had battled against the presidential project of immediate universal restoration of the South to full power. Johnson therefore sought to rid himself of Stanton. Congress saw to it that Stanton stayed. The tenure of office act, prepared and passed for this very emergency, balked the President, who, failing to induce the secretary to resign, would gladly have dismissed him. When Congress adjourned, however, after its stormy session of that summer of '67, Stanton was promptly suspended and Grant designated *ad interim* to serve in his stead. This was military duty and could not be evaded. In taking over the temporary duties Grant retained command of the army, keeping the offices entirely separate, spending a portion of each day in that of the secretary and a portion in that of the general. He also, at the outset, wrote to assure the Secretary, with whom he had been acting as much in accord as any man could with Stanton, of his full "appreciation of the zeal, patriotism, firmness and ability" with which Stanton had discharged the duties of Secretary of War, and Mr. Stanton, who well knew that Grant could not refuse to act as ordered, nevertheless seemed to think that he should have refused, in his reply to Grant rather implied that Grant was in accord with the President, which was by no means the case.

In accepting the duty imposed upon him, Grant behaved toward the Secretary with far more tact, courtesy and consideration than the Secretary had ever behaved toward him. As has been said, the moment Grant got back to Washington after the surrender of Lee, Stanton began giving him orders and instructions which as Secretary of War he had power to, but in which the General should have been consulted. Stanton had an exasperating way of sending a messenger for Grant, whose office as general of the army was across the way from the old War Department, thereby compelling him to drop his own work, don his coat and overshoes (this was before the days of Shepherd and crossable streets), plod over, climb stairs, and silently submit to criticism of acts or recommendations—not that Stanton had reason to find fault with them, but because he had the right and wished Grant to feel it. And so it is well remembered that after Johnson's total failure to force the bellicose Secretary from the Cabinet (the Senate refusing to concur in that *de*nomination), and Grant refusing longer to occupy the secretarial chair, Stanton's very first act on reseating himself therein was to send the War Department messenger across the way with the curt intimation that he needed at once to see General Grant.

And in refusing to remain in the office to which he had been ordered *ad interim,* Grant precipitated the rupture which ended at once and for all time his personal relations with Andrew Johnson and no less than three of his cabinet—notably Secretaries Seward and Welles. The President claimed that Grant had promised to hold that undesired office " until a successor could be appointed." Grant knew that Stanton, by the decision of the Senate on the 13th of January, had become, as it were, his own successor, and reminded the President that on Saturday the 11th he had assured him that " on no account " could he consent to hold the office " after the Senate should act." All that Saturday the President argued, urged and temporized, but Grant was firm in his stand. They parted with the President saying he would see Grant again, and Monday brought his mandate to the General to attend a cabinet meeting. Grant had already locked the office, handed over the key to the adjutant-general and gone to his own desk—that of the General-in-chief at headquarters of the army—when the message came. Obediently he repaired to the council chamber in the White House, but the instant the President addressed him as " Mr. Secretary " Grant protested. Then came the direct issue of veracity, and Grant, who never lied in his life, stood accused of a breach of faith by the highest, if not the best, authority in the land.

From that time forth Ulysses Grant never spoke to Andrew Johnson, nor to the Secretaries who rather ruefully and reluctantly, perhaps, supported the President in his contention; and Mrs. Grant, making, as she ever did, the General's cause her own, struck from her visiting list the names of four distinguished households.

And that breach was even more momentous than at first it might have seemed. It brought Grant into direct personal and political antagonism with the President; it made him the leader of the opposition—the candidate of the Republican party for President of the United States.

From the collection of F. H. Meserve

JULIA DENT GRANT IN 1866

Be this as it may, the spring of '68 found the General-in-chief at last committed to the project, and now, true to the Ulysses of old, having put his hand to the plough, his face was fixed upon the goal—having given that hand to the work before him it was to be done with all his might. And so it resulted that in May, '68, on the banks of the beautiful river of the middle West, only a short ride from that picturesque birthplace, only an hour away from the fields where, while yet a laughing urchin, he first rode into prominence, only twenty-four miles as the crow flies from the scene of his first boyish battle, and from that of the first admonition as to silence he ever laid upon his father, the Republican convention in session at Cincinnati unanimously ratified that old-time prophecy of the wandering phrenologist, and the lad who had never wished to be a soldier, yet had risen to be the greatest in the nation, the cadet who had blushed at his own vision of himself standing in the place of Scott, yet had lived to stand even higher—the young captain who had won such fame and commendation in his country's battles only to find himself defamed and condemned—the struggling, sickly farmer—the humble applicant for county office—the shabby, sorrowing, debt-burdened servitor in the village store—the unprotesting victim of a popular belief if not a personal habit, sustained through all by a woman's faith and devotion, and in spite of all, dauntless and confident of ultimate success, had risen step by step through the ordeal of battle to the topmost round of the ladder, for that nomination meant an overwhelming vote and his election in November to the presidency of the United States.

The chagrin of Mr. Johnson at this juncture was only exceeded by the calm (some called it the self-complacency) of the president-elect. As placidly as he received the surrender of Buckner, of Pemberton, even of the magnificent Lee, Grant now accepted the highest honors attainable in our country. From every State and from almost every community they came thronging upon him—the authorized delegations or the self-constituted delegates—to tender homage and congratulation, coupled, as frequently happened, with incidental suggestion as to appointments to office. Men high in the world of politics, men schooled in diplomacy and statesmanship, men skilled in the arts of flattery and dissimulation, men inspired by hope or curiosity came flocking to see him to suggest, and especially, if possible, to secure his promise as to public policy or personal or political patronage. And now there dawned upon the astonished vision of men hitherto sought and consulted a president-soon-to-be who asked no advice, who sat, smoked, listened, but spake not. To an extent little suspected until toward the very last, Grant had the faculty of hearing, of remembering all that was said, and, without giving a sign that he was so doing, of pondering long over everything said and forming his own conclusions. And now the men whom Lincoln had been wont to send for and consult—not so much that he needed their advice as that it made them think so, and therefore won their support—found themselves no longer in request, and when they came and sought to advise, found themselves heard in unresponsive silence. What seemed most to sting the statesmen was the fact that Grant still sought and cherished the society of soldiers. Ever about him were the men, tried and true, with whom he had borne the heat and burden of many a day in battle, and on whom he seemed now to lean, whereas he was not leaning at all.

Senators and representatives, office-holders and delegations, receiving no promise and in many cases no response as result of their suggestions, went away swearing he listened only to " swashbucklers " about him. This was one of Senator Sumner's bitterest complaints. As a matter of fact, he was listening to everybody and talking to nobody. It was not long before his soldier associates were becoming almost as sore-hearted as so many senators. Some few there were, like Ingalls and Horace Porter, who knew him well enough to know that he was carefully observing, deeply thinking and profoundly planning. Previous to the election, as though anxious to avoid the allurements and entanglements at Washington—the things Sherman so dreaded —he had cut loose from the capital, as he had when he marched away from Bruinsburg and into Mississippi, and had betaken himself to his old home at Galena, where he might reflect and think. Here he had received the notification of his election and made that modest reply. Then he had to return to his desk at Washington, where, though importuned every living minute by seekers innumerable, he pursued his relentless way, giving no hint whatsoever of his intentions or policies, even to men who had been his stanchest friends—even to two who might almost be called his benefactors—Rawlins and Washburne. Washburne felt so grieved that it well-nigh made him ill. Rawlins felt so hurt that it actually made him ill, and he took his leave and went Northward, cherishing a grievance against the man he had so devotedly served.

Former presidents-elect had consulted party leaders by the score as to portfolios, policies and the all-important inaugural address. The time was nigh when the announcements must be made, the names of the cabinet given to the press for dissection and to the Senate for confirmation, and not a syllable had been extracted from this soldier sphinx at Washington. Badeau, his military secretary, was with him hourly, opened all his letters, and wrote at his dictation most of his replies. Badeau was as much in his confidence at this moment as any man on earth, and yet Badeau knew next to nothing. Grant well understood that he owed his selection to the overwhelming demand of the people

—not to their political file leaders. It is improbable that men like Seward, Chase, Sumner or Horace Greeley, as Badeau declares, would ever have chosen Grant for President. It was to the people to whom he was accountable and to them he would speak direct, and consult no intermediary. It was a course which robbed him of counsel and of friendships that might have been of priceless value. But he played the game as he liked to do when playing euchre, and " went it alone." What is most remarkable, he did not even confide in her whose admiration he still most ardently craved. She, too, was worrying over the situation, the silence of her husband, the clamors of the press, the veiled comments of " society," the constant questioning of their kindred. She could not induce him to talk of the cabinet or of the inaugural address, which seemed to fret her most of all. In common with the women of Galena she believed him incapable of making a speech, and urged him to consult Mr. Conkling, Mr. Logan, Mr. Washburne and other gentlemen of eloquence and re- nown, and he quizzically asked her was it their speech or his he was expected to deliver, and reminded her still laughingly that he had Jesse, Jr., to fall back upon— Jesse who was as ready as ever had been his grand- father to make a speech on any occasion. In her anxiety she broached the matter to others, and one day Grant's prospective brother-in-law, Mr Corbyn, entered the office and placed in his hands an elaborate address which Corbyn had concluded it his duty to write for him and conceived would be the very thing—an effusion which Grant directed Badeau to lock up and let no one see until after the inauguration. Never having consulted a soul that Badeau could hear of, Grant finally sat down one afternoon three weeks before the 4th of March, and wrote every word of the address he expected to deliver, then told Badeau to read it and give him the benefit of his criticism. No one else was to be per-

From a photograph by E. W. Kempter

PARLOR OF THE GALENA HOME AS PRESENTED TO GRANT AFTER THE CIVIL WAR

mitted to see or hear a word of it until the day before its delivery, and until the 3rd of March, at least, no one did.

A more amazing, exasperating, intractable president-elect the old-style politicians had never known, the press had never encountered. Two or three departures from his self-imposed rules he finally permitted, one for business and two for personal reasons. Casting about for a suitable Secretary of the Treasury, he had settled on Mr. A. T. Stewart, the great drygoods merchant of New York. In view of his immense business affairs Mr. Stewart was confidentially notified of Grant's intentions, and delightedly made all preparations to accept. Then there were Washburne and Rawlins, hurt and saddened by his silence. Washburne unquestionably had hoped to receive the office of Secretary of the Treasury, and so far from being gladdened, was aggrieved when Grant summoned him to say that he was to be Secretary of the Interior. Rawlins, who knew that a man of Washburne's eminence would surely be in the cabinet, and who reasoned that there could not be two from Illinois, had feared there could be nothing for himself. Grant loved to spring surprises on his friends and he began with Rawlins. The once stalwart chief-of-staff came at his bidding, wondering what might be in store for him. He entered the inner office, pallid and sorrowing. He came forth with sparkling eyes and springy step, restored temporarily, at least, to life and vigor, but with his lips sealed to the fact conveyed to him alone—that he was to be the Secretary of War. These three men, only, were notified of the eminence in store for them. To the rest of the world, even Julia Dent, his wife, Grant refused all information.

Up to the last the retiring President sought to hamper and worry him, but Stanton had " ceased from troubling," having resigned in disgust after the failure of the impeachment proceedings. Mr. Johnson sent Rose-

crans as minister to Mexico, knowing well that Grant
would never do so, for in common with other generals
who had personally failed, Rosecrans, as Badeau declared, had first joined the " War is a Failure " party,
headed by McClellan, and later had met Mr. Johnson
in all his measures.

Johnson shrewdly reasoned, therefore, that the president-elect might expose himself to criticism by seeking
to prevent the confirmation in the Senate. Grant never
seemed to notice what was probably meant as a studied
affront. Rosecrans went to his station; was received
with the honors due an accredited envoy of the United
States, and there his powers ended. Grant and Romero,
Mexico's greatest statesman, were bosom friends, and a
few lines from the military secretary to Romero had
apprised the latter that it might be advisable to await
the wishes of the new administration before executing
any important diplomatic business with the newly accredited minister.

The momentous day drew nigh, and still no whisper
of Grant's prospective appointments had escaped him,
no line as to his policies been accorded to even the
friendly powers in the greatest of the editorial chairs.
Even the New York *Times* and *Tribune* were in
the dark. Even Julia Dent, anxious, indeed agitated
at times, could extract no word from him. He absolutely refused to share her worry as to that inaugural
address—the manner of preparation and the awful
probabilities as to the delivery of which so constantly
were the subject of her thoughts and the burden of her
song. Then the great day arrived and, refusing to ride
in the same carriage, as custom prescribed, with his
predecessor, the silent man of the nation, calm and unruffled as in the storm of battle, stepped forward in the
face of the immense throng at the Capitol, turning his
back temporarily upon the circle of dignitaries seated on
the platform—Julia Dent, quivering with mingled pride

and dread, seated in their midst—drew from his pocket
his carefully penned pages, glanced casually over the
sea of faces before him, and in the midst of a silence—
a strained interest—almost indescribable, the soldier
who never yet had made a speech slightly lifted up his
voice and began. And then the anxiety on the face of
his wife gave way to bewilderment, then to amaze, for,
in confident tone audible to every one upon the crowded
platform the new Chief Magistrate of these United
States delivered to the very last word his brief, sensible,
spirited address; then, even while receiving impulsive
congratulations, made his way as speedily as possible
to where, fluttering with pride and amaze commingled,
the wife of his bosom stood the centre of a bevy of
friends, and at the first convenient moment quietly observed, "And now, my dear, I hope you're satisfied."

CHAPTER XXXV

PRESIDENT AND COMMANDER-IN-CHIEF

Of the cabinet with which President Grant started on his eight years' incumbency not one remained at the close. For this there were various reasons: As originally laid before the Senate and promptly, though not too willingly, confirmed by that august body, Mr. Washburne was named foremost as Secretary of State, Mr. Stewart as Secretary of the Treasury, Mr. Borie as Secretary of the Navy, Mr. Cresswell as Postmaster-General, Mr. Hoar as Attorney-General, and Mr. Cox as Secretary of the Interior. The Secretaryship of War had been held for some months by General Schofield, in succession to Stanton—one of the best appointments President Johnson ever made. Nor was it the last time the government at Washington availed itself of the statesmanship and soldierly qualities of which Schofield was so remarkable a combination. It was General Grant's desire to retain Schofield there for a few weeks until Rawlins could learn something of the intricacies of the office, then the latter was to enter upon his duties.

Washburne, failing to get the Treasury and caring nothing for the portfolio of the Interior, asked that he be named Secretary of State—to start, at least, as premier, then to be sent to France. It was ungenerous in Washburne to ask it, and unwise in Grant to assent, for the Senate little relished the idea of confirming a merely complimentary nomination, yet did it to show its abundant good will toward Grant. It was unusual, but so was pretty much everything else about that cabinet. Mr. Stewart, who entered confidently upon his duties, was presently pointed out to be ineligible under an old

352

HON. HAMILTON FISH
Secretary of State, 1869 to 1877
From the collection of F. H. Meserve

HON. ELIHU B. WASHBURNE
Temporary Secretary of State, March, 1869;
then Minister to France

law prohibiting the appointment to that office of "any one engaged in trade," and Mr. Stewart, to his supreme regret and that of Grant, was compelled to retire. The mortification to everybody concerned might have been avoided had Grant consulted men of experience beforehand—yet the Senate was supposed to contain men of experience, and the Senate had confirmed.

Then came Mr. Borie, of Philadelphia, who having been in conversation with his friend, General Grant, on the 3rd of March, was not a little amazed on the 5th to find himself placed at the head of the Navy. It was an undesired appointment and, had he earlier been notified, Mr. Borie probably would have had none of it; but now, rather than further embarrass the already embarrassed President, he decided to remain for a little time, and did so. Then came trouble as to Massachusetts: Mr. Hoar being the attorney-general, there was prompt remonstrance when Mr. Boutwell, also of Massachusetts, was named, *vice* Stewart, for the Treasury. Hoar was later sacrificed, the Senate refusing to confirm him to the Supreme Court. Mr. Wilson, of Iowa, also had declined a secretaryship, and Mr. Sumner, who had ardently hoped and longed to be Secretary of State, was given nothing at all. The first statesmen to fall away from Grant were therefore those of the old commonwealth of Massachusetts.

When Lincoln was elected he dared to designate as his cabinet ministers the men who were his foremost rivals for the leadership of the Republican party, notably Chase and Seward. When Grant followed he preferred no fellow leaders. What he thought he needed was a staff, and he chose the men personally acceptable to himself if not to the country. It is safe to say that after his experience as President he never would have done it.

It was, however, a stroke of supreme good fortune at this juncture, if not of genius, that prompted him

23   353

to tender the State Department to Hamilton Fish, of New York. Therein he won to his cause and that of the nation a gentleman and a scholar, a strong and judicious mind. In many another way, however, the composition of that cabinet had bred dissension. Mr. Hoar never fully forgave the President for letting him out. Mr. Stewart never ceased to complain that he had been humiliated and later ignored. Mr. Borie, whose personal friendship never wavered, positively refused to serve longer than a few months, and so the civil administration became clouded from the start.

And if this were not enough, there were other sources of grievance. Lincoln, Johnson and most of their immediate predecessors—even courtly Mr. Buchanan—had been easy of access to public men, but now, said these latter, " we can't get in without the countersign." " The White House is a military camp." " The President has his sentries set and his staff on duty." " It is difficult to get a word *with* him, it is impossible to get a word *out* of him." Mr. Sumner was one of the senators who later worked himself up into a fury over this " odious, insulting, degrading, aide-de-campish" surrounding of the presidential chair. The simple truth of the matter was that Grant desired to have at his beck and call some of the men upon whom he most relied in times of stress and danger. He had parted from his military staff on the 4th of March, yet arranged with his successor as commanding general, his ever devoted Sherman, that three or four of their number should be continued nominally on Sherman's staff, but practically as aides to the President. Two of them, Horace Porter and Babcock, were ever about his desk as private and presidential secretaries, and Porter's supreme capacity for guarding his chief and his secrets exasperated not a few men of influence who sought to reach both. Babcock lacked the poise and impenetrability of Porter, but for a time followed the lead as far as possible of his senior. Badeau had a room to himself, withdrawn from politics and politicians, and busied with Grant's military Memoirs. Comstock, the frigid and unbending, remained but a brief time, and gladly resumed duty with the Engineers. Surely a President should be allowed to choose his secretaries as he pleases, and had these men not originally been soldiers no offense might have been taken. As to the fifth in attendance, brother-in-law and former chum, Frederick Dent, the most capricious of congressmen could hardly have found fault with that simple-minded, affable, approachable and utterly unmartial soldier. The geniality and joviality of General Dent in fact became proverbial, but failed to mollify. There were still others with whom Grant speedily surrounded himself as obnoxious in senatorial eyes as were the staff. Doing his utmost to be courteous, attentive and patient in his dealings with delegations and individuals, especially from " the other end of the avenue " where gleamed the great Capitol, it was soon evident to everybody that the President preferred the society of the men whom he had known for years and upon whose loyalty and fidelity he could count unerringly.

Sherman had come to be head of the army, *vice* Grant, become commander-in-chief. Rawlins was in the war office and living close at hand. Rufus Ingalls had been assigned to duty not far away, and, together with Stewart Van Vliet, of Sherman's class—Van Vliet of the snow-white hair, the rubicund nose, the jovial personality, the resonant laugh—these, and other old cronies would often assemble in the late afternoon, for an old time, camp-fire " powwow " on the shaded south porch of the White House. Then there were two or three prominent and well-to-do citizens—men who drove the best roadsters about Washington, and Grant, who had abandoned riding, dearly loved to hold the reins over a thoroughbred trotter when, as some indignant committeeman would have it, he should have been closeted with him and giving attentive ear as to this collectorship or that post office.

Elected on the Republican platform, he affronted certain conventionalists by the adoption of democratic planks. While he would not set foot in a street car, he would saunter at evening about the streets, sometimes chatting with a friend, sometimes gazing into shop windows, but always smoking. While former presidents had accepted no invitations to dinner or similar attentions, he liked to dine with his cabinet, enjoyed evening visits at the homes of Washington friends, and often with Mrs. Grant, yet sometimes without her, was quite accustomed when he felt in the mood for a chat, to take his hat, light a fresh cigar, and sally forth without so much as a word to even Crook, the faithful Fifth Cavalry door keeper. Indeed the Fifth Cavalry were kept in evidence about the White House longer than even other army folk thought justifiable. That sterling Pennsylvania soldier, " Jule " Mason, had captained the bodyguard of the General-in-chief at City Point, and he and his famous troop had followed him to Washington, supplying the innumerable orderlies and messengers still maintained about the White House and War Department, and long months after Grant had become President, and the rest of the regiment had been chasing Ku Klux or fighting Cheyennes and Sioux. Then Sherman shipped the bodyguard to Wyoming and speedily followed their exit by prescribing his own to St. Louis. The atmosphere at Washington had become charged with elements the man of the march to the sea declared intolerable.

It had been Stanton's imperious way, as we have said, to send for Grant when he wanted to see him, sometimes when it was unnecessary. It became presently noticeable that the President considered such methods beneath him. When he wished to see and talk with a Secretary or Senator he saw no reason why he should not do it in the simplest way, by stepping out in search of him. When full of a subject and desirous of clinching his point, the President set about doing it just as he would send Sheridan off on a raid or Meade in to headlong assault—by going over and saying so. This trait scandalized Charles Sumner—one of the ablest men that ever sat in the Senate of the United States, and unquestionably the most arrogant and domineering. It was one of the early sorrows of Grant's administration that he could never win the support of Mr. Sumner, for whose scholarship and statesmanship he had conceived sincere regard. Feeling this admiration for Sumner, although he would not make him Secretary of State, well knowing that the secretary would promptly strive to be the master, he had not scrupled, when the San Domingo question was up for action, to step round to the Senator's house one evening and say that the President would like to speak with him a minute. As luck would have it, the great chairman of the senate committee on foreign relations was entertaining friends at dinner and expounding on some pet theme when interrupted by the butler's announcement. He could not deny himself to the chief magistrate, nor could he conceal his sense of offended dignity. He never forgave Grant for what in his simplicity the latter deemed an evidence of his desire to personally consult the views and wishes of the great leader. Grant never sought him again.

Sensitive to the core, though silent as the grave, as to slights and indignities, Grant would not speak of a wrong or injustice done him. He ceased to speak to the dealer, as in the case of Johnson and certain of his secretaries, and he soon had other difficulties, not of his own making. Yet Sumner saw fit in his bitter speech to refer to him as "the great quarreler," holding that the President had no right to quarrel with anybody. In spite, therefore, of the happiness it gave him to see Mrs. Grant's high content in her station as " first lady " and leader of social Washington; in spite of the pleasure it gave him to keep many an old friend about him and of making many a new, Grant was often glad to get away from Washington, and during the five years in which his first-born was struggling through the Military Academy, the President frequently appeared and temporarily took up his abode, dwelling with his wife and his winsome little daughter at the old hotel, and, except for sympathetic anxieties on account of Cadet Fred, enjoying himself hugely.

Fred had little of his father's gift for mathematics, all of his failing in French, and more than his indifference to regulations. The lad brought with him to the Academy the traditions and mannerisms of that famous fighting command, the Army of the Tennessee. He had picked up the vernacular of the camp and the free-and-easy methods of their campaigning, and it speedily developed that Fred was going to have a hard time getting through. Moreover, these were his callow days, and he had been somewhat spoiled by a fond mother and a doting sister. The stern old régime of the Point was changing. Mahan was breaking mentally, Bartlett and Church were visibly aging. The rigid discipline of the scholastic Engineers had given place to the more elastic ways of the line. In former days deficiency in any branch meant dissolution—the cadet dropped out entirely. When Fred proved totally deficient in French, the new administration, headed by stanch old friends of the President, pointed out that in spite of shortcomings in languages and laxity in deportment, the Grant of '43 had later made an unparalleled record in soldiership; had ten thousand times over repaid the people the cost of his education and keep at the Point, and that now the nation could well afford to take a chance as to the Grant of the future. Everybody really liked the young fellow. He was frank, cheery, good natured, as the father ever had been, yet by no means as "cadet-wise." Like his father, he appeared to best advantage in saddle. His figure was fine, his seat was firm, and he rode straight and well. The elders of the Academic Board who had schooled his father through, strove hard to carry the son, but even the scion of the chief magistrate had to bow to the inexorable ruling of the Point, and to fall back into a lower class when he could not keep up with his own. Finally, by the "skin of his teeth" and in spite of academic "skins" and sins innumerable, Fred managed to squirm through and be graduated with the class of 1871, and great was the rejoicing of the household of Grant and the laughing delight of the corps. With his fellows he had put on no airs whatsoever, and from the start had been, if anything, almost too "hail fellow well met." The younger brother of Rawlins had been appointed, and dropped as hopeless within the six months; the sons of famous and beloved generals and admirals had entered, failed and vanished. The President must have felt a sensation of infinite relief when early in June, '71, he came to the Point to see Fred graduated, for during that summer he seemed at his best.

He sat at table at the old West Point Hotel, with Mrs. Grant and a bevy of her friends about him; he bloomed in the sunshine of her smile and the presence of attractive women; he laughed delightedly over good stories (he never would listen to a bad one), and in spite of his aversion to French he saw the point and shouted with merriment when told that some one at an adjoining table, selecting *ris de veau* from the day's *menu,* complained that though supplied with the veal she was refused the rice, and that was what she most desired. He was tickled immensely over a story then current about his new war secretary, Belknap, of Iowa, who, in '71, was in the pride and heyday of his administration. Belknap had just married a beautiful young widow, Mrs. Bowers, and was deeply enamored. To the War Department at this time came General Robert Williams, one of the most courteous, consistent and dignified soldiers of the old school then left to the army— its exemplar, in fact, of punctilio and deportment. Williams, some years before, had wooed and won the lovely relict of the late Stephen A. Douglas, and was as devoted a husband as he was *debonair* a soldier. Genially, jovially accosting him, when the new adjutant came to pay his respects, Belknap shouted: " Hello, Williams! Glad to see you! How is Mrs. Douglas? " And with unflinching gravity and aplomb came the answer: " Very well, thank you, Mr. Secretary, and how is—er —Mrs. Bowers? "

In those days the West Point Hotel was managed by Theodore Cozzens, a genial host, while the big establishment perched on the cliff above Highland Falls, a mile below the Point, was presided over by his brother, Sylvanus. The iron-clad rules of the West Point Hotel prohibited the sale of wines or liquors, but Theodore in his private rooms in the basement kept a choice supply for his chosen friends, and thither the President repaired when he wished to chat in comfort, perchance over a glass of wine and a cigar. Much of the time of the presidency he was a total abstainer, turning down his wine glasses at table even at diplomatic dinners, but always providing the best he could buy for the guests whom he honored with invitations.

And this basement branch of the executive office led to the first personal meeting of the present writer with his great admiration, the President. It was a breathless evening, warm, dark and moonless, and a bevy of young girls and officers were gathered on the north piazza. A bright gleam of light from the hanging lamps and the open hallway illumined the broad flight of steps leading from the piazza to the terrace below, leaving everything to the right and left of the stairs in blackness and gloom. Some laughing remark had led to a playful attack on one of the party, and in effort to escape, he went bounding down the steep flight, five steps at a jump, and with all the impetus of the rush, collided forcefully with a sturdy form in sombre black, just rounding into view at the foot of the stairs. A silk hat went spinning down the lighted pathway, a burning cigar shot into space, the burly form recoiled from the sudden impact, and the subaltern at fault, springing on after the hat, recovered it, brought it back, carefully wiping it with his handkerchief and, all contrition and confusion, began his hurried apology to the black object slowly heaving once more into view. He had got as far as: " I beg ten thousand pardons, sir; it was most careless, but I declare I never met anybody coming round that corner before " (it was the turn to Theodore's private apartments)—and just then the light fell upon the bearded features of the lately battered, and there, fumbling in his pockets for a fresh cigar before resuming the restored hat, stood, all unruffled in spite of the recent concussion, the Chief Magistrate of the nation, and all that eminent personage had to say, either by way of rebuke or remission of sins, he condensed in three monosyllables and nine letters: "' Got a light?' " It almost put the sorely disturbed subaltern once more at his ease.

CHAPTER XXXVI

STORM AND STRESS

Brief indeed were the days of happiness allotted to Ulysses Grant as President of the United States. Stanch, strong and true as were many of his adherents, there seemed to be an ever-increasing clamor against him or against those about him. For every important office at his disposal he had found rival applicants in embarrassing numbers. In any event far more could be aggrieved than appointed, and the aggrieved, with their backers, returned from Washington filled with bitterness. No President, of course, escaped this condition of things, but in the case of Grant it was made worse by the undoubted prominence of many of the applicants, and the doubtful merit of so many of the appointees. Senator Sumner and his admirers believed that eminent statesman the logical successor of Mr. Secretary Seward in the Department of State. Mr. Sumner had more than once expected to supplant Mr. Seward during the days of Lincoln, had counted on becoming premier of the cabinet upon the impeachment of President Johnson, and the resultant elevation of Mr. Wade. Mr. Sumner had personally disapproved, but publicly supported, the election of General Grant, and then, as it were, presented through his emissaries his bill for services rendered, and the virtual demand for payment in shape of the portfolio of state. This, as we have seen, was given temporarily to the man who had done more for Grant than all the Senate combined; but, having given preference thus to a mere representative over a senatorial applicant, and that senator The Senator from Massachusetts, the act was unpardonable in the eyes of Mr. Sumner, who forthwith found in almost every appointment of President Grant a bit of bargain and sale business reprehensible in the last degree. It cannot be denied that General Grant's original cabinet was selected very much on the same principle which prompted his selection of a military staff.

Mr. Sumner and Mr. Fish had been strong personal and political friends until the latter was named for the very portfolio Sumner so craved for himself, and though their friendship and intercourse continued a few months longer, it could not stand the test of Sumner's imperious temper and his venomous pursuit of the President. Mr. Fish, a gentleman "to the manner born," bore with Sumner long after Mr. Sumner had broken with the President. Mr. Fish sorrowed for his old friend and associate of senatorial days and had long striven to comfort and sustain him. Like Mr. Lincoln, Senator Sumner was most unhappy in his domestic relations. Unlike Mr. Lincoln, he could not manfully bear his trouble; and when Mr. Fish found him sobbing like a child over his wounded feelings, and besought him to take a run to Europe for a time and get away from the scene of his struggles and his sorrows, he added impulsively: "How would you like to be minister to England?" Now, this was but a year after Grant's inauguration. Sumner, after first seeming to acquiesce in the President's views as to Samana Bay and San Domingo, had taken to violent opposition. To the amaze and indignation of both General Grant and Mr. Secretary Fish, the papers were presently accusing them of seeking to bribe Senator Sumner to change his vote or his views. The authority for the statement was Mr. Sumner himself, the base of it Mr. Fish's impulsive and unauthorized proposition as to the mission to the Court of St. James. The next three years of Grant's first administration found the Chairman of the Committee on Foreign Relations in constant opposition to the President and the Secretary of State. The close of the first term found Senator Sumner Grant's most vehement opponent for a second nomination and election. The people by a solid majority vindicated Grant, and the Senate deposed Sumner from that all-important chairmanship. It broke the power, if indeed it did not break the heart, of Sumner, who speedily fell ill, and within the second year of the second term had succumbed to *angina pectoris*. When it is remembered that the basis of the Treaty of Washington, as proposed and insisted upon by Senator Sumner, was " the withdrawal of the British flag from this hemisphere—including the provinces and islands," one can well appreciate the descriptive of " far-reaching " as applied to his statesmanship. It is idle to speculate over what John Bull might have said and done had Sumner prevailed. It is singular that the apostle of peace in our country is sometimes author of a policy which can result only in bitter war.

The outcry against and opposition to Grant toward the close of his first term took shape in calumny of every kind in the public press, in assaults upon his honor, integrity and intentions, with Senator Sumner as head and front of the move in Congress. Pretty much everything said in the papers was but amplification of what Mr. Sumner said in the Senate. Let us briefly consider this:

Paraphrasing Lord Durham, Mr. Sumner had demanded the downfall of this " odious, insulting, degrading, aide-de-campish, incapable administration." Odious, insulting and degrading it might have seemed to Sumner, but the citizens at large did not so find, and declared against him. " Aide-de-campish " it may have been, though not to the extent practised openly in later years. No one hitherto seemed to have questioned the right of a President to choose his private secretaries. An officer is no less a citizen because of his soldiership.

In point of fact, he is more of a citizen since he can be expected and required to act as the government wishes—something the sovereign citizen often flatly declines. Surely the secretaries selected were as brainy and efficient as any of Grant's acquaintance who could be chosen from civil life. Moreover, they did the work on their army pay and saved to the state the salaries provided for civil incumbents. The papers, of course, made no mention of, and possibly saw no merit in, that. As for the politicians, it was simply a case of so much pay and patronage wasted.

The crux of that complaint may be found in the fact that most private and presidential secretaries, known to Washington society before the days of Grant, had been nominees or possibly pupils of men prominent in political life—schooled in the ways of, and in the observance demanded by, politicians. Even when men were chosen, as were John Hay and Nicolay by Mr. Lincoln, because of brains and qualifications of their own, there was sure to be a criticism, but Lincoln in his inimitable way could placate the complainant. One irate war governor who appealed to him, indignant at being detained a few minutes by Mr. Hay until the President could dispose of an importunate caller, furnishes a case in point. Lincoln listened all patience and apparent sympathy, then disarmed, or at least mollified, his angry visitor by the whimsical point of his reply: "Governor, you and I are in the same boat, and we will have to help each other out. Do you know that that young man has had to act for me and think for me so often, and has helped me so much, that the chances are that he sometimes thinks he *is* the president, and, Governor, I let him think so."

It was no more consolatory, perhaps, than Mr. Lincoln's response to the influential statesman who came to lodge furious complaint against General Sherman for threatening to hang a certain constituent of his if ever again that constituent showed himself within the lines of the Army of the Tennessee—" That is serious; that is *indeed* serious," said Lincoln, reflectively. " I know that fellow Sherman. He's a man of his word. Take my advice, Senator, and tell your friend to give him a wide berth, for if he said he'll hang him, he'll do it."

But Lincoln had been gifted as Grant had not, and the latter when assailed promptly showed fight or else stood mute. With the press he was widely at odds almost from the start, with the odds on the side of the press, the President and his defenders being confined to mere statement of facts. It mattered little now that he might be the most abstinent of men, that he had not always been so gave abundant opening for reportorial flights. It mattered little that Grant's admirations, those swift pacers or trotters, were the property of men high in business or professional standing, his old-time love for a good horse led to the newspaper claim that his boon companions were " horse jockeys " and " swaggering dragoons."

There was not a symptom of swagger about the four officers on duty: Badeau wore spectacles and a crippled foot, Dent a perpetual smile, Babcock the look rather of the politician than the soldier (and in due season developed some of the characteristics), and none of them wore uniform. As for Porter—Porter, with his inscrutable face, his consummate poise and *sang-froid*—Porter who, with sepulchral gravity, could say the most side-splitting things—Porter was a joy perennial to his chief and a tower of strength to his administration, but the fact remained that they were all four of the army and that was enough in the eyes of the fault-finders. Four long years Porter stood by his General, but at the close of the first administration he had the deep sagacity to look to the future and accept a more lucrative and far less hazardous employment.

"More reprehensible . . . more illegal than anything alleged against Andrew Johnson," declared Mr. Sumner, in his famous assault upon the President, and yet the only acts of alleged illegality as against the array charged to Johnson, was General Grant's tentative in sending a staff officer (Babcock) to sound the San Domingo officials as to a future connection with the United States. That Babcock should have announced himself as "aide-de-camp to the President," and should have had one of our prehistoric tubs from the navy to paddle him about the islands of the Antilles, were both ill-advised—not that there was anything much amiss in the use of either the title or the ship, but that Sumner made it so appear. And people of the good old Bay State, who long had sat and worshipped at the feet of Sumner, were now aghast at the revealed depravity of the general of their admiration, thus become exposed as a military despot. The legislature of his State, however, did not so comprehensively swallow Mr. Sumner's slander, and notwithstanding his eminence, resented his joining hands with the "anything-to-beat-Grant" element, and actually passed a vote of censure.

But there were two charges made by Mr. Sumner which the soldiers about Grant could not effectively combat, and against which Rawlins, in part at least, is known to have warned him—the acceptance of gifts and the appointment of relatives to office. As to the former there was absolutely no reason why Grant should have declined the gifts in the way of boxes of cigars, brands of tobacco, pipes of briar or meerschaum and all manner of little things that came from genuine and admiring friends. There was no reason why he should not have accepted the house and homestead tendered him by a grateful community, and having accepted one, was there reason why he should decline to accept those of others? The great trouble growing out of it all was that some gifts were not as innocuous, and some givers not as disinterested as others. Mr. Borie, of Philadelphia, was probably one of the subscribers, and possibly one of the prime movers, in the purchase of the Philadelphia homestead, and Senator Sumner did not scruple to declare Mr. Borie's appointment as Secretary of the Navy a *quid pro quo* on the part of Grant; whereas Mr. Borie never sought, never wanted, and speedily rid himself of that portfolio, and accepted it only to save Grant from temporary embarrassment.

Most of the gifts lavished upon Grant were just such as successful generals had accepted without reproach in days gone by, but Grant's came in swarms and continued after his nomination and election. Washington, under similar circumstances, had loftily declined, but these gifts gave infinite pleasure to that power behind our silent soldier's sword—his wife—and what Julia Dent very much approved, Grant could seldom deny. But that he did at times assert himself, and oppose her, was apparent in his declination of the third nomination suggested toward the close of the second term. Mrs. Grant ardently hoped and prayed that her husband would accept a third term, confidently believing it could be his. Sherman, Badeau and certain of his military counsellors, at least, were set against it. So were the wisest of his civil advisers—Secretary Fish, especially.

As to that charge of "nepotism" which Sumner exploited and the press had long proclaimed, it must be owned that to a degree achieved by the kith and kin, by blood or marriage, of no other occupant of the presidential chair, the relatives of Ulysses Grant succeeded in scrambling somehow into place. Early in his career as a general, as we have seen, they essayed to "work" him in the West. Once fairly installed at the White House it appears that he had not to be importuned, nor were the chosen ones to be charged in many cases to Mrs. Grant. There were brothers-in-law, nephews and cousins; and two of the brothers-in-law, at least, were given highly important posts. The claim that no less than thirteen—some newspapers put it at forty—of the President's appointees were family connections, injured him far more than their gratitude, if given, could ever have aided, and some of the results were injurious to the last degree.

" The New Orleans Custom House," declared Mr. Sumner, in open senate, " has a story much worse. Here presidential pretension is mixed with unblushing corruption in which the collector, a brother-in-law, is a chief actor."

It so happened, oddly enough, that the writer was brought into official and personal relations with this particular brother-in-law. Time and again during the year 1870–71 there came to West Point from New Orleans boxes for Cadet Fred, which, as regulations required, that young gentleman had to open in presence of the " officer in charge," and some forbidden or contraband luxuries not infrequently appeared therein, and had to be thrown out. The year after Fred's graduation this occasional " officer in charge " found himself in New Orleans as aide-de-camp to the general commanding the Department of the Gulf. Those were lively days in Louisiana. Two rival legislatures were in session, riots were frequent, wars and rumors of wars kept the wires hot and the aide-de-camp bearing messages between his general and the governor and the collector in question. It took less than half an eye to see that the latter was but a catspaw, a bewildered tool, in the hands of half a dozen shrewd and designing men. The *coup d'état* to which Mr. Casey lent himself in bidding a baker's dozen of the obstructive but legally-chosen legislature to dinner aboard the revenue cutter, and spiriting the entire party off to an undesired cruise in the Gulf of Mexico, proved a " boomerang " at Washington. These legislators were imperatively needed for

24   369

the passage of certain acts opposed by the "Custom House" faction, and this enforced absence, contrived by the aid of Mr. Casey, became in the hands of the congressional investigating committee, promptly sent to the scene, nothing short of abduction and kidnapping. The pitiable exhibition made by the collector in his examination by the Hon. Mr. Spear—a most suggestive name—was something no witness to the scene could soon forget. If ever man had cause at that time to echo the prayer, "Heaven save me from my friends," it was President Grant. The sorrows of his two administrations, the scandals of the "Star route" affair, the thunderclap that came to the War Secretary as well as to the President in the sudden charge of bribery and corruption (accepted in silence because that genial and *debonair* official proved far more of a man than the original Adam), the innumerable aspersions and calumnies—far too often were grounded in some one of the friends the unsuspecting President had favored. His own rectitude and fidelity stood unconquerable, no matter by whom assailed, to the triumphant yet sorrowful end.

In spite of all the alleged mismanagement the nation throve, the country prospered, the debt was greatly lessened, the people reasoned for themselves, and though many fell away from their allegiance, more stood firmly by the soldier-leader of their original choice. The responsibilities of the office, as he said, he had felt, yet never feared. The statesmanship which fathered the treaty of Washington, the settlement in favor of the United States of the Alabama claims, and the veto against such numbers, even of his own party, of the inflation act, will compare favorably with that which is ascribed to even the most gifted of our Presidents—something which Grant never thought himself to be. He found the country in turmoil when he took the reins;

he left it as he hoped, and in his inaugural he had
prayed, almost at peace.

But though that second term had come to him as
a vindication of the first, it closed in such a cloud of
calumny that he was glad to leave it; and Julia Dent,
loyal to his wishes when once announced, stifling her
own disappointment, graciously put everything about
the White House in order for her successor-to-be, prepared for the newcomers a welcome luncheon on their
arrival from the ceremony of inauguration, tactfully
took the arm of Mr. Hayes and led him to what was to
become his own table, and then, when the bright and
cheery repast was ended, as tactfully took her leave,
the arm of her own soldier-husband, and gracefully
retired from the scene of her social triumphs.

CHAPTER XXXVII

FOREIGN TRAVEL AND FINAL RETURN

YET in spite of those social successes there had been family anxieties and cares. The hearts of both father and mother were bound up in their winsome daughter. The child had been the object of no little attention everywhere; and now, even before she had donned the long garb of young ladyhood, attentions of more pressing nature were being lavished upon her. Several rivals were in the field. Mrs. Grant took alarm. The Bories were going to England, and she besought them to take Nellie with them and away from these young gallants who sought to woo and win her.

It was a case of fleeing from one evil to others we know not of. Several months were they gone and, on the homeward voyage, Princess Nellie met a young Englishman of excellent family, who proceeded to devote himself. The voyage was rough, the Bories were poor sailors and kept below. Proximity did the rest. The joyous welcome to home and White House took on a tinge of anxiety when Mr. Algernon Sartoris presently called, and it became obvious in spite of all precautions that love had laughed at locksmiths, that Nellie's heart was lost to this handsome young Briton. What it meant to the President no man was ever told. From the first, however, it is known that he looked upon the suit with apprehension if not aversion. Yet at the time no valid objection could be urged. Sorely against his will, the mother and daughter persuaded him to hear Mr. Sartoris. The young man was bidden to dinner and later invited to the billiard room, was tendered a cigar, and then the two were left alone, Grant in grim silence sitting and studying the abashed

372

and nervous suitor. There was, as Badeau tells it, only one way out of it: "Mr. President, I want to marry your daughter," said Sartoris, and so the ice was broken.

It was a beautiful wedding, say all the chroniclers, but men nearest the President could never forget the foreboding and sorrow in his face. From the very first he seemed to dread, even to foresee the outcome. But his beloved daughter and her mother had made up their minds and he could name no reason for refusal. Welcomed and beloved by all in her young husband's home, almost as in her own where she was idolized, our Princess had that at least to sustain and cheer her when, before very long, convinced that her father's fears had been too well founded.

Once away from the White House, spending a month or more as the guests of Mr. and Mrs. Fish, the Grants found themselves again the object of almost universal adulation. The wave of popular sentiment returned in full volume. The few mistakes, the many calumnies, of the eight years' reign were forgotten. Once again Grant was the great soldier of the nation, their hero, their foremost citizen, and he who had been so saddened by the manifold attacks was amazed to find the very papers that had assailed him as President, now lauding him as the typical American. He was going abroad. He was about to spend two or three years in travel and observation, and all the United States seemed bent on saying to Christendom and the far Orient, "This is a man, our most honored son and soldier; bid him welcome befitting his soldiership, his services, and his exalted station—the foremost republican of the foremost republic," and practically the world obeyed.

The departure from Philadelphia was an ovation the like of which even Grant never before had experienced, the voyage a joy to him. The landing in England, the public receptions in Liverpool, Manchester, Sheffield and so on, the deputations and addresses of the British workingmen, all proved a revelation. It dawned upon him of a sudden that to an extent never before accorded an American he was being received with honors and ceremonies approximating those prescribed for royalty.

Badeau, who for long years had been his close attendant at home, was there to meet and escort him. Badeau was then consul-general and thoroughly conversant with the ceremonial etiquette which hedges every approach to the throne. Badeau looked to see his shy and simple-mannered general of the sixties a trifle abashed and nervous, and was delighted to find him placid and self-poised. Badeau wondered what might be the outcome when the mayor and corporation at the great banquet at the Guild Hall should toast the guest of honor, and Badeau could hardly believe his ears when the speechless soldier of yore calmly arose, faced that brilliant assemblage and spoke freely, fluently and well. From that time forth our former President had found himself, as it were, and the faculty of terse and even felicitous expression of his views, no matter how public the occasion or how vast his audience. Badeau felt less concern, but some curiosity, as to the outcome of the ceremonial visit to the Queen at Windsor. General Grant was not the first of the family to be received. Her Majesty had been graciously pleased to welcome winsome Nellie " and the lady accompanying her " to Buckingham Palace, and now that the General had been the honored guest of the Prince of Wales, of Lord Beaconsfield and others, and Queen Victoria had finally returned from the Highlands to Windsor, a visit was arranged for General and Mrs. Grant.

It has all been told inimitably in Badeau's Memoirs, and variously described in the press. The customs of royalty and those of republics are so much at variance that it is difficult for the American mind to take a tolerant view of the Old World etiquette involved in this and certain other functions in honor of our foremost citizen. Yet, during the presidency of Washington, of Buchanan, of Grant and certain of Grant's successors, questions of precedence and ceremonial have come up in which our American sovereigns have been quite as tenacious as ever were court chamberlain or imperial master of ceremonies abroad. General Grant, who at first scoffed at White House formalities, white ties and " swallow-tails," became speedily a stickler for exact and punctilious arrangement of guests at every dinner or reception. President Grant declined to call upon Prince Arthur of Connaught—third son of Victoria of England—or to return the call of the Grand Duke Alexis, son of the Czar of all the Russias. Such a call, he reasoned, would be a recognition of royalty which the head of a democratic nation should avoid, and so when in turn he visited foreign territory, although all England arose to receive him, and the band played " Hail Columbia " at his approach, the Duke of Connaught would not come up from Aldershot to call upon Grant, and when Fred, the son of our President, appeared in the suite of General Sherman, and was presented to the Czar, that monarch, remembering the Washington incident which had given him such annoy, stiffly acknowledged the lieutenant's confidently good-natured salutation with, " I hope you are well, sir," and turned back to talk with Sherman, thereby reversing the proceedings of the head of the Ottoman empire, who descended from his throne, took Fred by the hand, led him up to a seat alongside, and left General Sherman to his ministers.

There is something really comical about the episode at Windsor. Baby Jesse, the family pet and prodigy, by that time a genuine American youth of nineteen, had accompanied his father and mother to Windsor, but when he found that only General and Mrs. Grant were to sit with Her Majesty at dinner—that General

375

Badeau and himself were to be assigned to a table with the lords and ladies of " the Household," *our* third son was up in arms at once, refused to sit with "the servants," and declared he would go back to London instanter if the plan were not changed. The fact that even the premier of England, even ambassadors and visiting members of the government always dined with "the Household" unless specially bidden to sit with the Queen—the fact that our American minister plenipotentiary and his distinguished wife were present and were not to sit with Her Majesty, had no mollifying effect upon our representative of Young America. Jesse stood squarely upon his rights as having been invited by the Queen to Windsor.

Here as elsewhere, what his wife or children demanded, had its weight with Grant. Badeau was sent to the Master of the Royal Household, and that courteous gentleman waited at once upon the Queen. Her Majesty, doubtless much diverted, heard of the young gentleman's ultimatum, and was pleased to order that he be assigned to her table, and then amused the General, who was in no wise fluttered by the incident or by the royal presence, by a most gracious manner. " She seemed to be trying to put me at my ease," he laughed to Badeau, later.

Perhaps the most amusing incident of the memorable evening, however, was when Her Majesty, striking a congenial topic, spoke to Mrs. Grant of the manifold cares which beset her as sovereign of the British Empire, and was promptly met with, " Oh, yes, I can imagine them; I, too, have been the wife of a great ruler." It is remembered that Mrs. Grant was a most difficult person to patronize in the least at Washington, and it is well within the bounds of reason to believe that Julia Dent considered the wife of Ulysses Grant, lately chief magistrate of the American nation, as quite the social equal of the Sovereign Queen of Great Britain and Ireland; moreover, that she rather rejoiced in an opportunity of expressing her views to that effect.

All the same, though other former presidents had visited England, none had been received with the honors and distinction accorded General Grant. Once only was there a slight, the offender being the Earl of Dudley, a peer who lacked the breeding of our tanner's son, and who could never have won from the lips of England's great divine and orator the tribute which publicly he paid to Grant.

In Belgium, however, the king and queen received General and Mrs. Grant in every sense as equals—the king delighting our General by personally leading Mrs. Grant to dinner. In London *our* General and gentleman gravely excused himself from taking his place with royalty in the court quadrille, to which he, but not Mrs. Grant, had been invited. In Belgium, in France, he could find no possible flaw in the honors accorded the " first lady " of his land and the only one of his heart. There the reception given them both was perfect in every detail, and Grant's happiness in her happiness was complete.

The expenses of the first administration had exceeded the presidential pay. Congress raised the salary in time for the second term, so that Grant had some thousands of dollars to provide for a long and protracted tour abroad. Then Ulysses, Jr., had married into millionaire circles in the far West, and had invested a few other thousands for his father. Those were the " bonanza " days, and Ulysses, Jr., was enabled to hand over to his father something like fifty thousand dollars in profit. Grant felt rich, free from care, full of content and health, and all through those delightful days in Switzerland and Italy he seemed renewing his youth. He could not, however, enjoy the glorious scenery, or endure the incessant music, except at the side of his wife. If any one else, even temporarily, took the seat

by Mrs. Grant in car or carriage the ride was spoiled
for him, and she, grandmother though she was, rejoiced in her dominion and openly and triumphantly
coquetted with him. It was a far cry from the palaces
of Windsor and of Buckingham, from the Elysée and
the honors of a queen, to the shaded porch of White
Haven and the arching foliage of the old Gravois road,
but the woman's heart within her beat in the fulness
of pride and joy that the "little lieutenant in the big
epaulets" who had become the greatest soldier of his
day, and the acclaimed ruler of sixty millions of people,
was to the very zenith of his fame and to the end of the
life accorded him her constant lover and devoted admirer.

Two years they journeyed leisurely through Europe
and the Orient, Grant especially impressed with what he
saw in China and Japan. Then homeward across the
blue Pacific they came, and California rose at their
approach and flocked to the Golden Gate to give them
welcome such as even California never yet had given
mortal man. It was in the fall of 1879, and it was a
year before the presidential campaign.

The close election in November, '76, and the subsequent administration of President Hayes had combined to make the Republican party doubtful of the
issue in 1880. Its old-time leaders believed there was
just one man capable of re-arousing the desired sentiment, and that was Grant. If only they could keep him
abroad until the psychological moment—hold him away
from our shores until just before the convention—the
blaze of enthusiasm which would surely kindle at his
coming would sweep the entire country and consume
all possible opposition. It is probable that, better managed, the scheme would have succeeded. It is hazarded
that had they sent some gifted emissary to lay the plan
before Mrs. Grant and induce her to persuade him that
there were still people and places that she might wish

to see (for he indeed would gladly have visited Australia), he surely would have yielded to her wishes. Thus the managers could have tided over that fateful winter and spring of 1879–80, and then, at the last moment, along in May, permitted him to reach our western shores, to receive his tumultuous and tremendous ovation, and, proclaiming him at Chicago as the one obvious and logical leader of the whole people, declare him the candidate of the Republican party for reelection to the presidency of the United States.

It might not have gone by acclamation as it did in Cincinnati in '68, but the chances are that it would have prevailed, and that, rather than humiliate their great leader, even many who opposed on principle a third term would have cast their vote and elected him.

But, Grant returned too soon. The enthusiasm and excitement died away. The scheme for his renomination became public, and instantly its opponents set to work against it. Ardently as Julia Dent desired to reign again in Washington; undoubtedly as Grant himself would now have been glad to return to office, refreshed by years of rest and reinforced by the opportunities of seeing for himself the rulers and the nations of the known world; unquestionably as he was far better fitted for the presidency than ever he had been before, even devoted personal friends disapproved the project, and—it was not to be. Far too many sturdy citizens held to the republican doctrine that eight years in that high office should be the uttermost limit accorded any one man, no matter what his character and qualifications, no matter what the eminence of his past. Grant, with his old Guard, the immortal three hundred and seven " Stalwarts," came nearer a third term than any other aspirant ever has or probably ever will. He in whose sight a thousand years are but as yesterday had reserved him for one more supreme test and sublime humiliation before according the final honors which overshadowed even those lavished on our martyred Lincoln.

They visited the Galena home a little while, but they had outgrown it. They spent some weeks in Chicago with Fred, now aide-de-camp to Sheridan, and with Fred's own little household. It would be untrue to say that Grant cared little for his defeat. Like any strong man he hated to be beaten and he felt that he was far better fitted for the office than ever he had been. Defeated, however, he was, and might now with entire propriety have sought retirement. He might, as others less injured have done, " sulked in his tent," but the party leaders who had compassed his defeat now had to beg of him and of Roscoe Conkling that they should help elect the successful candidate of the convention, or see the country fall into the hands of the opposing party. And he whom they had rejected turned to and worked for their success.

That luckless campaign, however, had embittered Grant against men high in public station, even one or two who had been his devoted friends—even Elihu Washburne. Unknown even to Mrs Grant, and at the urgings of John Russell Young, who had been his companion in the journeyings abroad, and who knew politics at home, Grant had written a letter warranting the withdrawal of his name as candidate, but that letter somehow was seen by only a chosen few, who pledged each other, probably, to secrecy.

Incensed with the men he thought had belittled him in permitting his name to be submitted when it was plain that the opposition was far too powerful, angered at the new president who, he believed, had slighted his wishes, and generally disheartened with politics for all time, Grant sojourned awhile in Mexico, spent summers at Long Branch, enjoyed the society of certain old friends and chums, and the growing belief that his investments with his banker-son were destined to make him a millionaire.

From the collection of F. H. Meserve

GRANT THE BANKER, 1883

Then President Garfield was shot, languished and died—a victim to our national laxity which thus far has cost us the lives of three of the best and kindliest of our chief magistrates and may yet cost us more—and Grant, who had mutely followed the pall of Lincoln, whom he honored and revered, of statesmen like Chase and Sumner, with whom he had seriously differed, appeared in the train of him he had helped to elect and later learned to distrust. Then came the administration of Mr. Arthur, with whom at first the former soldier-president seemed to have such influence that swarms of office-seekers implored his aid. Then that influence also waned. Grant was sensitive to a degree absolutely incompatible with political life or association. He would have lived and died a happier man had he, like Sherman, refused every offer that led to the presidential chair.

He had returned from Europe in '79, worth presumably, says Badeau, one hundred thousand dollars, and the owner of two or three handsome homes. On the income of this sum he and his beloved wife could live in comfort in some small city or the country, but they longed to live as they had been living, " in the limelight " and in town. It was then that Ulysses, Jr., the putative financier of the family, and whose investments had certainly doubled the father's little nestegg in the past, tendered the general a partnership in the firm of Grant & Ward, which was doing, as all could see, a wonderful business in Wall Street. The fact that the President had allied himself with the house would undoubtedly add to its prestige and prominence. The name was worth all it might earn—and more.

Then followed four years of prosperous ease, of a bank account that placed our late President " beyond the dreams of avarice " and blinded him as to the methods of the management. Then came the deluge. Then followed desolation.

CHAPTER XXXVIII

THE FINAL BLOW

LONG months before the melancholy failure of that ill-omened bank, the General had told Badeau of the fabulous profits the firm was realizing, and Badeau went to their old comrade of the war and White House days—to Horace Porter—and asked that reticent but experienced soldier-citizen his opinion, and Porter solemnly shook his head. Such profits, he said, were impossible in a business honestly conducted. But Grant saw on every side men by the dozen who had started with less than his modest capital and had gathered fortunes in Wall Street. He was so confident in the sagacity and judgment of Ulysses, Jr., that he invested his every dollar with the firm and reinvested every penny of the profits which he did not lavish on his loved ones or on his followers and friends. Like Thackeray's most lovable hero, Colonel Newcome, he thought to share his good fortune with many of his kith and kin and urged their sending their savings to be invested for them by brilliant young " Buck " and his sagacious partner—that wonderful wizard in finance, Mr. Ward. Aside from the chagrin of seeing some of his recommendations disregarded, and certain of his opponents rewarded first by Mr. Garfield and later by Mr. Arthur, General Grant was living in those years a life of ease, luxury and freedom from care such as never before he had enjoyed. Julia Dent was as ever first and foremost in his world, but the children were the source of pride and joy unspeakable. Devoted, dutiful and loyal they unquestionably were, but Grant believed of his first born that he was destined to become renowned as a general, and of " Buck " and Jesse that they were

382

born financiers and business men. As for Princess Nellie, the father's love and yearning for that one daughter of his house and name was beyond all measure. No man ever loved home, wife and children more tenderly, more absorbingly.

Although widely scattered at the time, this heart-united household had been anticipating a blithe and merry Christmas at the close of the year 1883. When alighting from his carriage just before midnight, with the welcoming chimes pealing on the frosty air, the General's foot slipped on the icy pavement, he fell heavily, a muscle snapped in the thigh, possibly one of those injured twenty years earlier, the day of that fateful stumble at Carrollton, and he was carried into the house, never thereafter to leave it in health or strength.

Crutches again, and later a cane, long were necessary. In March they took him to Fortress Monroe so that he could hobble about in the soft air and sunshine. In April he was back again in Gotham, able to drive his favorite team, but not to walk. On Sunday, the 4th of May, the wizard partner, Ward, came into their home and quite casually announced that the Marine Bank of New York, in which Grant & Ward had large deposits, needed perhaps one hundred and fifty thousand dollars to tide them over a temporary difficulty. If General Grant could borrow that much over Monday, Grant & Ward would not have to lose a cent; otherwise they stood to lose perhaps fifty or sixty thousand. Of course the lender would lose nothing, said Ward, as there was a million, at least, of securities in the vaults.

The world knows the rest—how unsuspiciously our General called on his friend and fellow horseman, Mr. William H. Vanderbilt, said that he needed one hundred and fifty thousand for a day or so, and came away with a cheque for that amount. For no other man probably would Mr. Vanderbilt have parted unsecured with such a sum. The cheque was promptly endorsed and turned over to Mr. Ward, who took it unconcernedly and then his leave.

Tuesday morning, May 6th, believing himself a millionaire and the brief indebtedness to Vanderbilt already cancelled, Grant alighted at the Wall Street office to find an ominous gathering. " Father, you had better go home—the bank has failed," said Ulysses, Jr., with misery in his eyes, but Grant stayed to investigate. Badeau, the faithful, hastening in at noon, found his old chief seated in the rear office, calm in the midst of stress and storm. " We are all ruined here," he simply said. Ward had vanished, the key of the vaults with him, and when they were finally opened, the boasted " securities " were found to be but shadows. The ruin was complete.

Everything they had—all the beautiful gifts, trophies, souvenirs, even the little houses owned by Mrs. Grant in Washington, and the repurchased Dent property about St. Louis, had to be sold. Grant insisted, though it left them, for the time at least, absolutely penniless. It had dragged down others with them; it involved his honored name in a whirlpool of censure, criticism and calumny that well-nigh crushed him. Fallen from such supremely high estate, the insults and indignities that beset him now far outweighed the slights and sneers that had been his portion in the days of his earlier humiliation. Over the depths of the misery that had come to him in his old and recently honored age let us draw the curtain. No man on earth could know the suffering it cost him. Only one woman could faintly see. Helping hands there were outstretched to him instanter, and money to meet the immediate need. Then, as the storm subsided and the extent of Ward's villainy and Grant's innocence became known, new measures were taken to provide against absolute want. A trust fund had already been raised. A measure was speedily set on foot to restore to Grant the rank and pay which he had surrendered on assuming the presidency, and a modest competence would thus be insured him and those he loved. There was a home in which to live. They could even spend the summers at the seashore. There were offers of congenial occupation that might have proved mildly lucrative. There was measurable return to hope and possible health. There had never been complaint or repining. To all about him he had been gentleness, consideration, kindliness itself. There was just one cause of new, yet slight anxiety:

All through that summer of '84, while at Long Branch, his throat had been giving him pain, and a Philadelphia physician, examining it for the first time late in September, advised, even urged, says Badeau, his consulting a specialist on returning to town. For a time he took no heed. He was writing now, long hours each day, but at last he called, as further urged by his own physician, upon that distinguished expert, Dr. J. H. Douglas, and that evening calmly admitted that the trouble in the throat was cancerous in tendency. And that this was true, the fact that he suddenly dropped the luxury of all the days that had followed Donelson— his cigar—and the sufferings that followed in November and December proved beyond possibility of doubt.

By mid-winter the torture had become incessant, the weakness so alarming that daily visits to his physician were abandoned, and he was now spending long hours of pain and distress, propped in a reclining chair. Fred, with his wife and children, had come to help and cheer him. Friends and old comrades were constant in their calls. The success of the few articles written for the *Century* had been so marked that the publishers urgently asked for more. For a time his suffering and weakness were such that he shrank from the effort, but when the offers (in which our great author and humorist "Mark Twain" had been a prominent adviser) took definite shape, and he was induced to prepare his own Memoirs for publication, it seemed as though new life and purpose were vouchsafed him, for in spite of that suffering and weakness he set sturdily to work, dictating so long as the condition of his throat would permit, reading over the copied pages, comparing records, reports and orders, and finding comfort unspeakable in his task and in the hope that the resultant book would find such a sale as to place his loved ones once again in ease and affluence.

Twice or thrice it seemed as though he might not be spared to finish it. Once in April they believed him going. Once, in the dead of night again, violent hemorrhage ensued, and the physician sleeping in the adjoining room and suddenly aroused, bent every effort to check the flow, yet thought his efforts vain. Death seemed so imminent that April night that even Mrs. Grant, who had never lost hope or courage, now, kneeling beside him, besought his blessing. They were all gathered about him by that time—even sorrowing Nellie from her distant home across the sea, and it had been sweet to see the joy in his fading eyes as they watched and followed her. And then he rallied as he had at Shiloh, and firmly, grimly faced the destroyer he had dared on a dozen battlefields. And the summer came and found him still laboring at those Memoirs, still suffering untold, almost unbearable, pain, fighting on to finish the work in hand before the ever-increasing force and fury of the destroyer should utterly prevail.

And meanwhile a nation stood with bated breath and watched and prayed. Crowds gathered about the house and importuned the physicians for tidings. Congress had passed amid scenes of emphatic popular approval the bill restoring him again to the generalship of old—almost the last act signed by Mr. Arthur before leaving, as it was almost the first commission signed by Mr. Cleveland after entering, the White House.

THE LAST DAYS
Grant and family at Mount McGregor

THE FINAL BLOW

Then presently, for quiet and for better air, as all remember, they bore him to the Drexel cottage at Mount McGregor, near Saratoga Springs, and here, his voice utterly gone, compelled to make his wishes known by signs, compelled to complete the pages of his Memoirs with pad and pencil, our stricken soldier indomitably held to his self-appointed task, once more " fighting it out on this line if it took all summer." Never even at Shiloh, in front of Vicksburg, or in the fire-flashing Wilderness was he more tenacious, determined, heroic, for now intense suffering accompanied almost every move and moment. Physicians were constantly at hand ; Fred, the devoted son, ever at his side. Here there came to see him and to sympathize old comrades—even old enemies—of the war days, all thought of rancor buried now. Here, just as thirty years earlier he had hastened to offer aid, came Buckner (and this time unprotesting) in unconditional surrender; for beneath the shadow of that hovering wing the last vestige of sectional pride gave way to fond memories of the old and firm friendship. Here, almost as the twilight deepened into the gloom of night eternal, they bore him the tribute of honor and respect from men whom he had vehemently opposed—foeman-in-chief to the Union, Jefferson Davis, and soldier-candidate and political foe, Winfield S. Hancock. Here they read him letters, telegrams, editorials from every corner of the Union he had striven to weld and secure, every line telling of world-wide sympathy, honor and affection. Here, almost at the last, he pencilled those farewell pages of those fruitful volumes, which, whatever his earlier defects in style, have been declared classic in modern literature. Here, ere the light went out forever, he wrote the pathetic missive, his final words of love, longing and devotion to the wife whom he held peerless among women, to the children whom he loved with such infinite tenderness, and for whose future comfort, even in face of such persistent torment and impending death, he had labored to the very last.

And then, as he completed the final paragraph—the story of his soldier-life and services—and with faltering hand signed the final letter, he closed his wearied eyes upon the group that hovered ever about him, eager to garner every look and whisper, and so the long fight ended, even as it had begun, almost without a sigh. Apparently without consciousness of pain, certainly without struggle or suffering, surrounded by that devoted household—wife, sons and only daughter—the greatest of our warriors passed onward into the valley of shadows, and to immortality.

Thirty years have passed since that which struck from our muster rolls the name of our first and foremost general—thirty years, as these pages are given to the light, since that summer day on which, with the highest honors and the greatest retinue ever accorded to American citizen or soldier, the flag-enshrouded casket was borne almost the length of all Manhattan; Hancock, the superb on many a battlefield, heading the league-long procession of soldiery, the world-garnered dignitaries from every state and clime. Amidst the solemn thunder of the guns of the warships moored along the Hudson, the farewell volleys of the troops aligned along the heights, in the presence of the President and cabinet, the supreme court and the diplomatic corps, the governors of nearly every commonwealth, eminent soldiers, sailors, veterans of the Civil War, the gray mingling with the blue, and all engulfed in a vast multitude of mourners, the final prayers were said, the last benediction spoken, and under the shadow of the beloved flag he had served with such fidelity and to such eminent purpose, they laid to rest the honored soldier whose valiant service had secured to them and to their posterity the blessings of union, progress and tranquillity, and whose crowning message to the nation

he had restored was the simple admonition, " Let us
have peace."

And in those thirty years the people of our land
have had abundant time to study and to reflect. Each
succeeding year adds to their reverence for their greatest
friend, leader and statesman, Abraham Lincoln. Each
succeeding year seems to increase their appreciation of
their greatest soldier, Ulysses Grant, and yet it sometimes seems as though in the magnitude of the obstacles
overcome, the immensity of the military problems
solved, the supreme soldiership of the man has blinded
us for the time to other virtues, less heroic, perhaps,
yet not less marked and true, virtues as son, as husband,
father and friend, not often equalled in other men, if
ever excelled.

And was there nothing more?

Of Newcome, his modest hero, his kindliest gentleman, Thackeray says, " The humblest in his own opinion,
he was furious if any one took a liberty with him," yet
our Western soldier suffered many an indignity, furious
only when one he loved was scorned or slighted. Newcome could blush to the temples at reference to his
deeds: Grant blushed to the roots of his hair when,
as in the case of the poor woman whose little children
he offered to see safely through their journey, he had
to mention his title and name. Froissart's Chronicles
he may never have read, but in all their pages is there
finer picture of soldier courtesy than that which followed the great surrender, that which Canon Farrar
proclaimed as " faultless in delicacy " when the Virginia Cavalier found his match, not only in the ranks
of war, but in all that makes the courteous, considerate,
consummate gentleman, in our silent soldier-citizen from
the hills of western Illinois.

And was not his a marvellous career? Cradled in
the cottage, he spoke for years from the seat of the
mightiest. Chosen and trained for his country's wars,

he best loved the arts of peace. Schooled as a regular, he to the fullest extent and from the very first believed in the volunteer. Ignored by book and bureau soldiers at the start despite the fine record of the Mexican campaigns, indebted to a Western governor for the opportunity refused him by the War Department, he held his modest way, uncomplaining, asking only to be made of use. One year had raised him from the twilight of a Western town to the triumph of Donelson; two years made him the victor of Vicksburg, the head of the armies of the West; three had set him in supreme command, deferred to even by those who late as '62 had sought to down him; four and the sword of the chivalric Lee was his to do with as he would—the rebellion crushed, the war ended, and then, with our martyred Lincoln lying in the grave ever watered by a nation's tears, small wonder was it that twice the people held Grant long years at their head, and when he had returned from that globe-circling triumphal progress, in large numbers would again have called him to the White House, an uncrowned monarch, the chosen of sovereign citizens. Was he greater then than in the chain of ills that followed? Tricked by those he trusted, himself unskilled in guile, ruined financially by those he had been taught to hold infallible, and finally confronted by the dread conviction that, though barely beyond the prime of life, his days were numbered—was he ever amid the thunder of saluting cannon and the cheers of countless multitudes so great as when, with the grim destroyer clutching at his throat, he fought for life that through those matchless Memoirs he might earn the means to wipe out every possible obligation and provide in modest comfort, at least, for those he loved and must so soon leave to mourn him? In those last heroic days at Mt. McGregor he stood revealed in his silent suffering, the ideal of devotion, endurance and determination, until, his great work done, his toil

THE FINAL BLOW

and trials ended, his sword long since sheathed, his pen now dropping from the wearied, nerveless hand, he could turn to the Peace Ineffable and sink to rest—our greatest soldier—our honored President—our foremost citizen. Aye, soldier, statesman, loyal citizen he was and yet more, for in purity of life, in love of home and wife and children, in integrity unchallenged, in truth and honor unblemished, in manner simplicity itself—though ever coupled with that quiet dignity that made him peer among the princes of the earth—in speech so clean that oath or execration never soiled his lips, unswerving in his faith, a martyr to his friendships, merciful to the fallen, magnanimous to the foe, magnificent in self-discipline, was he not also, and in all that the grand old name implies, Grant—the gentleman?

THE END

INDEX

393

INDEX

INDEX

398

INDEX

Springfield, Grant at, 142
Stanton, E. M., 179, 221, 222,
239, 250, 255, 256, 257, 273,
275, 285, 294-296, 298, 307,
327, 329-331, 338, 339, 349
Stevenson, 257-259
Stewart, A. T., 349, 352-354
Stone, Charles P., 183
Stoneman, General, 281
Stuart, General, 280, 281
Sumner, Charles, 346, 353, 354,
357, 362-364, 367-369, 381
Swinton, Mr., 303-305
Tacubaya, 109, 120
Taylor, Dick, 342
Taylor, Zachary, 54, 81, 89, 99,
100, 343
Tender of service, Grant's,
143, 144
Tennessee, Army of the, 225,
230-232, 249, 258
Terrell, General, 202
Thayer, Sylvanus, 49
Theft of $1000, 119
Thirteenth Army Corps, 225,
230-232, 248
Thomas, George H., 66, 82, 170,
179, 192, 193, 207, 221, 222,
249, 255, 257, 260-266, 268,
269, 289-299, 315, 324-326,
331
Thomas, Grant orders him re-
lieved, 296, 297
T. I. O., the, 68, 116
Tod, Judge, 16
Torbert, General, 282
Trist, Nicholas P., 105-117
"Unconditional surrender," 174
Union League, 311
Upton, Emory, 288, 307
Vanderbilt, William H., 383
Van Vliet, Stewart, 355
Vera Cruz, 100

Vicksburg, 224, 230, 233 *et seq.*,
238, 248
Victoria, Queen, 374-376
Wade, Benjamin F., 362
Wallace, Lew, 197, 200, 201
Wallace, W. H., 199
Warren, Gouverneur K., 281,
284-287, 314-317
Washburne, Elihu B., 137,
147, 160, 206, 252, 271, 303,
347, 349, 352, 380
Wedding, Grant's, 120, 121
Welles, Gideon, 339
West Point, 35, 36, 40-48, 57-
61, 73, 88, 114, 117
heavy losses of, 92,
116
Scott's tribute to, 114
White Haven, 96, 119, 120, 310
Wilcox, Cadmus, groomsman,
120
Wilderness, Grant's emotion in,
279
Willard, aide, 262
Williams, Robert, 360
Williamsport, 240
Wilson brothers, 216, 217
Wilson, James H., 216-219,
224, 227 *et seq.*, 235, 244, 251,
253, 257, 258, 262, 269, 273,
274, 281, 282, 284-286, 290-
293, 295-299, 307, 311
Wilson, Mr. (of Iowa), 353
Winchester, 282
Winthrop, Fred, 317
Wood, General, 264
Worth, W. F., 45, 89, 100, 111-
114
Wright, General, 314, 316
Yates, Richard, 141, 142, 160,
224, 227, 271
Yellow Tavern, Va., 280
Young, John Russell, 380